Things I've Been Silent About

Azar Nafisi is a visiting professor and the director of the Dialogue Project at the Foreign Policy Institute of Johns Hopkins University. She has taught Western literature at the University of Tehran, the Free Islamic University and the University of Allameh Tabatabai in Iran. In 1981 she was expelled from the University of Tehran after refusing to wear the veil. In 1994 she won a teaching fellowship from Oxford University, and in 1997 she and her family left Iran for America. She has written for *The New York Times*, *The Washington Post*, *The Wall Street Journal*, and *The New Republic* and has appeared on countless radio and television programmes. She lives in Washington, DC, with her husband and two children.

ALSO BY AZAR NAFISI

Reading Lolita in Tehran: A Memoir in Books
Anti-Terra: A Critical Study of Vladimir Nabokov's Novels
Bibi and the Green Voice (Bibi e la Voce Verde)

Praise for *Things I've Been Silent About*

'[*Things I've Been Silent About*] transports us to a world that is at once enchanting and threatening; it is a tale that mixes family feuds, politics and literature and holds our interest from the first to the last page. [It] may be read by some for its historic context. Others will be intrigued by what it says about the condition of women in the Islamic republic. To me, it was above all, a touching portrait of a troubled childhood in a family torn apart by a seductive father and an overbearing mother . . . But as the narrative unfolds against a complex and at times tragic political background, it is a political statement on Iran's modern history as much as a personal attempt to come to terms with a past by unravelling its secrets.'

Financial Times

'A companion memoir to the bestselling *Reading Lolita in Tehran*, this is Azar Nafisi's more personal account of growing up in Iran . . . an intriguing memoir.'

Metro

'Nafisi's account is rarely shrill or self pitying, preferring to let her stories tell themselves.'

Independent

'This powerful memoir, from the author of the global hit *Reading Lolita in Tehran*, is a bewitching story of Azar's relationship with her brilliant, beautiful, romanticising and fictionalising mother. Set against the background of change before the Islamic Revolution, it is a complex, provocative story of family life, lies and loves – and of a desire to work out the past.'

Good Housekeeping

'Nafisi proves a compelling, and moving, witness.'

New Statesman

'If you enjoyed the wonderful *Reading Lolita in Tehran* by this author, you have another treat in store.'

Waterstone's Books Quarterly

'A portrait of a family and a country that are at once alluring and deeply dysfunctional.'

Economist

'This is a remarkable insight into a fascinating period in Iran's recent history, and a touching portrait of astonishing tenacity and integrity in the face of adversity that few in the Western world could imagine.'

Good Book Guide

'*Things I've Been Silent About* is a kind of companion volume to Nafisi's 2003 memoir *Reading Lolita in Tehran* . . . giving us finely etched portraits of her tempestuous authoritarian mother, and her doting, unassertive father, who was a mayor of Tehran under the Shah.'

Scotland on Sunday

'This is a poignant memoir: part therapy, part chronicle.' *Catholic Herald*

'A gifted storyteller with a mastery of Western literature, Nafisi knows how to use language both to settle scores and to seduce. Her family secrets pour forth in a flood of revelations of anger, humiliation and deceit.'

The New York Times

'An utterly memorable memoir'

The Washington Post

Things I've Been Silent About

Memories of a Prodigal Daughter

AZAR NAFISI

 WINDMILL BOOKS

Published by Windmill Books 2010

2 4 6 8 10 9 7 5 3 1

First published in Great Britain in 2009 by William Heinemann

Windmill Books
The Random House Group Limited
20 Vauxhall Bridge Road, London SW1V 2SA

Addresses for companies within The Random House Group Limited can be
found at: www.randomhouse.co.uk/offices.htm

The Random House Group Limited Reg. No. 954009

Permission credits can be found beginning on page 335.

www.rbooks.co.uk

A CIP catalogue record for this book
is available from the British Library

ISBN 9780099487128

The Random House Group Limited supports The Forest Stewardship
Council (FSC), the leading international forest certification organisation. All
our titles that are printed on Greenpeace approved FSC certified paper carry
the FSC logo. Our paper procurement policy can be found at:
www.rbooks.co.uk/environment

Mixed Sources
Product group from well-managed
forests and other controlled sources
www.fsc.org Cert no. TT-COC-2139
© 1996 Forest Stewardship Council

Book design by Barbara M. Bachman

Printed and bound in Great Britain by
CPI Cox & Wyman, Reading, RG1 8EX

In memory of my parents, Ahmad and Nezhat Nafisi

To my brother, Mohammad Nafisi,
and my family, Bijan, Negar, and Dara Naderi

CONTENTS

PART ONE | FAMILY FICTIONS

PART TWO | LESSONS AND LEARNING

PART THREE | MY FATHER'S JAIL

All illustrations courtesy of the author unless otherwise noted.

MOST MEN CHEAT ON THEIR WIVES to have mistresses. My father cheated on my mother to have a happy family life. I felt sorry for him, and in one sense took it upon myself to fill the empty spaces in his life. I collected his poems, listened to his woes, and helped him choose appropriate gifts, first for my mother and then for the women he fell in love with. He later claimed that most of his relations with these other women were not sexual, that what he yearned for was the feeling they gave him of warmth and approval. Approval! My parents taught me how deadly that desire could be.

As a family we were fond of telling stories. My father left behind a published memoir and a far more interesting unpublished one, and over fifteen hundred pages of diaries. Mother did not write but she told us stories from her past, usually ending them by saying, But I never said a word, I kept silent. She genuinely believed that she never talked about her personal life, although in her own way she often spoke, it seemed, about little else. She would not have approved of my writing a memoir, especially a family memoir. Nor did I imagine that one day I would find myself writing about my own parents. It is such a strong part of Iranian culture to never reveal private matters: we don't air our dirty laundry in public, as Mother would say, and besides, private lives are trivial and not worth writing about. Useful life stories are what matter, like the memoir my father finally published, a cardboard version of himself. I no longer believe that we can keep silent. We never really do, mind you. In one way or another we articulate what has happened to us through the kind of people we become.

My father started to keep a diary when I was four years old. The diary is addressed to me. He gave it to me decades later, when I had children of my own. The first few pages are about how to be good,

*My father and mother,
Nezhat and Ahmad Nafisi.*

how to be considerate toward others. Then he starts complaining about my mother. He complains that she no longer remembers that she once liked him and enjoyed his company. He writes that, although I am just a child, I am his only solace and support. He advises me that if I ever marry I should seek to be a true friend and companion to my husband. He describes one incident when he and my mother were quarreling and I, like "an angel of peace," tried to distract and entertain them. My empathy was as dangerous as any clandestine activity: here was a sin Mother could not forgive. My brother and I tried to please them both, but no matter how hard we tried—and we

tried very hard—they were never happy. My mother would turn her head away from us and gaze into the distance with a knowing nod to some invisible interlocutor, seeming to say, Didn't I tell you? Didn't I?, as if she knew my father would be unfaithful to her long before he even considered it. She acted upon this knowledge as an accomplished fact and seemed to take a perverse pleasure when it all became true.

When my mother was very ill, a few years after my family and I had left Tehran for the United States, I was told that for many days she had refused to go to the hospital unless the lock to her apartment was changed. *That man* and his floozy would break in just as they'd done before, she muttered, and loot what was left of her possessions.

"*That man* and his floozy" were my father and his second wife, whom she blamed for all of her misfortunes, including the mysterious disappearance of her collection of gold coins and two trunks of silver. No one, of course, believed her. Accustomed as we were to my mother's fictions, we indulged her without paying much attention.

She would evoke shadowy figures who, one by one, had been lost to her—her mother, her father, her first husband—and hold us responsible. Ultimately, not one of us was able to step out of her invented world. She demanded that we remain faithful not to her, but to her story.

My father's fictions were more straightforward, or so I believed for a long time. He communicated with us through stories about his life, his family, and about Iran—a subject he was almost obsessed with—drawing on the classic texts of Persian literature. This is how I first discovered literature and learned about my country's history. He also told us his version of my mother's fictions, so that we constantly vacillated between two shadow worlds.

All our lives my brother and I were caught by the fictions my parents told us—fictions about themselves as well as others. Each wanted us to judge the other in his or her favor. Sometimes I felt cheated, as if they never allowed us to have a story of our own. It is only now that I understand how much their story was also mine.

THOSE WHO ARE CLOSE TO US, when they die, divide our world. There is the world of the living, which we finally, in one way or another, succumb to, and then there is the domain of the dead that, like an imaginary friend (or foe) or a secret concubine, constantly beckons, reminding us of our loss. What is memory but a ghost that lurks at the corners of the mind, interrupting our normal course of life, disrupting our sleep in order to remind us of some acute pain or pleasure, something silenced or ignored? We miss not only their presence, or how they felt about us, but ultimately how they allowed us to feel about ourselves or them.

How did my mother allow us to feel about her? The only way I can bring myself to confront her loss is to ask this question. At times I have wondered if she wasn't always lost to me, but when she was alive I was too preoccupied with resisting her to realize it. There was something touching in the way she talked about herself and her past as if she too were an invention, occupying the body of another woman who teasingly appeared to us in glimmers, like a firefly. I am after those firefly moments now. What did they reveal of my mother and of us?

In my last years in Iran, I became fixated on my mother's memories. I even took from her several photographs. It seemed the only way of gaining some access to her past. I became a memory thief, collecting her photographs alongside pictures of the old Tehran in which she grew up, married, had her children. My curiosity veered into the realm of obsession. Yet none of this really helped. The photographs, the descriptions, at some point even the facts, are insufficient. They reveal certain details, but they remain lifeless fragments. What I am searching for is the gaps—the silences. This is how I see the past: as an excavation. You sift through the rubble, pick up one fragment here, another there, label it and record where you found it, noting the time and date of discovery. It is not just the foundations I am looking for but something at once more and less tangible.

I DO NOT MEAN THIS BOOK to be a political or social commentary, or a useful life story. I want to tell the story of a family that unfolds against the backdrop of a turbulent era in Iran's political and cultural history. There are many stories about these times, between the birth of my grandmother at the start of the twentieth century and my daughter's birth at its end, marked by the two revolutions that shaped Iran, causing so many divisions and contradictions that transient turbulence became the only thing of permanence.

My grandmother was born when Iran was ruled by a destabilized absolutist monarchy and was under rigid religious laws that sanctioned stoning, polygamy, and the marriage of girls as young as nine. Women were scarcely allowed to leave their homes, and when they did they were chaperoned and covered from head to toe. There were no schools for women, although some among the nobility provided their daughters with private tutors. And yet there was another side to this story, pale flickers of a future revealing itself through the cultural and political crisis that would upend all those old rules. My grandmother witnessed the Constitutional Revolution of 1905–11, the first of its kind in the Middle East, which helped usher in modern Iran, galvanizing different strata of society, including the progressive clerics, minorities, intellectuals, some members of the nobility, and women, some of whom had started to support the revolutionaries, setting up underground groups and demanding access to education. By 1912 Morgan Shuster, an American financial advisor to Iran, marveled at the leaps Iranian women had made in such a short period of time, embracing new freedoms that had taken years, even centuries, for Western women to achieve. "The Persian women since 1907 had become almost at bond the most progressive, not to say radical, in the world," he said. "That this state-

ment upsets the idea of centuries makes no difference. It is fact."

How can I describe the fragile, conflicted nature of my mother's childhood and youth in the mid-1920s and '30s, by which time the flickering possibilities had taken over to such an extent that she could appear in public without a

My daughter, Negar (second from left), with her classmates in Tehran. All the female schoolchildren were forced to wear the veil after the revolution.

veil, go to a French school, and meet and fall in love with her first husband while dancing at a wedding—all impossible two decades before. Yet there was another aspect to her times, a refusal to relinquish the vanquished past. When, in 1936, Reza Shah Pahlavi, in his efforts to hasten the process of modernization, issued a mandate that made the unveiling of women mandatory and banned traditional clothing for men, my paternal grandmother, like so many other Iranian women, refused to leave her home. Reza Shah's edict was finally rescinded in 1941, although its memory still ignites fresh questions and divisions.

By the time I was growing up, in the 1950s and '60s, we took our education and our books and parties and movies for granted. We witnessed women becoming active in all walks of life, governing in Parliament—among them, briefly, my own mother—and becoming ministers. But then, by 1984, my own daughter, born five years after the Islamic Revolution, would witness the return of the same laws that had been repealed during my grandmother's and my mother's lifetimes. My daughter would be forced to wear a veil in first grade and would be punished for showing her hair in public. Her generation would eventually find its own brand of courage and resistance.

In this book my interest is not in a general recitation of historical times but rather in those fragile intersections—the places where moments in an individual's private life and personality resonate with and reflect a larger, more universal story.

THOSE INTERSECTIONS BETWEEN the private and the public were what I was looking for when I started to write my first book, in Iran, on Vladimir Nabokov. I wanted to discuss Nabokov's novels in light of the different times I had read them. That was impossible, not just because I could not frankly write about the political and social realities of life in the Islamic Republic of Iran but also because personal and private experiences were treated by the state as taboo.

It was around this time that I started making a list in my diary entitled "Things I Have Been Silent About." Under it I wrote: "Falling in Love in Tehran. Going to Parties in Tehran. Watching the Marx Brothers in Tehran. Reading *Lolita* in Tehran." I wrote about repressive laws and executions, about public and political abominations. Eventually I drifted into writing about private betrayals, implicating myself and those close to me in ways I had never imagined.

There are so many different forms of silence: the silence that tyrannical states force on their citizens, stealing their memories, rewriting their histories, and imposing on them a state-sanctioned identity. Or the silence of witnesses who choose to ignore or not speak the truth, and of victims who at times become complicit in the crimes committed against them. Then there are the silences we indulge in about ourselves, our personal mythologies, the stories we impose upon our real lives. Long before I came to appreciate how a ruthless political regime imposes its own image on its citizens, stealing their identities and self-definitions, I had experienced such impositions in my personal life—my life within my family. And long before I understood what it meant for a victim to become complicit in crimes of the state, I had discovered, in far more personal terms, the shame of complicity. In a sense, this book is a response to my own inner censor and inquisitor.

Perhaps the most common of all narratives is one about absent parents and the urgent need to fill in the void created by their deaths. The process does not lead to closure—at least not for me—but to understanding. It is an understanding that does not necessarily bring with it peace but perhaps a sense that this narrative might be the only way through which we can acknowledge our parents and in some form bring them back to life, now that we are free, at last, to shape the boundaries of our own story.

PART ONE | FAMILY FICTIONS

A dim capacity for wings
Degrades the dress I wear.

—EMILY DICKINSON,
"From the Chrysalis"

CHAPTER I

Saifi

I HAVE OFTEN ASKED MYSELF how much of my mother's account of her meeting with her first husband was a figment of her imagination. If not for the photographs, I would have doubted that he had ever existed. A friend once talked of my mother's "admirable resistance to the unwanted," and since, for her, so much in life was unwanted, she invented stories about herself that she came to believe with such conviction that we started doubting our own certainties.

In her mind their courtship began with a dance. It seemed more likely to me that his parents would have asked her father for her hand, a marriage of convenience between two prominent families, as had been the convention in Tehran in the 1940s. But over the years she never changed this story, the way she did so many of her other accounts. She had met him at her uncle's wedding. She was careful to mention that in the morning she wore a flowery crêpe-de-chine dress and in the evening one made of duchess satin, and they danced all evening ("After my father had left," she would say, and then immediately add, "because no one dared dance with me in my father's presence"). The next day he asked for her hand in marriage.

Saifi! I cannot remember ever hearing his last name spoken in our house. We should have called him—with the echo of proper distance—Mother's first husband, or perhaps by his full title, Saif ol Molk Bayat, but to me he was always Saifi, good-naturedly part of our routine. He insinuated himself into our lives with the same ease with which he stood behind her in their wedding pictures, appearing unex-

Mother's first wedding, to Saifi.

pectedly and slyly whirling her away from us. I have two photos from that day—more than we ever had of my own parents' wedding. Saifi appears relaxed and affable, with his light hair and hazel eyes, while my mother, who is in the middle of the group, stands frozen like a solitary centerpiece. He seems nonchalantly, confidently happy. But perhaps I am wrong and what I see on his face is not hope but utter hopelessness. Because he too has his secrets.

There was something about her story that always bothered me, even as a child. It seemed not so much untrue as wrong. Most people have a way of radiating their potential, not just what they are but what they could become. I wouldn't say my mother didn't have the potential to dance. It is worse than that. She wouldn't dance, even though, by all accounts, she was a good dancer. Dancing would have implied pleasure, and she took great pride in denying herself pleasure or any such indulgences.

All through my childhood and youth, and even now in this city so far removed from the Tehran that I remember, the shadow of that other ghostly woman who danced and smiled and loved disturbs the memories of the one I knew as my mother. I have a feeling that if somehow I could understand just when she stopped dancing—when she stopped wanting to dance—I would find the key to my mother's riddle and finally make my peace with her. For I resisted my mother— if you believe her stories—almost from the start.

I HAVE THREE PHOTOGRAPHS of my mother and Saifi. Two are of their wedding, but I am interested in the third, a much smaller picture of them out on a picnic, sitting on a rock. They are both looking into the camera, smiling. She is holding onto him in the casual manner of people who are intimate and do not need to hold onto one another too tightly. Their bodies seem to naturally gravitate together. Looking at the photograph, I can see the possibility of this young, perhaps not yet frigid, woman letting go.

I find in the photograph the sensuality that we always missed in my mother in real life. When? I would say, when did you graduate from high school? How many years later did you marry Saifi? What did he do? When did you meet Father? Simple questions that she never really answered. She was too immersed in her own inner

Mother and Saifi on a picnic.

world to be bothered by such details. No matter what I asked her, she would tell me the same stock stories, which I knew almost by heart. Later, when I left Iran, I asked one of my students to interview her and I gave specific questions to ask, but I got back the same stories.

No dates, no concrete facts, nothing that went outside my mother's set script.

A few years ago, at a family gathering, I ran into a lovely Austrian lady, the wife of a distant relative, who had been present at my mother's wedding to Saifi. One reason she remembered the wedding so clearly was the panic and confusion caused by the mysterious disappearance of the bride's birth certificate. (In Iran, marriages and children are recorded on birth certificates.) She told me, with the twinkle of a smile, that it was later discovered that the bride was a few years older than the groom. Mother's most recent birth certificate makes no mention of her first marriage. According to this document, which replaced the one she claimed to have lost, she was born in 1920. But she maintained that she was really born in 1924 and that her father had added four years to her age because he wanted to send her to school early. My father told us that my mother had actually subtracted four years from her real age when she picked up the new birth certificate, which she needed so that she could apply for a driver's license. When the facts did not suit her, my mother would go to great lengths to refashion them altogether.

Some facts are on record. Her father-in-law, Saham Soltan Bayat, was a wealthy landowner who had seen one royal dynasty, the Qajars (1794–1925), replaced by another, the Pahlavis (1925–79). He managed to survive, even thrive, through the change in power. Mother sometimes boasted that she was related to Saifi on her mother's side and that they were both descendants of Qajar kings. During the fifties and sixties when I was growing up, being related to the Qajars, who, according to the official history books, represented the old absolutist system, was no feather in anyone's cap. My father would remind us mischievously that all Iranians were in one way or another related to the Qajars. In fact, he would say, those who could not find any connections to the Qajars were the truly privileged. The Qajars had reigned over the country for 131 years, and had numerous wives and offspring. Like the kings that came before them, they seemed to have picked their wives from all ranks and classes, possessing whoever caught their fancy: princesses, gardeners' daughters, poor village girls, all were part of their collection. One Qajar king, Fath Ali Shah (1771–1834), is said to have had 160 wives. Being of a judicious mindset, Father would usually add that of course that was only part of the story, and since history is written by the victors, especially in our country, we should take all that is said about the Qajars with a grain of salt—after all, it was during their reign that Iran started to modernize. They had lost, so anything could be said of them. Even as a child I sensed that Mother brought up this connection to the Qajars more to slight her present life with Father than to boast about the past. Her snobbism was arbitrary, and her prejudices were restricted to the rules and laws of her own personal kingdom.

Saham Soltan, mother's father-in-law, appears in various history books and political memoirs—one line here, a paragraph there—once as deputy and vice president of Parliament, twice as minister of finance in the early 1940s, and as prime minister for a few months, from November 1944 to April 1945—during the time my mother claims to have been married to Saifi. Despite the fact that Iran had declared neutrality in World War II, Reza Shah Pahlavi had made the mistake of sympathizing with the Germans. The Allies, the British and the Soviets in particular, who had an eye on the geopolitical gains, occupied Iran in 1941, forced Reza Shah to abdicate, exiled him to Johannesburg, and replaced him with his young and more malleable son, Mohammad Reza. The Second World War triggered such upheaval in Iran that between 1943 and 1944 four prime ministers and seven ministers of finance were elected.

Mother knew little and seemed to care less about what kind of prime minister her father-in-law had been. What was important was that he played the fairy godfather to her degraded present. This is how so many public figures entered my life, not through history books but through my parents' stories.

HOW GLAMOROUS MOTHER'S LIFE with Saifi really was is open to debate. They lived at Saham Soltan's house, in the chink of time between the death of his first wife and his marriage to a much younger and, according to my mother, quite detestable woman. In the absence of a lady of the house, my mother did the honors. "Everybody's eyes were on me that first night," she would tell us, describing in elaborate detail the dress she had worn and the impact of her flawless French. As a child I would picture her coming down the stairs in her red chiffon dress, her black eyes shining, her hair immaculately done.

"The first night Doctor Millspaugh came . . . you should have been there!" Dr. Millspaugh, the head of the American Mission in the 1940s, had been assigned by both the Roosevelt and the Truman administrations to help Tehran set up modern financial institutions. Mother never saw any reason to tell us who this man was, and for a long time, for some reason I was convinced that he was Belgian. Later, when I reviewed my mother's accounts of these dinners, I was struck by the fact that Saifi was never present. His father would always be there, and Dr. Millspaugh or some other publicly important and personally insignificant character. But where was Saifi? That was the tragedy of her life: the man at her side was never the one she wanted.

My father, to bribe my brother and me into silence against my mother's impositions, and perhaps to compensate for his own compliance, would tell us over and over again how she was imprisoned in her father-in-law's house, where Khoji, the domineering housekeeper, was the real woman in charge. Even the key to the larder was in the hands of the indomitable Khoji, whom mother had to flatter and cajole to get as much as a length of fabric to make herself a nice dress. Father would remind us that she was treated more like an unwanted guest than as mistress of her father-in-law's house.

Mother presented herself as a happy young bride, the proud heroine wooed by Prince Charming, and Father painted her as a victim of other people's petty cruelties. They both wanted us to confirm their own version. Mother flung the past at us as an accusation of the present, and Father needed to justify her tyrannies on all of us, by provoking our compassion. It was difficult to compete with Saifi, a dead man, and a handsome one at that—the son of the prime minister, with the potential to become whatever she could imagine him to be. My father's intelligence and goodwill, his future prospects and ambitions as a promising director at the Ministry of Finance, even the fact that he and my mother came from different branches of the same family, appeared poor seconds to what Mother believed Saifi had to offer her. Later she seemed to begrudge Father's successes in public life, as if they were fierce rivals rather than partners.

The problem was not what she said but what she left out. My father filled in the gaps: Saifi, the favorite first son, had an incurable disease—nephritis of the kidney, they called it—and the doctors had given up on him. Let him do whatever he wants in these last years of his life, one had recommended. Indulge him, let him have his way. Provide him with all the fun he desires, because he has so little time to enjoy life. When his family proposed to my mother, they conveniently neglected to tell her that he was ill. She discovered it on her wedding night. According to my father their marriage was never consummated. Instead, for two years she nursed a sick husband, watching him die every day. And this was the romance of her life, the man whom she brandished to remind us of our own inadequacies!

Mother.

Sometimes, when she went on and on about Saifi with that absent look of hers, I wanted to shake her and say, No, that's not the way it was! But of course I never did. Did he care what would happen to her when she discovered his condition, or what would become of her after he died? She was too proud and too stubborn to have much interest in the truth. And so she transformed a real place and history into a fantasy of her own creation. Ever since I can remember, my brother, my father, and I tried to figure out what it was exactly that she wanted from us. We tried to travel with her to that other place that seemed to beckon, to which her eyes were constantly diverted as she gazed beyond the walls of her real home. What frightened me was not her rages but that frozen place in her that we could never penetrate. While she was alive I was too busy evading her and resenting her to understand how disappointed and alone she must have felt, how she was like so many other women about whom her best friend, Mina, used to say, with an ironic smile: "Another intelligent woman gone to waste."

rotten genes

MOTHER OFTEN SAID THAT I resisted her from the moment I was born. Apparently right at birth I coughed up blood and was given up for dead. She liked to tell the story of how in my infancy I refused to nurse and later declined to eat, giving in only under threat of the doctor's needles, or a dreaded colonel friend's sword. She wouldn't let me eat cucumbers, for some reason, or nuts. Once she gave me so much cod-liver oil that I broke out in hives. When my brother and I were sick with scarlet fever we were confined to a darkened room for forty days, because she believed light caused blindness in children with scarlet fever. Later, as an adult, I would sometimes tell the story of how she fed me so much grape juice one morning that I threw up. I wouldn't touch grapes for almost thirty years, until one night at a friend's house, when I dropped two on a whim into my wineglass and discovered the pleasure of crushing them with my teeth.

We often quarreled about my toys, which were usually locked in a closet. She always chose my toys and every once in a while I would be allowed to play with them briefly, before having to put them back. There was a small doll who crawled on all fours and a rabbit I was particularly fond of that her friend Monir joon had brought back from Paris. It played drums and was white and fluffy, but because of the drums it couldn't be properly cuddled. How I adored the soft white fur of that inaccessible rabbit! Long after I left home my mother continued to add to the doll collection, which she claimed would someday be mine. When she died, no one could find the dolls. They were gone, along with her rare antique carpets, two trunks of silver, her gold coins, the china from her first marriage, and most of her jewelry.

The first time I was allowed to play with one of my favorite dolls,

a blue-eyed porcelain number with long blond hair and a turquoise dress, I threw her up in the air and caught her again and again until she fell to the ground, her face smashed into fragments. Over the years I will lose or destroy objects that are dearest to me, especially those given to me by my mother. Rings and earrings, antique lamps, figurines—I can see them all clearly. The loss of these objects, what does it mean?

I loved this porcelain doll so much, but I broke it as soon as I was allowed to play with it.

Was I just that way, the kind of careless person who loses people and things?

I can trace our first real battle of wills to when I was about four years old. This particular fight was over the location of my bed. I wanted it near the window—I loved that window, with its large ledge where I could arrange my dolls and my toy china set. Mother wanted it by the wall, next to the closet. And every time she conceded, in a day or two she would revert to her original plan. One evening, when I came home from playing with the Armenian neighbors' daughter— a shy four-year-old from whom I was inseparable—my mother had moved my bed back to the wall. I cried and cried and cried that night and refused to eat my dinner. Any other night she would have forced me to eat, but that night she made an exception and I cried myself to sleep.

The next morning I wake up on the detested far side of the room, filled with tearful resentment. Father comes to my bedside, smiling.

My father and I had begun to develop a routine: every night he would tell me a bedtime story. But this particular morning he offers me a special treat. He says—as he places on the bedside table a small china plate which he had filled with chocolates—that if I am a good girl and give him the biggest smile I can muster he will tell me a secret. What secret? He cannot divulge secrets to unhappy girls with big frowns. But I am obstinate and refuse to comply; he has to tell me the secret without getting anything in return. Okay then, he says, but I bet you will smile when you hear my plan.

Let's do something new, he says conspiratorially. Let's make up our own stories. What stories? I ask. Our own stories; we can make up anything we want. I don't know how to do that, I say. Yes you do, think of what you want most, and then make up a story about it. What do you want most right now? I say, Nothing. He says, Perhaps right now you want to have your bed back by the window, but do you know what your bed wants? I shrug my shoulders. He says, Why don't we make up a story about a little girl and her bed. . . . Have you ever heard of a talking bed?

Me when I was five years old.

And that was how a new ritual was created: from that day on, my father and I developed a secret language. We made up stories to communicate our feelings and demands, and built our own world. Sometimes the stories we made up were very mundane. Whenever I did something he disapproved of, he would convey his disapproval in a story form, saying, for example, "There was a man who loved his daughter so much, but he was so hurt when she promised him she would not fight with the nanny . . ." In time we developed other secret means of communication: whenever I did something wrong in company, Father would put his index finger to his nose as a sign of warning. If I wanted to remember an important task, I should strike my nose with my finger seven consecutive times, each time repeating what I had to do, a device I use to this day. In this secret world my mother had no role. This is how we took our revenge on her tyrannies. I would learn, over time, that I could always take refuge in my make-believe world, one in which I could not only move the bed over by the window, but fly with it out the window to a place where no one, not even my mother, could enter, much less control.

IN THE EARLY NINETIES, my father published three children's books based on classic texts. One of these was a version of the *Shahnameh*, known in English as *The Book of Kings*, written by the epic poet Ferdowsi. In the introduction to his book, my father explains that he first told these stories to us, his children, when we were about three or four years old, and that he continued his tutelage by acquainting us with other great classic Persian masterpieces: Rumi's *Masnavi*, Saadi's *Golestan* and *Boostan*, and *Kelileh va Demneh*. He writes that later we continued to read them on our own. What he emphasizes in this introduction is that Iranians of his day should learn more about their ancestors and their values through a careful reading of the *Shahnameh*. He says he is happy that through such a medium "Iran is seen, heard and felt in our house today and it warms our hearts . . ."

My father's voice would take on a reverential tone whenever he spoke about Ferdowsi. He taught us that poets demand a special kind of respect, different from the respect we owe our teachers or our elders. Once, when I was very young, perhaps around four, I asked my father to tell me more stories by this Mr. Ferdowsi. Not Mr., he corrected me. He is Ferdowsi the Poet. And for a long time after that I asked to hear stories by the Poet Ferdowsi. My first notion of Iran was formed by my father's tales from the *Shahnameh*.

Ever since I can remember, my parents and their friends spoke of Iran as a beloved but prodigal child whose welfare they constantly quarreled about. Over the years Iran acquired for me a paradoxical identity: it was a concrete place, defined by where I was born and lived, the language I spoke, the food I ate, and at the same time it was a mythical notion, encouraging all manner of virtues and values, a symbol of resistance and of betrayal.

For my mother there was no other country. She sometimes spoke of other places to which she had traveled. She admired them, but Iran was her home. Whereas my father constantly wrangled and struggled with what it meant to be an Iranian, Mother had no such problems. Certain things were immutable for her. Being Iranian seemed to come with her genes—like her beautiful dark eyes, so dark that they appeared black, or the light olive color of her skin. She criticized Iranians the same way she disapproved of certain members of her clan, but she never related what she perceived as their shortcomings to Iran.

Mother respected Ferdowsi, as any Iranian would, but she scorned our preoccupation with literature, considering it a waste of time. Later I found a more colorful explanation for her hostility to fiction makers: it occurred to me that she did not want rivals. She had created her own world and her own mythology and had no need for others who made a living of such things.

WHEN I THINK OF MY FATHER, the first thing that comes to mind is his voice. In different places, walking the streets, sitting in the garden, driving the car, and at bedtime, I can still experience the calm that came over me whenever he would tell a story. I paid attention to these stories and internalized them in a way I never did with real life experiences. Later my father broke my heart, and because I loved him and trusted him as I loved and trusted no one else, I also hurt him and broke his heart. What partly exonerates him now in my mind is his stories. Only those shared moments have remained untainted by our mutual plunderings and betrayals.

While I feared my mother's cold outbursts and her persistent de-

mands, I was deeply and constantly afraid of losing my father. I remember so many nights sitting by the window waiting for him to
come home, listening for his footsteps in the hall before I could finally
sleep. In time I became his most faithful ally and apologist. I felt that
he, like me, was a victim of my mother's tyranny and thus exempt
from blame. She resented our shared sympathy and every once in a
while burst out in fits of anger. "*You*, you are made of the same rotten
genes as your father," she told my brother and me in her moments of
rage. "You are all waiting for me to die so you will get my inheritance." I sometimes wondered if she might not after all be right: Was
I not made of those same rotten genes?

If Mother commanded and demanded, my father lured and seduced much like Tom Sawyer enticing his playmates to paint his
fence. My relationship with him always had the intimacy of a shared
secret, whether we were walking the streets as I listened to his stories,
or planning how to please or appease my mother. My father and I
were bound by our secret world, and by the intimacy created by our
shared moments of storytelling, which simultaneously freed me from
the reality around me and transported me to a new realm composed of
teasing figments shaped by his voice.

On Friday mornings, Father would wake me up early and take me
for a long walk. To stem my complaints about the length of these
walks, he bought me a special cup that we would fill up from a favorite
fountain along the way. He called this our special time, when he
would tell stories, and occasionally stop to buy ice cream. With time
the characters in Ferdowsi's *Shahnameh* became as familiar to me as
my own family. I could not imagine life without them, and the book
itself became a place I loved to visit, knowing that I could knock on
that door at all hours of day or night and roam around without restrictions or inhibitions. Later it became a habit, one that I have kept to this
day, to open it at random and read a story here or there. I never studied the *Shahnameh* properly, and never thought of writing anything
scholarly about it, perhaps because I wanted to preserve the sense of
wonder that came over me when I first heard my father tell its stories.

Over a thousand years ago Ferdowsi composed a mythical tale of

Iran, partly woven out of snatches of history. His epic spanned from the creation of the world up to the Arab conquest in the seventh century, a most humiliating defeat that marked the end of the ancient Persian Empire and the shift of our religion from Zoroastrianism to Islam. Ferdowsi's aim was to rekindle his countrymen's pride in their past, and to restore their sense of dignity and heritage. Father kept reminding my brother and me that the history of our country was fraught with wars and conquests—the Persians fought with the Greeks, Romans, Arabs, Mongols—and, later, after the Islamic Revolution, he said we faced the worst conquerors of all because they were enemies from within, who nonetheless treated Iranian citizens like conquered subjects.

The Arabs were pervasive conquerors. The legend was that they insisted on an almost perfect annihilation of Persian culture, especially the written word. Fed up with the decadent rule of the Sassanid kings and their powerful priests—the last Sassanid king, Yazdegerd III, was murdered in 651 by a mill owner at whose home he had taken refuge—many Persians turned to embrace those whom they considered wild barbarians. I remember, as a child, hearing stories about how the Arab caliph Omar ordered his soldiers to burn all the books they found in Iran since the only book people would need was the Koran. My father taught us that much of Iranian nationalism was based on anti-Arab sentiment. He said, We Iranians are too worried about our good image and want to appear blameless in the eyes of the world. So, many of us blame the Arabs. Few question our own role in our defeat. After all, who opened the gates of the kingdom to those barbarians, who facilitated their conquest?

In his epic poem Ferdowsi sought to conserve and interrogate an irretrievable past, both celebrating and mourning the passing of a great civilization. He brought the old Persia* back to life, recasting its

---

* The name Iran, meaning the land of Aryans, has existed for centuries. The Greeks knew as Persia the region that was in ancient times the seat of the great Persian Empire. The British also referred to the region as Persia. In 1931 Reza Shah, the founder of the Pahlavi dynasty, officially changed the name to Iran.

mythology in the first part of the *Shahnameh* and its real history until the Arab conquest in the second, gathering the orphaned fragments of our culture and history and giving them a new home in his poetry. Ferdowsi's impossible achievement was not just to portray the biography of a whole nation, but to foretell the future. After the victory of the Islamic Revolution, I would return time and again to our poets—especially this poet—in order to trace the invisible thread that had led to the creation of the Islamic state.

As a child my favorite tale of all from the *Shahnameh* was that of the beautiful Rudabeh and her love affair with the white-haired warrior Zal. Father preferred the story of Feraydun and his three sons, a story that was as personal to him as Rudabeh's story was to me. It was as if through it he could convey something about himself that he could not otherwise properly articulate.

No matter how many times he told a favorite story, Father always got so caught up in it that I felt as if he were simultaneously saying and hearing the story for the first time. I can picture him once more, holding my hand as we walk the wide avenue called Shemiran, which stretches northward toward the snowcapped mountains whose silhouettes I have memorized and can summon up in my mind from wherever I am in the world, just as I can conjure up my father's stories.

Feraydun was the king of the world, he would begin, having saved mankind from the Arab-born demon-king Zahak, who with Satan's help had killed his father and conquered Persia. From Zahak's shoulders, on the spot that had been kissed by Satan, two vicious serpents sprouted who had to be fed every day the brains of two young Persian men. Feraydun staged an uprising against Zahak, and when he defeated him he kept Zahak in chains at the foot of Persia's highest mountain, Damavand.

Feraydun had three sons, Salm, Tur, and Iraj. As he grew old and the time came to divide his kingdom he decided to test their courage and he attacked each of them at night. The two older sons fled, but the youngest, Iraj, invoking his father's name, prepared to fight. Having learned what he wanted to know, Feraydun disappeared into the night.

Feraydun decided to divide his kingdom into three parts and distribute the parts among his sons. "Do you remember what he gave each of his sons?" Father would ask, turning toward me. "Yes," I would respond eagerly, trying to mimic his words: "To the oldest, Salm, he gave the West. To the middle son, Tur, he gave China and the land of the Turks. And to the youngest, Iraj, he gave Persia."

"Yes," my father would say with approval, "he gave to Iraj the most precious of his possessions: Persia, the land of the warriors."

The two older sons were envious of Iraj, because he had received the best land, and they nursed a jealous rage day and night. They sent a messenger to their father, demanding that he "snatch the crown" off Iraj's head and "give him some dark corner of the earth to live." Feraydun responded with anger, advising them,

> *the heart that's freed*
> *From gnawing passion and ambitious greed*
> *Looks on kings' treasures and the dust as one.*

When his father complained about his brothers' jealousy, Iraj responded:

> *Our lives pass from us like the wind, and why*
> *Should wise men grieve to know that they must die?*

My father loved this line and he usually repeated it, more to himself than to me.

Iraj decided to pay his brothers a visit and try to reason with them. But blinded by jealousy and greed, Salm and Tur did not heed Iraj's offer of peace. "You remember what Iraj told them," my father would say, turning to me and giving my hand a light squeeze. "He tells them not to kill him," I would say. "Not exactly," he would respond. "Iraj tells them, Don't make yourself murderers. Iraj pleaded with his brothers when their intention became clear: You have a soul yourself, Iraj told them—how can you take another's soul away? But his brothers did not hear him. Tur pulled out his dagger and split Iraj's body in two. Salm and Tur stuffed Iraj's head with camphor and musk and sent it to their father with a gleeful message, celebrating the fact that Iraj's royal line was no more."

For Father, the real hero of this story was not Feraydun, but Iraj. "You should remember that Iraj was one of the best men in the *Shahnameh*," he would tell me, breaking into his story again. "Iraj was ready to give up Iran not because he was afraid of fighting, but because he felt worldly goods were not worth causing rancor and divisiveness between brothers. He had not just physical courage but moral courage, which is much harder to obtain."

Later, when I reread Ferdowsi on my own, I understood why the first story my father chose to tell us from the *Shahnameh* was that of Iraj. He was one of the few characters who did not seek revenge. He was not only brave and just, but, more important, he was good.

My father had a weakness for goodness in the same way that my mother was fixated on correctness. When my brother was young, Father wrote a story for him and called it "The Man Who Wanted to Be Good." It was the story of my father's own life, of how he had always been obsessed with injustice and had tried to be a good man. All his life our father kept reminding us of our duty to be good, a term he assumed to be self-explanatory, though it was, of course, impossible to define.

"Iraj's brothers did not understand that the world can be equally cruel to the unjust. Iraj's wife, Mah Afrid, gave birth to a beautiful daughter who brought Iraj's grandson, Manuchehr, into the world. Manuchehr, in a mighty battle, beheaded first Tur and then Salm, whose head he put on a spear and sent to Feraydun with a message of victory," my father would say, giving me a sidelong glance to see how I was taking it.

When Feraydun heard that Iraj's death had been avenged, he abdicated his throne to Manuchehr and spent the rest of his days mourning his dead sons.

And so, heartbroken, weeping for the past,
He lived tormented till Death came at last.

O world, from end to end unreal, untrue,
No wise man can live happily in you—
But bless'd is he whose good deeds bring him fame;
Monarch or slave, he leaves a lasting name.

At this point I should have felt happy because the good guys had finally won, but almost every time my father told this story he added that while Iraj's name and legacy were restored, from that moment on the land of Iran saw no peace. "This is how the world gave birth to Iran," he concluded, "and the conflicts continue to this day. In the *Shahnameh,* the Iranians were mostly good men, followers of Iraj, courageous and just. I wish I could say the same for Iran today, for in actual fact our country is sometimes more the land of Salm and Tur than of Iraj." We would walk in silence for a while, until Father would say, "How about an ice cream?"

Ferdowsi's Iran was the magnificent paradise I came to believe in as a child. It was an endless green pasture, populated with heroes and queens. I was for some time under the illusion that my country was as splendid as the edifices its classical poets had built out of words.

Not just Damavand with its snowcapped peak, but all those mountains toward which my father and I walked almost every Friday during my childhood are forever associated in my mind with figures he conjured up. It never went away, that other world just behind the mountains, where Feraydun and his three sons, the White Demon, the legendary bird Simorgh, and the beautiful Rudabeh all lived side by side, reenacting the same tales over and over.

learning to lie

MANY YEARS AGO, A PSYCHIATRIST TOLD me that my problems could be traced to my brother Mohammad's birth. He said that this event, diverting my mother's attention from me, caused me to experience "death." He was a follower of the Melanie Klein school of psychiatry and I was rather irritated by the way Klein, like so many others, reduced everything to one component—in her case, death. How could we ever cure ourselves of death? Soon I started arguing with him, taking on Melanie Klein instead of focusing on my own problems.

All the same, my brother's birth must have been traumatic. I was not yet five, but I remember the night my mother was taken to the hospital. I was left behind with the housekeeper, whom my mother loved and revered and we all called Naneh. She had taken me to the front steps, where we sat until dawn, waiting for my father to come home with the news. Naneh had packed her bags, ready to leave if the new baby was a girl. She hated girls and for a year she had made me feel that hatred. She would go around the house saying, "A girl is like a candle in the daylight and a boy is a lamp at night." She refused to call me by my name, and referred to me as "girl." Mother was so devoted to her that she never paid attention to my complaints and always took Naneh's side.

I believed my mother loved Mohammad in a way she never loved me. Although she later denied it, she used to say that when he came into the world, she felt here was the son who would protect her. I was always amazed that my mother, who had suffered so much at the hands of men, could have such confidence in them.

From then on we were seldom alone or intimate. She resented what she called my stubbornness and I was hurt by the burden of her impositions. She froze me out, and I tried to remain impervious to her complaints.

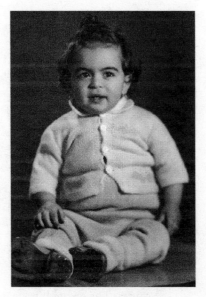

My baby brother, Mohammad.

I craved her approval, which she never gave. She praised my achievements, grades, and such, but I felt that I had in some indescribable way disappointed her. I wanted her to love me. I resisted her, but went out of my way to attract her attention. Once when I was barely seven I threw myself down a flight of stairs leading from the house to the backyard. Another time, not long after that, I heard her talk with a friend about someone who had committed suicide by slashing his wrists, so I tried to slash mine with my father's razor, in my own bedroom, in front of the mirror, when the detested Naneh walked in and, rather than stop me, left the room to call my mother. Unimpressed by my desperate act, Mother banished me to my room for the rest of the day.

I AM ABOUT FIVE, Mohammad is a few months old, and we have just moved to a new house. The windows are shaded and the room on the ground floor is cool, semidark, and very quiet. My mother sits me on the floor and places herself opposite me. Now, she says, tell me where you and your father went last Thursday. I say, We went to the movies. Who was with you? No one. She asks me the same question, again and again. She tells me how she hates liars. One thing, she says, one thing I have always tried to teach you is never,

never lie. I say I am not lying. I feel cold and frightened. I want her to hold me and kiss me, but she is frowning. She says people saw me with my father and a woman. Tell me, she says, tell me: Who was the woman?

Mohammad and me, when he was about two years old.

There was no woman. We had gone in secret to see one of my father's close friends who had recently married a woman my mother disliked. My mother had decided that she did not wish to interact with them anymore. But my father loved this friend, and continued to see him on the sly.

For a few days after this she would not talk to me. I remember that they were fighting for the first time in a new way. They would shout and didn't care about me or the servants overhearing. I listened at the doors. I listened to her hushed conversations with her friends, her conspiratorial telephone calls. The "woman" she suspected us of having seen was in fact married to my father's friend. This woman, Sima Khanoom, was very attractive, sexual in an obvious way that my mother never was. She had apparently been half-engaged to my father at one time and then, suddenly, while he was away on a business trip, she got engaged to and later married his best friend—it was Father's first real heartbreak. My mother, suspecting my father's secretary as a go-between, kept asking me about her too, and wanted to know whether I had ever been out with my father and Sima Khanoom.

I hear the venom in my mother's voice without understanding what it means. I am five. I don't know, even now, if I understood what this betrayal she had accused my father of entailed. What concerns me is their open quarrels, my mother's hostile glances, my father's absentminded patting of my hair and his stressed voice at night when he tells me bedtime stories. Then she suddenly picks up my brother and leaves home, leaving me with Father and the detested Naneh. I feel left out and neglected. My father is distracted and sometimes when he talks to me I feel as if he is talking to himself. Some days he takes me to his office, where I look at the wicked secretary with new eyes.

That, I think, is when I told Mother my first lie. It was a simple lie, but it took some ingenuity on my part. She was staying at a friend's house and I was there on a visit. There was no anger anymore. In a sense it was worse. She peppered me with questions, determined to gather evidence. Her questions were not direct, but sly. Every once in a while she and her friend exchanged glances. I felt miserably lonely and distant. Her attempt to drag things out of me, her conspiratorial glances, were more frightening than the direct accusations in that cold, dark room. I so much wanted her to be my mother again, to smile at me, to hold my hand, that I decided to lie and bring her back home. I invented a story about my father confronting Mrs. Jahangiri—his secretary—at the office, telling her he wanted her never to mention her friend again. Did she not realize that he only tolerated Sima Khanoom because of his friendship with her husband?

I⸺T IS AMAZING HOW we predict our own futures, especially in relation to others—how often we determine their behavior toward us. When my mother accused me of lying and of complicity with my father, I was innocent. But it would not be long before what she said became true. In a sense, she left us no choice. No amount of loyalty was ever enough. In reality she desired something we could not give her. She soon returned home, but nothing was ever the same again. I would go with my father to his friend's house, and later I would accompany him on his assignations. I became his most trusted accomplice, our relationship cemented by the mutual misery we felt we suffered at my mother's hands.

That first time she took me aside, that day has stayed with me. I did not resent her—I think I was too young for that. She never laid a hand on me, but I felt bruised all the same. I remember wanting so badly to cry. I didn't know how to defend myself and had a vague sense that I was somehow guilty. Also that if I admitted to what she wanted me to say, if I started to bad-mouth my father, saying, for example, that he had forced me to visit Sima Khanoom, I would be okay. But I didn't. Later I stopped listening to her—it became a practice. I simply pretended to listen and nodded and never heard a word. Her voice would come in and I would push it back and start a conversation with an imaginary friend, retelling the stories I had heard or read or making up new stories. I had found in my imagination one place where I could be the queen of my own vast and variable kingdom.

I AM ABOUT FIVE YEARS OLD. It is early evening. Father is just home from the office. He and my mother are arguing in the living room behind a closed door and I lurk in the hall but I know their argument is about me. My mother and I had an argument of our own earlier today. The devil that grown-ups often claim tempts children seemed to have taken residence in me, egging me on as I sat there on the swing and refused to go in for lunch when my mother told me to. I knew I was wrong and I knew I would pay for it, but I could not help myself.

I can still savor the taste of those few moments of disobedience as I leaned back on the swing and enjoyed the mild breeze on my face, swinging back and forth, back and forth. When I finally went in, washed my hands, and appeared at the lunch table, my mother was furious. She would not allow my playmate, our neighbor's son, to eat with me, although she had given permission before. She sent him home. Humiliated, I sat at the table and refused to eat. The more she insisted on my eating, the more unable I was to comply. I played with the spoon and the fork. I made shapes out of the bread. When I made for the door, she ordered me back and told me to go to my room. "Wait until your father comes home," she said, "and we will solve this problem once and for all, since your highness will not listen to me. Who am I to tell you what to do and not to do?"

All day I stayed in my room. I tried to make up stories to cheer my-self up: Once upon a time there was a girl who was unhappy . . . then what? Once upon a time . . . I soon gave up. Instead, I cried and cried and looked at my picture books.

When my father emerges from the living room, his face is full of thunder. But I can sense, as I always do on such occasions, that his heart is with me, that he is putting on this face in order to appease her. Why did you disobey your mother? he says. I say nothing. You must apologize, he says. Still I remain silent. Do as I tell you or you will be confined to the cellar. Mother does not appear but the door is ajar and I know she is listening. I say nothing. So he marshals me toward the stairs. I don't want a rebel in my home, he says loudly and a little lamely. After all your mother has done for you. . . . Why, he asks, why? On our way down the stairs his voice becomes softer, almost pleading. If you apologize, then that is another matter, he says quietly. Come on, Azi, be reasonable.

He knows how scared I am of the cellar. It is damp and dank, with very little light. We use it for storage, and during winter there is a rope from which the laundry is hung. On the far side is the coal cellar, where I imagine there is a presence, malignant and threatening, lying in wait for me. Father makes me stand there with my back to the coal cellar. I keep feeling that the creature is watching me while I have no power to see him. You will stay here until I come for you, he says. I stand frozen in place and some part of me registers his incomprehensible abandonment, as it will future instances of betrayal.

M Y BEST MEMORIES of my mother are of our wandering about the streets of Tehran. There is one street in particular that will always represent the Tehran I love and long to return to, even now as I sit at this desk in a city that has been far more generous to me, and, by the same token, is emptier of memories. As I remember it I am struck by the irrelevant fact that the name of that street is the same as my husband's last name: Naderi.

Most of my childhood seems to have been spent on Naderi Street and on the network of side streets that branched off from it. There was the piroshki store and the place for nuts and spices, the fish market, a perfume store called Jilla where my mother would buy Nina Ricci's

The intersection of Lalehzar Avenue and Istanbul Street, in the 1940s.

L'Air du Temps and where the shopkeeper always kept a few free samples for me (*échantillons* we called them: such things were always French). And the coffee shop, which had a foreign name (in a sudden leap of remembrance it comes to me: Aibeta), where Mother bought her chocolates. Of all the smells and fragrances of that enchanted street, what has remained most imprinted in my memory is that of chocolate, which we pronounced like the French, *chocolat*. There was a small chocolate factory next to the clinic where I got my vaccinations, and after each visit my mother would reward me with chocolates from the factory. That was where I first discovered white chocolate, which I loved not because it tasted better but because it was so unexpected.

Naderi Street changed into Istanbul, which branched off on the left to Lalehzar—Avenue of the Tulips. During the Qajar kings' rule in the late nineteenth century, this strip of land had been an immense tulip garden. The government cut a boulevard across the garden and turned it into one of the busiest business sections of Tehran, interspersed with theaters and movie houses. What a name for such a commercial street! Lalehzar was always filled with the smell of leather. My mother and I would step in and out of overcrowded lingerie shops, fabric stores, and purveyors of leather goods. In each place she exchanged pleasantries and gossiped with shopkeepers while I wandered around and peered into the back rooms, eager to catch a glimpse of those dim workshops where strips of fabrics and leather were transformed into bras, negligees, shoes, and bags.

Once a month we would make a trip to a toy store called Iran, on Naderi Street, which my mother thought was the best toy store in Tehran. She selected a new toy or a doll for me, which would then be locked in the closet back home with the other toys. I remember vividly the neon sign above the door of the toy store: a big, jolly Santa Claus, driving his reindeer. This did not surprise us, nor did the names of so many of the restaurants and movie houses: Riviera, Niagara, Rex, Metropole, Radio City, Moulin Rouge, Chattanooga. For me Santa Claus was as familiar as Iran; we called him Baba Noel. We accepted all this as part of modern Iran—"modern" being another adopted foreign word. My father, with a hint of sarcasm, used to call it the surprising flexibility of the Persian language, which he likened to the unfortunate flexibility of its people. But how flexible were we really, and what price would we pay for all this flexibility?

On Naderi Street and in the surrounding area, most shopkeepers were either Armenian, Jewish, or Azeri. Many Armenians were forcibly removed to Iran in the sixteenth century, during the reign of the powerful Safavid king Shah Abbas. Some Armenians and Jews migrated from Russia after the revolution; some came from Poland and other Soviet satellites after the Second World War. Just as it was natural to buy sweets and ice cream from Armenian shopkeepers, or fabrics and perfume from Jewish stores, it was also natural for some families to shun the minorities because they were "unclean." The children knocked on their doors, singing "Armenian, the Armenian dog, the sweeper of hell." The Jews were not just dirty, they drank innocent children's blood. Zoroastrians were fire worshippers and infidels, while the Baha'is, a breakaway Islamic sect, were not just heretics but British agents and spies who could and should be killed. Mother was hardly touched by these matters; despite a vast array of other prejudices, she obeyed the rules of her own universe, where people were judged mainly by the degree to which they acknowledged her mores and fantasies. Most people seemed to accept their place in the stratified scheme of things, although every once in a while tensions erupted to the surface, until the bloody nature of this hidden discord was fully revealed several decades later, after the Islamic Revolution, in 1979, when the Islamists attacked, jailed, and murdered many Armenians, Jews, and Baha'is and forced restaurants to carry signs on their windows announcing "religious minority" if their owners were not Muslims. But we cannot blame everything on the Islamic Republic, because in some ways it simply brought into the open and magnified a preexisting bigotry.

On Thursday nights—the start of our weekend—I roamed the same streets with my father. We usually paid a visit to the huge deli next door to the leather shops, where we would pick up sausages and sometimes ham or mortadella for our special Friday morning breakfast. Afterward, we strolled around in search of a film or a play. The sights and sounds of those streets changed at night. All across Naderi, Istanbul, and Lalehzar were a number of restaurants, theaters, movie houses, and Persian-style cabarets, each with its own special clientele that varied in class and cultural background. The one we frequented most was Café Naderi, run by an Armenian. It had a beautiful garden, and in summer there was always music and dancing in the garden. That was one place my parents took us to frequently, even as small children. I don't ever remember my parents dancing, although at times my mother would remind us of what a perfect dancer she used to be. But sometimes I and other children joined the grown-ups onstage, moving to the music of the cha-cha or of slower dances like the tango.

A few blocks away there was a more traditional café whose name I have forgotten; its clientele was mainly men, and the music was Persian, sometimes Azeri or Arabic, far more erotic than the cha-cha or tango of the Café Naderi. This café and others like it were always full, serving mainly beer and vodka with kabob. Men who frequented them were devotees of certain favorite female singers, some of whom became legendary in their own right, their images now beckoning to us from YouTube, reminders of a vanquished but not vanished past. Yet a few streets southward there was another Tehran—religious, pious, and resentful of what it perceived as excesses of a heathen culture.

The enticing cacophony of the street would gradually fade into the quiet drone of my father's voice, as he told me one of his tales. I was taken to that other world where Ferdowsi's heroes and demons, his raven-haired heroines, lived alongside the naughty Pinocchio, Tom Sawyer, La Fontaine's animals, and Hans Christian Andersen's poor little match girl, whose specter still lives after so many years because I could never accept that all her pain and suffering on earth would be rewarded only by death.

Once, when I was about four years old, I lost my mother on the way back from my ballet class. We paused by different shops and somehow, during one stop, I walked on and when I turned around she was gone. I continued to walk, crying quietly. I knew the street well, each shop a bread crumb leading me to safety: the toy shop, the chocolate shop, the fishmonger, the shoe shops, the movie houses, the jewelry stores, until I reached my favorite place of all, the pastry shop, called Noushin. I loved everything about Noushin, especially its chocolate-covered ice cream, which was called Vita Crème. Every time we entered the shop, we were greeted by the jolly Armenian owner, who liked to tease me by saying that he had his eye on me as a future bride for his son. This time, before he had a chance to greet me, I blurted out that I had lost my mother and started to cry. He tried to calm me and offered me a free Vita Crème, but I was a polite girl and never accepted anything without my parents' permission, and anyway I was too frightened to want even ice cream.

The expression of anxiety in my mother's eyes canceled the excitement in her voice as she sighed my nickname: "Azi!" I will never forget that look of panic because, over the next decades, it would return in the context of much smaller incidents: when my brother or I stayed out a little late, when Father did not call exactly on time, or we were not home when she returned from a party. Later, her grandchildren were subjected to the same anticipation of tragedy, which I unconsciously internalized and made my own.

After the revolution, when I went back to Tehran, one of my first pilgrimages was to those streets. I felt as if I had stepped into the pages of Ferdowsi's *Shahnameh*—one of those recurring scenes in which the protagonist, anticipating a hospitable feast, finds himself instead in a witch's snare. I could never have imagined in my wildest dreams that one day Naderi and Lalehzar would become the scenes of bloody demonstrations and that I would find myself running away from the militia and vigilantes, past the toy shop, the chocolate shop, the nut and spice shops, the corpse of the cinema where I saw my first film, with no time to pause for reminiscences.

coffee hour

OVER THE YEARS, EVER SINCE I can remember, my mother invited a medley of people to our house in Tehran, sometimes to eat at her table but more often just for coffee and pastries. She had several collections of cups, which she chose according to the occasion: solid colors with thicker rims for intimate friends and family, and more delicate ones—cream with floral designs, or white porcelain with golden rims—for more formal events. Journalists, society types, taxi drivers, her hairdresser—all were ushered in at different times of the day as Mother presided with majesty over her small coffeemaker. Discussions would vary according to the company in a ritual that mesmerized me as I sat in a corner of the room, watching my mother deliver coffee to everyone present, including me. Later she served my children when they were as young as four, dismissing my vehement protests with a shrug. "*Please, please,*" she would say. "Don't *you* teach me how to feed the children." She would then turn to my amused offspring with coffee, which they did not like, and chocolate, which they did, and say, "Don't listen to your mother. Go on, go on. Drink your coffee and eat your chocolate."

As a child I lurked in the background, sometimes playing with my paper dolls, later amusing myself with a book or magazine. On days when Mother was pleased with me, every once in a while she would throw a smile my way, or offer up a pastry, telling me how unnatural it was for a young girl to spend her time reading. Even when I was in her ill graces I was not banished from these sessions. In fact, I think she took a certain pleasure in having me there. Her anger was of the type that needed a constant audience. It thrived on demonstration.

At least twice a week she invited her female friends over around

Mother and me,
at a relative's wedding.

ten o'clock to share gossip, stories, and fortune-telling. Being a day person, she crammed as much social activity into her mornings as possible. In these forums there was little trace of the dictator I knew. Mother's coffee sessions had a carnivalesque aura about them, as if all assembled had gathered to reveal momentous secrets. "She can't actually be sleeping with him?" "Does *she* really deserve to marry so well?" "How could men be at once so cruel and so stupid?" It was all in the tone: a spouse's vicissitudes, a nasty divorce, news of a death, was shared in a way that made the pain and scandal seem remote, or at least conquerable. At times they would throw warning glances in my direction and lower their voices. One, pointing to me, would repeat a Persian proverb—Let's not forget that the walls have mice and little mice have ears—signaling that they should be careful what they said in front of me.

Some of the sharpest memories I have of my mother are of her knitting. She and Monir joon, a friend and former neighbor, would exchange gossip and patterns in the same breath and with equal zest. She would knit in all seasons, even in summer, though the results of these endeavors were always uncertain. She seldom followed patterns, preferring to choose her own colors and invent her own designs, which added to the unpredictability of the results.

My mother's hairdresser, a young divorcée called Goli, was often part of this entourage. One of her functions was fortune-telling, a skill

Mother dabbled in. When the coffee had been drunk, the women would turn their cups down—toward the heart—and leave them in the saucers until the grounds began to dry. Goli picked each up in turn and, with immense concentration, she transformed the lines and swirls formed by the coffee grounds into amazing tales of past, present, and future woes and conquests. She had a square-shaped face, big eyes, and thin lips; as she turned the coffee cup in her hand she had a way of pursing her lips that made them disappear into the flesh around her mouth. I liked to watch this disappearing act, waiting for her lips to return.

My glance rapidly passes over Monir joon, a thin spinster with a sharp nose, blue eyes, and faded, frizzy red hair who speaks in short, clipped sentences. I see the indolent, overweight Fakhri joon, herself a remarkable fortune-teller, who would turn and turn the coffee cup between her plump hands with their surprisingly long fingers, and the pious Shirin Khanoom, whose presence usually provoked hostility, as few could abide her self-righteous pronouncements. I want to pause on my aunt Mina, who always chose a chair in the least conspicuous place and seldom offered up a comment. Usually, when the others left, she would stay behind for lunch. My brother and I called our parents' close friends and relatives aunt or uncle, but Aunt Mina was the most special, "The *real* sister I never had," Mother would say. As it happened, she did have a real sister—at least a half sister, Nafiseh—with whom she carried on a precarious love-hate relationship.

Aunt Mina and my mother had been classmates at Jeanne d'Arc, one of the few schools for girls in Tehran, managed by French nuns. They were both top students, and fiercely competitive. This, over time, morphed into a begrudging respect; they started to study together and became inseparable friends. For many years, until they had a falling-out, we would see Aunt Mina almost every day. Dinner was either at her house or ours, and on most weekends and holidays we planned shared activities.

Aunt Mina was slightly overweight, making the rest of her body incongruent with her legs, which were elegant and slim. Mostly she kept her hair long, neatly gathered at the back of her neck in a bun or a French roll. But none of this makes tangible the aura she created around her. She seemed as if she were constantly recoiling from unexpected blows. As a child she lost both her parents and was taken in, with her sister and two brothers, by an older uncle, a formidable politician who had been an influential ambassador to Russia and who had two daughters of his own. Every once in a while my mother

Mother (front, center) in her school picture. Ozra Khanoom is seated behind her, in a white sweater. Mother was sent to school without the proper covering for the photo, and she had to borrow a jacket from the girl at the end of her row.

would say, with sympathy, that Mina was plagued by bad luck. Her cousins went to university and became prominent academics, but she was unable to pursue her education beyond high school. At the time, she had no money. She was married off to a man much like her uncle: ambitious, inflexible, and unapproachable. What he lacked was her uncle's stamina and that ineffable quality that goes by the name of backbone. Two of her siblings—her older sister and brother—died very young, in their early twenties, and the third died twenty years later of a heart attack. With her younger brother's death, Aunt Mina inherited everything. Only by then it was too late.

Aunt Mina's husband's ambitions were only half realized and, perhaps because of this, he chose to exercise his authority at home. My mother admired him a great deal and, despite his condescending manner toward my father, hung on his every pronouncement, an attitude that did not escape Aunt Mina, who would mock Mother's sympathies for authoritative men. "Nezhat is blind to their weaknesses," she would say. Personally, I disliked him because he had far too great a liking for me. Whenever he found me alone, taking an afternoon nap or talking on the phone to a friend in the hall, he tried to embrace me and tell me what a wonderful girl I was and how much he liked me. I could not complain about his attentions to my parents; I merely tried to avoid him. At times I felt a strange satisfaction in knowing how wrong my mother was in her admiration for him.

Years later, this strong authority figure would one morning go to the garage, put a gun to his head, and kill himself. In the note he left behind for his startled wife and children he explained that he could no longer tolerate the burden of their financial difficulties. He had in his last years come to rely on my father and confide in him. After his death it was my father who took care of the funeral arrangements and tried to use his influence as mayor to keep the suicide out of the papers.

Despite her orphaned state, Aunt Mina had a better childhood than Mother, whose own mother died when she was quite young, leaving her at the mercy of the capricious will of her stepmother and the careless attentions of a father who confused discipline with affection. While her half siblings lived in great comfort and luxury, Mother was relegated to an attic room and made to brush her teeth with soap and water. What made life intolerable for her was being treated like a poor relative in her own home. The only way she could cope with her deep resentment and bitterness against her family was to develop an inordinate sense of pride. Aunt Mina once told me that she and my mother shared her books (my grandfather forgot to give Mother money for them) and they got into a habit of studying together. "That is how we became so close," she said. "Nezhat was always first in the class, she was so competitive. She couldn't compete with others in terms of clothes or things. The only area in which she could compete—and one at which she excelled—was her studies, especially mathematics." While her siblings were sent abroad to study, Mother was forced to stop her schooling after high school.

"I wanted to be a doctor," my mother would say. "I was the most brilliant pupil in class, and the most promising." Time and again Mother reminded my brother and me of how she had sacrificed her career to stay at home. She seemed to pride herself on the fact that I was not a "housewife type," and when I married boasted to my husband that I couldn't even make my own bed. "My daughter," she announced on their first meeting, "was brought up to be an educated woman, not a drudge." But she never stopped reproaching me for working and not spending more time at home with my children.

After Mother's death I was surprised to learn from the same Austrian lady who had been present at her wedding that my mother had worked for a while as a bank clerk. The Austrian lady told me how impressed she had been with my mother, who seemed to be so unlike other women of her class. Nezhat was intelligent, eloquent, spoke fluent French, and most impressive of all, she worked in a bank. In those days if girls from her background worked it was mainly as a teacher, sometimes as a doctor. Apparently, after Saifi's death, my mother, unwilling to be solely dependent on her father and hated stepmother, had chosen to work. But she who so proudly talked of her ambitions to be a doctor, and her desire for independence, never once mentioned this. Instead, time and again she talked about how a family friend, Mr. Khosh Kish, who later became head of Iran's Central Bank, was one of her ardent suitors and admirers.

I think my mother's constant restlessness was partly due to a sense of deep homelessness. Not just because she was never made to feel at home, but also because she belonged neither to the category of women who were content to stay at home, nor to that of career women. Like many women of her time she was an in-between woman who felt that her capabilities and aspirations were stifled by her condition. When she told us stories about her grades and the bright future her teachers predicted for her, she would often end up shaking her head and saying, "If only I were a man!" The Alice James syndrome, I would call it, thinking of Henry James's intelligent and sickly sister—her capabilities and aspirations were far ahead of her actual condition.

Aunt Mina was brilliant too. She didn't have the means to continue her studies, so instead she married; "another intelligent woman gone to waste." Aunt Mina never raised her voice, laughed loudly, or displayed emotions. Unlike my mother, she did not pick fights or engage in open rebellion. She withdrew even from those closest to her, as if to hide something precious from a world that had denied her so much. She chose her outlets deliberately: she gambled obsessively, and she smoked. Mother, who boasted that she enjoyed both but had chosen to abstain because they were wrong (although she did dabble in the occasional game of gin rummy), engaged in an ongoing crusade to make her friend give up these vices. Aunt Mina would smile her ironic half smile and say, "I'm not a masochist like you, Nezhat." She was a little irritated when Mother sided with Mahbod, Aunt Mina's husband, in these matters. She avoided open confrontations and went her own way, even if it meant hiding her actions from the two people who were closest: her husband and her best friend.

A bond grew between my father and Aunt Mina, based on common concerns and common resentments. Yet Father could not lure her with his charm. "Ahmad Khan, I am not one of those women you would want to win over!" she would say. She liked him very much and later she too would turn to him for support, but she never gave much heed to his complaints.

As I was growing up, Mother repeated time and again how in "those days" the popular wisdom had been that only girls who were not marriageable continued their education. Educated women were considered ugly and were generally picked on. Some families claimed that reading and writing would "open a girl's eyes and ears" and turn her into a "loose woman." My grandfather was progressive enough not to heed such nonsense. Mother's younger half sister, Nafiseh, was sent to America to study, but Mother herself was never offered such an opportunity. "I had no one to defend me," she would say, "no mother who cared about what happened to me." Mother and Aunt Mina never got over their unrealized potentials, what Emily Dickinson called "a dim capacity for wings." Perhaps this is what made them stay together for so many years, despite their enormous differences in temperament and despite the fact that, in some respects, they very much disapproved of or, more accurately, could not tolerate each other.

Mother liked to make a scene. She prided herself on being "completely frank and open." Sometimes, in utter frustration, she would call Aunt Mina sly. "It appears to be part of Mina's nature," she would say, "for her to hide things. She knows how much I value honesty, and yet she lies or simply won't tell me the truth." "Your mother has her head in the clouds, she has no idea how to live her life," Aunt Mina would say. "This woman is an idealist through and through. She's as naïve as a two-year-old child."

Aunt Mina had no patience for my mother's indulgent recollections of her more perfect first husband. "To think of how Saifi treated me," Mother would say, "from that very first moment he had eyes for no one but me. And now . . ." her voice trailed off. "And now what?" Aunt Mina would snap back with a half-ironic, half-indulgent smile. "Now you have a good husband and two healthy, wonderful children. Nezhat, will you forever live with your head in the clouds?"

EVERY FRIDAY A DIFFERENT kind of crowd gathered in our living room. These were more serious affairs. Guests usually began to convene in the late morning, and these sessions were presided over by both my parents. The numbers varied, but some people were fixtures. Aunt Mina sometimes attended but seldom spoke. I think she came partly out of curiosity, and partly out of loyalty. Every once in a while she would drop a word or two, usually to oppose and contradict a statement or claim.

I remember Mr. Khalighi, a colleague of my father's in the civil service, his senior both in rank and years. He had watched Father rise while he himself remained in the same position, as a minor government functionary, until his retirement. I believe they had met when Father was a director at the Ministry of Finance and kept their friendship when Father moved on to become the deputy head of the Planning and Budget Organization. He celebrated my father's public successes with a rare generosity of spirit. Mr. Khalighi was in the habit of writing humorous bits of poetry for different occasions, which he insisted on reading aloud whenever he visited us. He usually came earlier than the others and seldom missed a session. It seemed to me that he never aged—he just gradually shrank and shriveled until one day he disappeared and I was told that he had died.

Another fixture of those Friday sessions was an army colonel who retired early because he wanted to enjoy life. He was good-looking in an old-fashioned movie-star way, with a Clark Gable mustache, which he dyed black along with his hair. Unlike Mr. Khalighi, the colonel was usually silent, a permanent smile lurking under his mustache. He listened to the sometimes heated arguments without much apparent interest in participating.

Shirin Khanoom, the colonel's wife, started coming too, first to make sure the colonel wasn't off with some "slut," as she put it, and later because she was engaged by the discussions. Unlike her husband, she took a strong interest in all the discussions. She was a big woman—big boned, as they say—much larger than her husband. She had a low voice, and every time she spoke it seemed to boom, perhaps because, burdened with such an overflow of energy and personality, her large body could not contain her urges and demands. The colonel was not well-off and Shirin Khanoom had to work. She had a sewing school, where she bullied the poor young women who came to her to learn a craft and make a living. Some doubled as her maids, though as far as I know they were never paid for this honor. Shirin Khanoom and Aunt Mina did not like each other and, both being frank in their own way, took little trouble to hide their feelings.

There were always a few young ambitious men in attendance on Fridays, distant relatives hoping to cultivate high connections and former functionaries who had fallen from grace. All of this mixing of have-beens and not-yet-arriveds made Shirin Khanoom uncomfortable. She mistrusted everyone and claimed that Mother was too kind, too unsuspecting of other people's evil intentions. Loafers, she called them, with a finality that even my mother did not challenge. "Nezhat Khanoom," she would say, "has too good a heart. Trouble," she added knowingly, "is what she is asking for."

family ties

For years my father worked on his memoirs. The first draft was interspersed with anecdotes about his childhood. He described how his four-year-old sister was killed while resisting a man who was tearing a pair of gold earrings off her ears. To stifle her cries, the man knifed her. This event led my father, at a young age, to rebel against the basic injustice of life. It was a heartbreaking story, told poignantly, but when it came time to publish his memoirs he was advised to delete the personal parts—after all, what is important about a life is not the murder of your sister but what great deeds you have achieved in the public domain. When, later, I read his book, which was published in the nineties, I noticed how empty and contrived it seemed without those personal stories. The book, filled with important political developments, is devoid of the voice that dominates his unpublished memoirs. It gives much information about his political career but few of his deeper insights.

I so regret not having paid more attention to my father's memoirs when he was alive. He gave me an early draft after the revolution. At the time I mainly ignored it, feeling a slight condescension toward his literary efforts. It was only after his death, when my brother sent me his diaries and copies of the original manuscript, that I realized how much I had missed. In his unpublished manuscript he is surprisingly frank about the vagaries of his upbringing, including his sexual dalliance at the age of eight with the neighbor's daughter. Later, he unabashedly recounts his many flirtations with women who, despite social and religious restrictions, were open in their urges and desires.

The book begins with a genealogy tracing the family back six hundred years to Ibn-Nafis, a physician, a man of knowledge, a hakim. For fourteen generations the men in the family were physicians trained in philosophy and literature, some of whom wrote important treatises. My father gives a detailed account of our various ancestors' accomplishments in the realms of science and literature. (When I first started to teach at the University of Tehran he suggested that a portrait of Ibn-Nafis hanging on the wall at the Faculty of Law and Political Science should remind me of my own difficult task as a teacher and a writer.) I never knew quite what to do with these distinguished ancestors. My brother and I belonged to a generation that shrugged off the past and considered ancestry more of a burden and cause for embarrassment than a point of privilege. Only after the revolution did my family's past suddenly become important to me. If the present was fragile and fickle, then the past could become a surrogate home.

My paternal grandfather,
Abdol Mehdi Nafisi.

My father's father, Abdol Mehdi, was a doctor who displayed no political or worldly ambitions. Family lore had it that upon the death of his first patient he gave up his practice, tried to teach for a while, and then made a disastrous choice: he went into trade. He was said to be a good doctor and a terrible businessman, and barely made enough to support his large family. He married a young girl, my grandmother, from a strict religious background who was nine at the time and gave birth to her first child at the age of thirteen.

Abdol Mehdi was a stern man. His somber attitude toward the world seems to have been shaped by his unrelenting demands on himself. In a photograph I have of him he is withdrawn and impenetrable: a man who will reveal nothing of himself to the world. Father's family were Shaykhis, members of a dissident sect that challenged the orthodox Shiism, Iran's official religion. My grandfather was the group's intellectual mentor in Esfahan. His connection to the sect marginalized the family, which as a result shaped itself into a tight-knit and seemingly self-sufficient intellectual community, fostering the illusion that through this they would be immune to the decadence and wiles of the outside world.

My grandfather's Esfahan was an austere place, full of fear and pent-up emotions, but in his unpublished manuscript my father unveils another Esfahan, with a pageant of surprising sexual transgressions. A high official sleeps between his two beautiful wives; another seduces young boys, including my father, taking them swimming in his garden. Father pauses here to digress on the impact of sexual deprivation in Iran, especially among young men, which, as he sees it, ultimately leads to pedophilia.

He describes with affection the colorful religious festivals, especially that of Muharram, when the Shia Muslims mourn the martyrdom of Imam Hussein at Karballa in Iraq. During these rituals, people would crowd the streets to watch the processions, those hundreds, perhaps thousands, of men parading through the streets, flagellating their backs with thin chains in empathy with the martyred Imam and his followers. Some wore black shirts with slits on the back where the chains had come down. Others wore white shrouds. It was one of the rare times when men and women could mix and mingle in public without fear of punishment. Mourning a man who has been dead over thirteen hundred years may seem an unlikely forum for the expression of aborted desires, but everyone crowded the streets to watch the ceremonies and theatrical reenactments of the martyrdom of Hussein. Father's cousin Yusuf insisted that this was the best time to flirt with girls, and regaled my father with tales of conquest, sometimes no more than a stolen touch of hands. Until the early years of the twentieth century, my father would tell us, the clerics were guardians not just of religion and morality but also of our senses and private lives.

How could we foresee, he would ask, what would happen when other sights, sounds, smells, and tastes, when wine and restaurants, dance and foreign music and open relations between the sexes, came to compete with and even overtake the old rituals and traditions?

My paternal grandmother, talking with Uncle Hassan, in the 1980s.

In his manuscript, Father describes those who populated his world—his shy and kind young mother, who seldom looked her own children in the eye; his fanatical uncle, constantly trying to save his wayward nephew from the fires of hell; the pious pedophiles who preached modesty in public and molested their own nephews and nieces in secret. What amazes me now is not so much that a city like Esfahan contained so many contradictions—what city doesn't?—nor even the hypocrisy of religious fanatics, but the fact that my father seriously contemplated publishing these stories. It took a certain courage—or innocence, call it what you will—for a public man of his generation to wish to expose himself in this manner.

Had my mother paid more attention to my father's stories, she might have found in him some of what she yearned for. His life seemed to me far more romantic than what I knew of Saifi's. Father was the rebel in that large family. His older brother, Abu Torab, brilliant and much indulged by his parents, went into the medical profession, married appropriately, and loved his wife, Batoul, a good pious woman from his mother's side of the family. My father was the second child, caught between Abu Torab and Karim, who was obedient and obsequious as a child, and who grew up to be the most devout and inflexible of the nine children. My father was the wayward son, endlessly punished for small transgressions. In his unpublished memoirs he describes rebelling against his ultrareligious uncle, his strict teacher, even his father, and later against the government. He some-how came to associate a good conscience with rebellion. He told us that when he decided to leave Esfahan, at age eighteen, he was tired of the closed society there and of his father's narrow teachings. He wrote to his fanatically religious uncle that he could not believe in a God who allowed only the few hundred Shaykhi Muslims into heaven. Nor did he want to marry a woman in an arranged marriage. Perhaps his views of marriage developed when he tried to reconcile his puritani-cal religious upbringing with his own more romantic aspirations. His parents had already found a "suitable" wife for him. He refused to consider her and later she married his younger brother.

Ironically, it was thanks to my mother's father, Loghman, that my father's life was radically transformed. My paternal and maternal grandfathers were second cousins and had the same last name. Logh-man Nafisi visited Esfahan as the head of a special governmental agency on official business. At the time, Father was working in his fa-ther's shop and the family was going through a period of financial dif-ficulties. Impressed by my father's intelligence and energy, my grandfather encouraged him to apply for a job at the local branch of his agency. Unlike my paternal grandfather, Loghman was a sociable man, if temperamental, wealthy, and ambitious, with a beautiful young wife. He gambled and drank but considered himself a devout Muslim who paid his religious dues and performed his prayers. His way of life must have presented a welcome alternative to the sober and ascetic life in Esfahan. Father took his advice, much to his own fa-ther's displeasure. It wasn't long before he was persuaded by his col-leagues that his future lay not in Esfahan, but in Tehran. Father applied for a transfer, hoping both to work and to continue his studies in Tehran. At eighteen he left home, against the wishes of his parents, with no money, rejecting a safe way of life and not knowing what he would find to take its place.

In Tehran he lived at first with his mother's aunt. He worked full time to support himself and taught himself both French and English. He studied at nights, pushing himself to the edge of his physical ca-pacity. To stay awake, he would sometimes sit in a shallow pool in his aunt's house, holding the book up high, reading by the dim light in the yard. Eventually Loghman invited him to his house. But that was not where he courted my mother. After Saifi's death, Mother left Saifi's father's house but, feeling unwelcomed by her stepmother, she moved in with some relatives, a childless couple who adopted her. It was in their house that my father first met my mother. He was taken by her beauty and her sadness, and perhaps by the potential that a match between them might offer a young and ambitious man such as himself.

Both families were unhappy about my mother and father's decision to marry. His parents had hoped for a more traditional girl and Loghman, who could be unpredictable, also opposed the match—perhaps on account of his wife, or perhaps he did not consider a penniless cousin the best match for his daughter. In the end he refused to attend the ceremony, which was held at the house of Ameh Turi, the relative who had introduced them.

Father's brother Abu Torab sent a telegram from Esfahan saying that their father had consulted the Koran about the wedding and the answer had come back against the marriage. My uncle added that, despite this, their family would be content with whatever decision Father reached and they gave him their blessings. The telegram arrived on the day of the wedding. For the marriage to be legal, the bride's father had to give his written consent, and since they could not get Loghman's signature, my father pretended that the telegram—also signed by a Nafisi—was from Loghman. And so their life together started with a lie.

the holy man

HAJI AGHA GHASSEM WAS SO holy that his name was a testament to his zeal. Everyone in Esfahan knew him as Haji Agha, an honorific bestowed on those who have made the pilgrimage to Mecca. He was a distant relative, a close associate of my father's uncle in the city of Shiraz. Ascetic and thin, like a scholar, he had a way of talking that seemed to impart meaning to the most insignificant utterance. He stated things with finality and with some contempt for his interlocutor. He was not an intellectual like my many uncles who analyzed Islam and sought to relate their faith to philosophy and life. Haji Agha had no time for recondite knowledge and reserved his energy for frequent terse pronouncements: There is to be no music at home. Baha'is are the spawn of the devil. The Constitutional Revolution was a British plot.

Thin-lipped, with a slight stubble (a staple of pious Muslim men), he wore muddy brown suits with a white shirt that buttoned up to the neck. He disapproved of my father and never looked my mother in the eye, another mark of piety. Once, when we went to the bazaar with him and my cousins saw some silver spoons they wanted to buy, he sternly reminded them that to eat from silver is banned in Islam. Despite his extreme piety he seemed—perhaps was—deceptively sweet.

I can picture him now as he was when we first met him on one of our visits to Esfahan. He speaks to Mother about religion, about Fatimah, the Prophet's daughter, her obedience to her father and husband, her tragic death at the age of eighteen, and her modesty. You will agree, he says softly but with finality, that modesty does not prevent a woman from being useful, or important. A woman's duty

The Mother's King madrasa, Esfahan.

is sacred in Islam. My mother is surprisingly receptive. It is the mixture of attentiveness and inflexibility that appeals to her—that and a stifled urge to spite my father, who cannot help but show his disdain for such nonsense. She agrees with Haji Agha: no one appreciates the burden of a wife's responsibilities these days—especially not her children. Not your children, I hope, he says with ingratiating concern. She shakes her head. At the time I was six, my brother one, yet already she foresaw a bleak future.

My father cynically teases Haji Agha. If religion is about the love of mankind, then why are Jews, Christians, Zoroastrians, Baha'is, Buddhists—even atheists, for that matter—why are they considered unclean? Is it really true that we Shaykhis are the only ones who will be allowed in heaven? He is almost childish in the way he goads the pious man. But he cannot shake him. My younger uncles chime in, while Mother tries to silence Father with her eyes. Before we leave Esfahan, to my father's surprise, she invites Haji Agha to stay at our house the following month, when he will be in Tehran for business.

W HEN I WAS A SMALL CHILD, Esfahan loomed large in my imagination. Even now I remember its wide and dusty tree-lined streets and the magnificent filigreed bridges over the Zayandeh Rood—the River of Birth, as it is known. Esfahan was once the capital of the Safavid dynasty and the home of its most powerful ruler, Shah Abbas, who built magnificent monuments, mosques, and bridges, and the wide leafy avenues for which the city is still famous. A testament to Safavid power and glory, the city was known as Esfahan, Half of the World. It was the Safavids, to distinguish themselves from the Ottoman foe, who decided in the sixteenth century to change Iran's official religion from Sunni to Shia.

Esfahan was as different from Tehran as my father's side of the family was from my mother's. In Esfahan, layers of the ancient past existed side by side in a sort of asymmetrical harmony: ruins of a Zoroastrian temple, the perfect blue dome of a mosque, monument to the glorious Safavid kings. Unlike Tabriz, Shiraz, or Hamedan, Tehran could boast of little history. It was a small village known for its fruit orchards and fierce citizens until the founder of the Qajar dynasty, Agha Mohammad Khan, chose it for his capital in the eighteenth century. Tehran had little memory of ancient conquests or defeats and was only developed into a modern city in our time by Reza Shah Pahlavi and his son Mohammad Reza. Tehran was free of the weighty magnificence of Esfahan, creating the illusion that because it had no past to compete with, it could be transformed according to anyone's imagination. It played the reckless rogue to Esfahan's austere beauty.

Six of my father's seven brothers lived in Esfahan (his one sister was in Shiraz). We were closest to Abu Torab, who had nine children, five sons and four daughters, and we moved back and forth from his house to my grandmother's small house, with its grapevines and pomegranate trees. I had no memory of Grandfather, who died in 1948. I remember a blue-tiled fountain in my uncle's cool basement where, in summer, we were forced to take afternoon naps.

My father's family indulged in an elaborate asceticism, as intimidating in its own way as my mother's family's insistence on manners and social prestige. My mother was never completely accepted by my father's family, who had a way of being meek and hospitable while remaining aloof. She was not treated badly—in fact, she was accorded a great deal of courtesy—but there was no escaping their silent disapproval. She, in turn, treated them with dutiful condescension. She entered their domain a little gingerly, and with some defiance.

You share the same rotten genes, my mother liked to remind Mohammad and me when she was displeased with us, or with Father. And in Esfahan it was obvious which genes we had chosen to identify with. The sheer number of uncles and cousins—it was not unusual for twenty to be at any given lunch or dinner—diminished her authority. Over time my mother's visits to Esfahan became increasingly rare while ours, despite her protests, grew more frequent.

I AM SIX YEARS OLD when Haji Agha Ghassem first visits us in Tehran. He follows me around the house with his eyes. You have to excuse my insolence, he says, cautiously and politely to my mother, but I think of you as my own sister. My mother smiles obligingly, handing him a cup of Turkish coffee. This child, he says, turning to me, is at a dangerous age and many are not like us, God-fearing men. I see you have men servants about, and perhaps this child, he says, should wear more modest clothes, to cover herself.

My mother is visibly surprised. Had it been anyone else she would not have tolerated such conduct, but she tells Haji Agha not to worry, to rest assured that the first thing she taught me was how to look out for myself ("Be careful of strange men. Don't let them touch you. Ever"). My parents are both on their best behavior. Father, as host, maintains a polite attitude punctuated by an occasional sardonic glance as Haji Agha serenely utters his pronouncements. Mother is surprisingly docile. "I like a person who is honest about what he is," she tells my father that evening over dinner. "I wish everyone were as firm in their beliefs." She mistakes inflexibility for strength, and confuses zeal with principle. Even Abu Torab, deeply religious but with a scientific turn of mind, does not meet with her complete approval.

He stands behind me as I am trying to do my homework and bends down to look at my notebook. What are you writing? he asks, and as he reaches down and picks up the book he rearranges my skirt, his hands casually brushing my thigh.

That night my parents go to a party. Haji Agha retires to his room early. My one-year-old brother is sleeping in Naneh's room and I, as is my habit when my parents are out, sleep in their bed. I developed this routine after my brother's birth. He always slept in Naneh's room when they were out and I felt left out and alone. Somehow sleeping in their room and being carried to my room when they returned gave me a sense of security. I like their big roomy bed, and enjoy pushing my bare legs across the cool places on the sheet.

I am woken up by the sound of irregular breathing at my side. Someone is holding onto me lightly from behind, touching me below the waist. Soft pajamas touch my bare legs. More than the touch I am frightened of the breathing, which seems to gain momentum, and the panting that accompanies it as he grips me tighter. I try to keep very still, almost holding my breath, and press my eyes shut. Maybe if I keep them shut and don't move, he'll go away. I am not sure how long he holds onto me but I don't move when suddenly he gets up. I can hear him walking for a while very softly as if in circles on the thick carpet, and then leaving the room. I don't open my eyes even then, afraid that I will conjure him back.

Ever since that night I cannot sleep alone in the dark. My parents think I am trying to draw attention to myself and make sure the lights are turned off in my room at night. I sleep badly. He stays at our house one more night. I cannot tell my parents but I try to avoid him. When he asks me if I have more homework, I pretend not to hear. When it is time for him to leave, my mother calls for me to come and say good-bye but I go to the bathroom and lock the door. She rebukes me for my rudeness. What have I taught you? she says, exasperated. Haji Agha Ghassem is a very nice man. He said to say good-bye to you. He said you are a bright child.

He came to our house two more times after that. I always tried to escape him, even when others were present in the room. What is amazing to me now is how he never acknowledged his actions with a look or gesture. He always had the same remote and kindly expression. Once he caught me unawares. I was in my usual haunt at the back of the garden by a small stream. I loved the small wildflowers that grew on the banks of the stream. That day I was busy with a favorite pastime: picking up pebbles and watching them change colors as I put them in the water. He came silently and squatted behind me, saying softly, "What are you doing? Shouldn't you be studying?" I was startled and made a move to get up, but he held me by the waist, stretching his hands to touch the pebbles, "Oh, how pretty," he said, as his hands moved to and fro over my bare legs. When I finally got up he rose with me, still groping me with gestures too painful to describe even now. At first I thought, I will invent an imaginary character to whom this happened who isn't me. But the game my father and I had invented was too light for such a story. The shame would remain. Later I learned that it is not unusual for a victim to feel guilty, mainly because she becomes complicit through her silence. And then there is the added guilt of feeling some vague sense of sexual pleasure out of an act that is imposed and feels reprehensible.

"DON'T LET STRANGERS TOUCH YOU." And yet it is seldom strangers, I learned long before I was a teenager, who do you harm. It is always the ones closest to us: the suave chauffeur, the skillful photographer, the kind music teacher, the good friend's sober and dignified husband, the pious man of God. They are the ones your parents trust, whom they don't want to believe anything against.

My father describes in his memoirs the prevalence of a certain form of pedophilia in Iranian society, one that arises from the fact that, as he sees it, "contact between men and women is banned and the adolescent male cannot be close to any women other than his mother, sister, or aunts." His view is that "most lunacies are rooted in sexual deprivations." He goes on to explain that such deviancies are not limited to Iran or to Muslim societies but occur wherever sexual repression exists—for example, in strict Catholic communities.

I cannot be quite so forgiving. Intellectually I can understand the complexities—I know that at one time marrying nine-year-old girls was the norm and not a taboo, that hypocrisy within such confines was not a vice but a way of survival. But none of this is a consolation. It does not erase the shame. I am thankful that societies, people, laws, traditions, can be changed, that we can stop burning women as witches, keeping slaves, stoning people to death; that we are attentive now to protecting children against predators. My parents' generation lived in the twilight of this transition, but my generation grew up in a world different from the one Haji Agha Ghassem represented. His way of life had become taboo in the same way that incest, once the accepted norm among ancient societies, became a crime.

Haji Agha was my first experience and the most painful; the others were more casual and fleeting, although they each added to my sense of shame, anger, and helplessness. I could not talk about any of them to my parents, who were, after all, adults, like my molesters. Would they believe me, or believe Haji Agha, a man whom my mother listened to and respected? As I grew older I learned to distance myself from the experience by placing it within a larger context. Analyzing it as a social malaise rather than a personal experience had some therapeutic effect: it made me feel as if I had some power over the reality I could not control. It was both soothing and disturbing to know that what happened to you was common, not just in your own country but the world over; that you shared the same secrets with a young girl or boy living in places called New York or Baghdad. But it did not modify the pain and the bewilderment of the experience. I did not talk about it to anyone for a long time. I never wrote about Haji Agha in my diary, although I have reviewed the experience so many times in my mind that all its details are vivid even now.

MANY YEARS LATER I did finally talk about my experience to one of my cousins. He told me Haji Agha was notorious for fondling children, although, in his defense, there were many others like him. It was worse with boys, he told me, because he could handle them far more easily. He would make you sit on his lap behind a desk, with a book in front of him, and as he pretended to go through the lesson he would fondle you and keep you rooted to his lap. That was two decades after the incident in my parents' bedroom.

In his memoir, my father wrote about how this conduct was particularly prevalent in Iran among those who catered professionally to youth, especially bicycle-shop owners who rented out bikes to young boys. He mentions a certain Hussein Khan, who owned a bicycle store next to his father's shop in the bazaar. Until the mid-seventies, he says, Hussein Khan was still a pedophile, still managing his shop.

It took me some time to accept the fact that my father's family had its own secrets and untruths. They were at once intellectually adventurous and extremely puritanical. When I told my brother that it seemed wrong to suppress one's feelings to such a degree, he said, "Maybe that's how we grow up." "What do you mean?" "We define ourselves not through what we reveal, but what we hide." He did have a point, but then it has always seemed to me that what is not articulated does not really exist. And yet at some point the unarticulated, that which is silenced and stifled, becomes as important as what is said, if not more so.

The terrible thing was not merely that such things happened. I am aware that sexual abuse and hypocrisy, like love and jealousy, are universal. What made it more intolerable—what still makes it intolerable—was that it was not talked about and acknowledged publicly. Airing the dirty laundry, this was called. In private, in their coffee sessions, my mother's friends swapped stories about girls who, before marriage, had their virginities restored by being sewn back up. Scandals were constantly alluded to, but on the surface there was a smooth veneer, glossed over with rosy phrases. Protective fictions were more important than the truth.

Decades later I found it easier to stand up to the militia patrolling the streets of Tehran than to sleep alone at nights. If Haji Agha Ghassem were alive today, would I be able to confront him? Our personal fears and emotions are at times stronger than public danger. By keeping them secret, we allow them to remain malignant. You need to be able to articulate something if you want it to go away, and to do that, you must acknowledge that it exists. Political injustice I could talk about and resist, but not what happened that afternoon in my parents' garden. For decades, after I came of age myself, sex was an act of compliance, a form of disembodied appeasement. And for decades I felt an inarticulate feeling of anger at my parents, especially my mother, for not protecting me. My anger was not without some sense of irony: she tried to protect me by preventing me from seeing boys my own age and yet she trusted all those men she admired for their strength of character, who did in fact harm me.

a death in the family

Ｆｏｒ ｙｅａｒｓ ａｆｔｅｒ my mother's father died, my parents—each from a different perspective—brooded over how different things might have been had he lived longer. Mother had performed certain perceived duties to her father, whom she loved and at the same time resented: to meet him once a week, to call him every other day, to be polite to his second wife, and to demonstrate her bitterness with a show of pregnant silences. Suddenly, he was gone.

He died unexpectedly, near dawn, of a heart attack. He was sixty-two and I was about twelve. Father was away in Germany on some official business. I had been pouting all through breakfast because the night before, Mother and I had had a big fight over a sweater she had knit for me. She'd forced me to try it on, despite the fact that the sweater did not fit properly and I hated the color. Halfway through breakfast Mother was called to the phone. Who could be ringing at this hour?

She didn't return to the table but the servant came back, her face tinged with excitement. "Be good now, children," she said. "The missus is busy right now." We looked up, fidgeted, threw a few pieces of bread at one another, drank our orange juice, and went upstairs, looking for our mother. I was astounded to see her tear-drenched face. She said, without releasing the phone, "Go wait for Aunt Mina." Which we did without the usual questioning, stunned by her tears.

How do you tell a child of a close relative's death? I am grateful to Aunt Mina for being honest and straightforward. She told us gently that our grandfather had died, that our mother was very upset. We needed to think of her and to be considerate, especially since Father was not here to help. Could we see her? we wanted to know. "Not just now, you have to go to school." "But we're late for school already," we complained. "You needn't worry about that," she said, "there will be a letter for the principal."

The excitement of unusual circumstances, the sense of some tragedy not yet digested, fuses in my mind with a shameless feeling of self-importance: pride at showing off your wounds. I am late this morning because my grandfather died, I can tell the teacher and my classmates, drawing sympathy and curiosity. Later I wrote an essay about it ("The Event That Most Changed My Life") and to this day I am somewhat ashamed of the high praise I received for that essay. Did I love him? Did his death make me sad? Did I learn from it? In my essay the answer to all three questions was in the affirmative. My teacher had me read my essay to the class. Mother kept the notebook in which I had written it for a long time. She would sometimes dig it up and read it to her guests, tears gathering in her eyes as she enunciated my carefully chosen words.

That day we did not go home. After school we were taken to Aunt Mina's house, where we were entertained by her daughters, Mali and Layla, who did their best to divert us. I was always a little in awe of them. Mother often reproached me for not being more like them. They were everything I was not: they played the piano and were educated but also very correct and conventional. They were well-read but not excessively bookish, independent but at the same time gifted cooks and immaculate housekeepers.

We ate a lot of ice cream. We told silly jokes. We put makeup on my sweet and compliant brother, placed a straw hat decorated with flowers and a pink ribbon on his head, and made him parade around the house with a handbag. When Aunt Mina returned, a little before dinner, we all sobered up. She said, "Nezhat is still there, trying to help." "She's just doing her duty," said her husband. "Nezhat never shirks her duties," Aunt Mina said. "If anything, she overdoes it . . ." She interrupted herself and turned to her daughter: "Layla," she said,

"take this child to the bathroom and wash that muck off his face."
Looking at my brother, her voice softened. "You don't have to take
this, you know? You are not their toy."

When a few days later I saw the picture of my grandfather in the
newspaper that was lying on the table in Aunt Mina's house, I burst
into tears. Layla said, "A bit late for crying, isn't it?" In a clumsy way
I tried to explain how his death had not hit me until I had seen it there,
alongside his picture, in the papers. That was as true as my sentimental essay had been questionable, but her doubt aborted my display of
grief.

Two days after his death, we all went to Grandfather's house. It
was early in the morning and the house was relatively quiet. My step-
grandmother's younger sister, a kindly lady whom my mother liked a
great deal, was there along with her daughter and an elderly gentleman, a distant relative of my step-grandmother's. For a while we sat
in the cool, darkened living room. I kept smoothing my skirt. My
brother sat politely next to me and, when offered, we each took one
small pastry which we left on our plates, untouched. Mohammad
softly banged his legs against the chair. I stared at the pictures on the
mantelpiece. There was my grandfather in a dark suit and bow tie; my
handsome uncle Ali smiling at the camera; Aunt Nafiseh with her hair
down to her shoulders, in a black dress with a diamond brooch. There
she was again with my cousin in her arms, and again with her husband. My eyes fell on an old photo of my step-grandmother taken
years earlier, when her hair was still light brown, showing off her bare
shoulders, her head thrown back, not just smiling but laughing.
Nowhere was there a single picture of my mother or of us, her family.

After a few desultory attempts at conversation my step-grandmother, who had been telling the elderly gentleman about "how it had
happened," got up and led us upstairs to the room where my grandfather had died. She walked ahead and we followed in a procession, as if
we were being given a tour of the house. Apparently he had felt uncomfortable around dawn. He left the bedroom and came to the small
room adjacent to theirs—or was it his bedroom and they slept in different rooms? In this room, filled with sunshine, there was a small bed

next to the wall. She said he called her, saying he did not feel well. My step-grandmother insisted on telling us how he had come to her room, waking her up, how she had called the doctor, and how in this room, on this narrow bed, with the blood-pressure equipment still connected to him, he had died.

*My mother's stepmother.
Her own mother died when
Nezhat was very young.*

Decades later this scene rushed back to my mind. It was the day after my father's death and I had called Tehran to convey my condolences to his second wife. She accepted my words of consolation but never said how sorry she was that my father was dead, how sorry for me and my brother. Instead she went into a long and detailed description of how he had held her hand and told her that she should not worry and how grateful he was for her care and support. She described his look, and her own grief. Her tone was filled with something besides grief, perhaps greed. She was taking possession not just of his worldly belongings but of him. *She had been there.* That room, his last words, his helplessness, were all hers. We others were strangers, left out in the cold.

Father returned after a few days, but even then he and Mother were so busy with the funeral arrangements that we were left more or less to Aunt Mina. I would walk from room to room accumulating fragments of conversation. "He was a good man, but naïve and impressionable, like Nezhat," I heard my father tell Aunt Mina. "He was influenced by his wife, but lately he had come to regret his treatment of Nezhat and was making amends for it."

"Your mother is throwing herself into this with such fervor," Aunt Mina said. "She has always been too proud to admit it, but she never had a real home. They treated her like a poor relation, but those days are behind her now, she doesn't need them anymore. Maybe if she had openly expressed her anger, her father would have paid more attention. Eat your apple," she said a minute later with a sly smile. "Just because your mother isn't here doesn't mean you can get away with misbehaving!"

Later, I understood the wisdom of Aunt Mina's point of view. At every turning point in her life my mother squandered opportunities to transform or transcend her relationship with her stepfamily, not so much because they refused to alter their attitudes toward her but mainly because she could not change hers. To the end she deliberately perpetuated their ability to hurt her. The resentment and pride inside her had become a malicious and malignant entity.

A FEW WEEKS AFTER my grandfather's death, we were driving toward his house when Mother said something about how she had lost her only protector in the world, and Aunt Mina lost her patience. My grandfather had been supporting a few poor families in secret, a fact he hid from his own family. The discovery further confirmed my mother's esteem and persuaded her of his innate unselfishness. Later she would claim (with a wrathful sideways glance at us) that "people" took advantage of her trusting nature, much as they had taken advantage of her father's generosity. "What did your father do for you after Saifi's death?" Aunt Mina said sternly. "He was a good man, but he was not a good father to you. Let it go." "I can't let it go," my mother shot back. "I owe him everything. He was the one who protected me when I was young. Now I have no one in the world." Aunt Mina rolled her eyes.

"I hope you will live your own life," Aunt Mina told me, after we had dropped my mother off and were making our way home. "Nezhat seems to have forgotten everything. This good father sent her to school with a chauffeur but forgot to buy her decent clothes. I remember once we were taking a school photograph and your mother was the only one in the class with no jacket. She had to borrow someone else's jacket for the photo. She made the best of it, but I remember how humiliated she felt."

Later, Father told me that in his final year, Grandfather had felt increasingly guilty about his treatment of my mother. A delayed sense of responsibility had compelled him to try to make amends. He had offered to transfer yearly stipends to my parents' account and had even financed the building of a new house, as they had never owned one. "Nezhat has no luck," Father said. "Had he lived longer, things might have been different."

So long as her father was alive, my mother's resentment had a live target, and her favorite tale was the romance of Saifi. He was the prince who had rescued her. She loved her father but there were barriers of mistrust and of hurt. She was the virtuous and neglected daughter who never demanded anything. So long as he was alive there was a room for her in her father's house, but what would happen now that he had died? "That house," she would tell Aunt Mina, "is no longer mine." "Nezhat, get your share and get out," Aunt Mina told her. "They won't ever give you what you believe is yours." After his death, Mother's father gained a sacred status for her and she could no longer blame him for past injustices, so she blamed her husband instead.

On the Friday after my grandfather's death, a crowd gathered in our living room to pay tribute. His philanthropy was praised and his failed political ventures cited as examples of his integrity. His hot temper was a sign of a frank nature, an inability to tolerate any form of hypocrisy. My mother held forth on how good a father he had been, how he had paid more attention to her upbringing than that of her siblings. I will never forget the touching way she cited, as proof of his love, the punishments he meted out to her alone, and how he had, just last year, called her in private to tell her he would pay for the house she wanted to build. Don't spare any expenses, he had said. I want you to have the house you deserve. "Now," she said tearfully, "I will never live in that house; I can't bear it!"

The house had become a metaphor for my mother's relations to those closest to her. The whole family put long hours into its creation.

Every corner was discussed, every space negotiated time and again between my parents and with the young architect. It became a habit for us to visit the unfinished structure, as if we were calling on an old friend. I even wore a special shirt to show the painter the exact color I wanted for my room. I remember sitting by the newly painted swimming pool, mesmerized by a white mouse in a corner intoxicated by the paint fumes. Once the house was finished my mother made up any excuse she could think of not to move in. When she said she could not live there because it reminded her of her father, my father suggested that she had more memories in our current house. She countered that the new house was too far from the center of the city and therefore inconvenient. In the end they first rented out and finally sold the house and we never moved into it.

At this point, in the summer of 1960, my father was rarely home. He was an ambitious young man, steadily on the rise in the civil service, and had been appointed by the Shah to the post of deputy mayor of Tehran. My mother and I were by now fighting almost every day. She refused to let me go out with my friends. My diary is filled with feelings of frustration, of being left out. In one entry, on the 21st of March, just before the Persian New Year, when we were supposed to go to a place called Sefid Rood for a vacation with Aunt Mina's family, I wrote: "When I was brushing my teeth in the bathroom I heard Mother telling my brother, I can't take it anymore, she's ruining my reputation. I won't go to Sefid Rood with her. She doesn't love me, she's waiting for me to die."

PART TWO | LESSONS AND LEARNING

But are not all Facts Dreams
as soon as we put them behind us?

—EMILY DICKINSON

leaving home

I F AT HOME I WAS SUBDUED INTO COMPLIANCE, at school I quickly developed a reputation as a difficult child. My uniform was always ink-stained. My grades were good, but I liked literature, history, and algebra and paid little attention to the rest. A few friends and I created a secret group called the Red Devils, whose mission was to take revenge on teachers. I organized a walkout on the English teacher when, distracted by her own affairs, she insisted on talking all through class about her husband.

My friends and I made up songs about Dr. Parsay, the stern, pug-nosed principal, which we went around the school yard singing during breaks and at lunchtime. She would stand every morning in front of the entrance to the school and examine us as we came in. Those whose uniforms were too short, those who wore nylon stockings instead of white socks, or who had on makeup or nail polish, were reprimanded or sent home. We made fun of her appearance, and speculated as to whether she had a sex life to speak of with her husband. How could anyone love her? Once, when a friend was expelled from another class, I and three Red Devils boycotted the class. Our boycott did not last more than two days. My father was called to school almost every week, but this latest offense was serious. We were told that we could be suspended.

For a long time whenever I heard about Dr. Parsay, the same feelings of rancor were evoked. Like my mother she was an authority figure I was instinctively provoked to disobey. I was reminded of her stern expression, her uncompromising attitude, the commanding tone that made me want to disrupt class and stir others to rebellion. It was only with her death years later, in 1979, that I would become intrigued

Dr. Parsay.

about her life. In time I learned that her mother had been among the first women to fight for women's rights in Iran; for that she had been attacked and even exiled for a while. Dr. Parsay would be one of the first women to enter Parliament. She was a senator for several years and in the seventies became minister of education. She was credited with changing the schoolbooks, purging them of derogatory representations of girls and women. After the revolution she was arrested and, in a summary trial, she was found guilty of corruption on earth, warring with God, spreading

prostitution, and working for the imperialists. Rumor had it that because she was a woman and was not to be touched, she was put in a sack. The method of her murder was not clear; some said bullets had been fired into the sack, others that she was stoned to death. According to a recent biography she was hanged along with a prostitute, but her death certificate cites "the reason for illness: gunshot wounds." Was this to be the end in store for those intelligent women who did not go to waste?

LIKE SO MANY OF LIFE'S TURNING POINTS, my parents' decision to send me to England began as small talk. Father told me that Dr. Parsay had recommended that I go abroad, to protect me from "bad company" at school. Later he said he wanted to protect me from my mother's hostility, from her endless anger and spite. In truth, there must have been a number of reasons for my parents' decision to send me abroad. They wanted me to get the "best education," but they insisted that their motives were different from those of the upper-class families who had begun to send their children to fashionable boarding schools in Britain and Europe. They made sure I understood that even if they *had* liked the idea, they just didn't have the money for that sort of thing. They would be making a sacrifice as it was. Not having the money would become a symbol of worth in our family. I never really would find out how much money was enough money.

The subject of my studying abroad was first brought up when I was in eighth grade, and every day there was a new debate about where I should be sent. America was considered for a short time. My father liked the United States. He'd been sent to the American University in Washington, D.C., for a master's degree in accounting and finance while he was working at the Ministry of Finance in the early fifties. He had been impressed by the good nature and hospitality of the people he had met, and, more than anything else, by their freedom to be who or what they wanted to be. He felt America was a good place for a girl like me.

Mother was against my going there: she said the people were rude, the distance too far. Switzerland was considered and rejected as too expensive. Every once in a while she would say, "It's a shame Azi can't speak French; my brother, Ali, could have looked after her." He lived in Paris, where he got his medical degree. I had a feeling she didn't actually want me to go to France or even to learn French because she felt it was her territory. "*Please*, not another word," she would say when I finally took French in college, "*Not* with that accent. You either speak French with the right accent or you don't speak it at all." Then she would repeat what she had said so many times before: when she had visited Paris two years before, everyone had been so impressed with her command of the language that she had been taken for a native speaker. Ultimately, French became a citadel I never could conquer. Around the French I blushed and became a little gauche: I never did feel comfortable enough to respond to the simplest sentence.

The French were our superior relatives, especially men like Napoleon and de Gaulle, but it was the British she admired most. They were wily, polite but also sly, never revealing what was really in their minds. How else could they, from their small island, have conquered the world? I still remember an argument between my parents after a reception in honor of Lyndon Johnson, then vice president of the United States. My father was mayor of Tehran at the time and they were invited to the event by the foreign ministry. Mother asked Johnson if he could recommend any top schools in America where one could receive a solid British education. "Don't you see that this is rather insulting to the vice president of the United States?" my father asked in exasperation. "He should feel privileged," my mother shot back. "Most probably he himself was sent to a good British school."

My mother's passion for British correctness may have persuaded her that in Britain I would be bent back into shape. Finally it was Ameh Hamdam, a beloved cousin, who solved the problem. Her husband's children had boarded at the house of a respectable Englishman, a Mr. Cumpsty, who had a large house in the town of Lancaster called Scotforth House. I could stay with him and be under his guardianship and go to a local school. It was agreed that my mother would accompany me for three months, to see that everything was in order, and decide if the place was suitable for me.

Father proudly told me one afternoon, as we were walking up and down the spacious terrace of Aunt Nafiseh's house, that I was lucky, my mother and he had never had such an opportunity, they never had anyone who would worry about their future to the minutest detail. He wanted me to be educated and independent—both my parents were very keen on the idea of my education and independence. He reminded me again of his own decision to leave Esfahan, penniless and knowing no one. "Your position in society and the respect you will earn," he said, "should have nothing to do with what you have inherited. You're going there to get an education, but we expect you to come back and serve your country—your place is here, in this country that has given you so much." Position in society, service to country—everything in our family was burdened with significance.

Amoo Said.

THE MONTH BEFORE I left was spent in a flurry of goodbye parties. We visited different relatives and family elders to pay our respects. On one particularly memorable evening, my parents took me to visit Ameh Hamdam's older brother, Said Nafisi, whom we all called Amoo Said, or Uncle Said. Amoo Said had been schooled in Europe. He was well versed in both literature and history, and was one of Iran's best-known modern intellectuals. In addition to his numerous works on Iran's history and literature, he had several works of fiction, a French-Persian dictionary, and many translations, including Homer's *Iliad* and *Odyssey*, to his name. His main weakness was his prolific pen, for he could be simultaneously insightful and shallow, meticulous and careless.

My parents would often take me to his house, at the end of Nafisi Alley, a seemingly forsaken side street with a dry stream running down the middle. The house was a little cold and damp during winter. It had a sooty quality, as if no matter what the time of day, it was forever evening. The furniture seemed to fade into its surroundings, creating the illusion that the shabby couches and chairs were ghostly objects, as insubstantial as the secrets I imagined lingering in the shadows of that wonderful home.

The only bright room in the house was the library, where stacks of books filled the shelves and were piled precariously on the floor. The books seemed alive to me, like turtles with square backs and invisible legs. Whenever we visited, Amoo Said would at some point, with a rare smile partially hidden under his full beard, send me to his library with the exact location of a specific book that I was to bring to him. Perhaps it was because of this that I always imagined enchanted places not as glorious edifices but as penumbral ruins, their magnificence confirmed by the secrets hidden in their dark corners.

Amoo Said himself was suited to the role of wizard, commanding riddles that I hungered to discover. He was tall and slim, his body curiously elongated—he seemed to be almost elastic. His face was neither kind nor cold but receptive, with large brown eyes that appeared, from behind his horn-rimmed glasses, to be perpetually drawn to some unknown and invisible point or destination. Because he so seldom looked at anyone directly it always shocked me to see how attentive he had been.

Amoo Said was about twenty years older than my father. As a young man he had lived through the Constitutional Revolution, which had radically curtailed the power of the absolutist monarch and orthodox clergy, and he had seen the Qajar dynasty toppled by a Cossack officer later crowned as Reza Shah Pahlavi. Reza Shah set out to create a cohesive nation-state, building modern institutions, establishing a secular judicial system, centralizing power with the help of a network of railroads, and improving the military. Iran was thrust forward, but the old absolutism never completely disappeared: it reemerged in modified form as a modern political dictatorship that constantly undermined its own established institutions, especially Parliament and the judiciary.

In 1921, Amoo Said and a handful of fellow-writers and intellectuals founded Iran-e Javan (the Young Iran Club)—a group whose aim was to bring about a democratic Iran. It called for the cancellation of all legal and judicial privileges for foreign nationals; building railroads in various parts of the country; a ban on opium; compulsory public education; the easing of restrictions so that more young Iranians could study abroad; building museums, libraries, and theaters;

women's emancipation; what they called "the adoption of the progressive aspects of Western civilization"; and, finally, the establishment of a secular state and the separation of civil laws from religious laws. It is a measure of how things changed that the next generation of Iranians—my parents' generation—were members of that same Young Iran Club, but it had by then been transformed from a vibrant cultural and political society into a fashionable social and gambling club.

Amoo Said was a constant source of controversy within our family. He gained a great deal of notoriety when he published a roman à clef, *Halfway to Paradise*, exposing the decadence and political incompetence of Iran's elite and their dubious loyalties to foreign powers, especially the omnipresent British. The prominent Iranians who had been accepted into the order of Freemasons were portrayed as agents of the British government. The book strained relations with his brother, a minister of finance, whose friends (some quite unjustly) he had targeted in the novel. His views on this matter were at times exaggerated, bordering on paranoia.

Amoo Said was an impossible person to deal with. His family was proud of his literary reputation but constantly exasperated by his attacks on their friends and peers. Later he was forced to praise the Shah and retract his critical remarks so as to be able to write and earn his meager living. Despite this, and the fact that most of his years were spent in constant anxiety over financial difficulties (resulting in family conflicts and marital tension), Amoo Said was spoken of in our family with so much awe and reverence that his way of life presented itself as an alternative to the wealth and power my parents both coveted and shunned. Neither his financial, personal, or political problems took away from the image I formed of him as some kind of wizard.

That evening, when we went to pay our respects to Amoo Said, he turned to me, keeping his eyes cast down, and said, "You may not know this, but when I was sent to Europe only a handful of people had ever gone abroad. The world, our world here, was so much smaller. Education was what we hungered after. I hope you won't take what you have for granted." Not waiting for a response, he added, "Well, you'll be on your own from now on. Have you thought of what you want to be?"

I wanted to say, I want to be like you, but that seemed too ingratiating, so I said that I didn't know. "You must have some sort of a role model," he said. I whispered that I had none. And immediately as I said it, even before having said it, I knew I was in trouble. "Well, there must be someone you admire, someone you want to be like?" "Rudabeh," I blurted out at last, thinking of my favorite heroine from the *Shahnameh*.

"Well, well, not Rostam but Rudabeh, not a bad choice," he said. "Strange that you thought of her. Go to the library," and he gave me the location of a particular book. "This is my going-away present," he said, giving me the book. "One day, you will read this book and you might thank me for it. I am giving it to you because you admire Rudabeh." The book he gave me was *Vis and Ramin*, by Fakhredin Gorgani, who lived around the same time as Ferdowsi.

THAT EVENING, AS WE WALKED toward the car through the narrow curving alley with its dry stream, I could sense my mother's displeasure. I should have said she was my role model. She never differentiated between great and trivial matters. In the car she was silent and so was I, she because of her anger and I because I knew I was the cause of that anger. My father tried to break the tension in his usual conciliatory manner.

"You should know," he said, taking on his preaching tone, "that when Amoo Said was a child there were no proper schools in the country. Children of the upper classes were educated either at home or in *maktabs*, small rooms where students of different ages were crammed from early morning to evening and taught by a low-ranking cleric. Amoo Said was among the first to go to a modern school. In fact, his father, the king's personal physician, was among the first to found such a school." There was no response either from Mother or me, and he continued more casually, as if we were listening. "There is so much wisdom in your mother's insight that you should know your country's history. You've reached an age when you need to take these matters seriously. It's not enough to know the *Shahnameh;* you'll have to start paying more attention to real history." I hated it when he took on that tone just to please her—and he seldom succeeded in pleasing her. She shot him a hateful glance and turned her head to the window.

That night, when I tried to kiss her good night, my mother turned away, saying, "Go and kiss your imaginary role model, Rudabeh." I walked to my room, resisting the tears and holding the book Amoo Said had given me in my hand. It was the tale of two star-crossed lovers, like Rudabeh's story. What was I to do with several hundred pages of a poem written several hundred years ago? I tried to read it in bed. But it was difficult and soon I turned to another, more familiar one. It took me two decades and a revolution before I realized what a rare gift he had given me that day.

CHAPTER 9

rudabeh's story

I LISTENED CAREFULLY TO ALL MY father's stories, but with some I would hold my breath and remain very still in anticipation. That was how I felt—how I still feel—about the story of Rudabeh. I was not aware then of its deeper implications, but like certain recurring motifs Rudabeh would keep reappearing at different times throughout my life. I had forgotten until I started writing this book that I had chosen her name for my imaginary friend, whose memory suddenly leaped out reproachfully and irrelevantly, demanding full attention.

Rudabeh and Zal were the parents of Rostam, the main protagonist in the *Shahnameh* and perhaps the most important mythical hero in all of Persian literature. Rostam lives for four hundred years, is possessed of Achilles' courage and Ulysses' guile, and is far more important than the kings whose empires he defends and protects. And yet it was never Rostam who held my interest, but rather his parents, the white-haired Zal and Rudabeh.

> In purdah, and unseen by anyone,
> He has a daughter lovelier than the sun.
> Lashes like ravens' wings protect a pair
> Of eyes like wild narcissi, hidden there;
> If you would seek the moon, it is her face;
> If you seek musk, her hair's its hiding place.
> She is a paradise, arrayed in splendor,
> Glorious, graceful, and elegantly slender.

Her eyebrows were like a "bow," her nose a "silver reed," and her small mouth like "the contracted heart of a desperate man." I forced my father to repeat the tale of the lovers Rudabeh and Zal so many times that I knew it almost by heart. Rudabeh is perhaps the first in a long line of literary characters over whom I would find myself obsessing and with whom in one way or another I would identify.

When my father told the story, he began something like this: Sam, the son of Nariman, was the strongest warrior in the land of Iran. His wife gave birth to a child who was as handsome as any infant being could be, with a face "as bright as the sun," but he had the white hair

An illustration of Zal and Rudabeh, from my father's children's book.

of an old man. Sam was so dismayed by his son's white hair that he gave instructions for the infant to be abandoned in the woods. His mother tried to save him by leaving him in the vicinity of a high mountaintop where Simorgh, a great mythical bird, lived. Simorgh took pity on Zal, provided him food and shelter, and raised him with her own offspring until Zal grew to be a fine young man, strong and fearless. The traveling caravans passing through the mountains caught sight of Zal and soon his fame spread.

Since, as Ferdowsi tells us, "neither good nor evil remains hidden," one night Sam, who had felt some remorse, dreamed that his abandoned child was still alive. The next night he dreamed that a banner was raised on top of a mountain and a youth was leading an army, with a high priest and a wise man riding on each side. Sam regretted his rash deed and after consulting with his wise men set out to search for his son. He discovered him in the land of the magical Simorgh and invited him back to his court, asking for forgiveness. Zal was reluctant to leave Simorgh. But the great bird gave him some of her feathers and told him that whenever he was in trouble he should throw a feather into the fire, and summon her, and she would come to his aid in the shape of a black cloud.

When King Manuchehr, Iraj's grandson, commanded Sam to go to war, Sam left Zal to rule his lands. "Enjoy life and be generous," Sam advised Zal. "Seek knowledge and be just." Zal took his father's advice and gathered men of knowledge from all parts of the land and studied with them for a long time. Then he decided to make a tour of the vast lands he ruled over. In his travels Zal finally came upon Kabul (in modern-day Afghanistan), which was the capital of the kingdom of King Mehran.

King Mehran's daughter, the lovely Princess Rudabeh, eavesdropped on a conversation between her parents, heard of Zal's handsome looks, his courage, and heroic exploits, and fell in love with him. "I'm in love, and my love is like a wave of the sea that's cresting up toward heaven," she confided to her servants. "I sleep he never leaves me. The place in my heart where I should feel shame is filled instead with love, and day and night I think of his face. Now, help me, what do you think, what do you advise? You must think of some scheme, some way to free my heart and soul from this agony of adoration."

"Have you no shame?" the servants admonished her. "Have you considered what this would mean to your father?" They wondered if Rudabeh was really ready to embrace "someone who was brought up by a bird in the mountains, who is a byword among men for his strangeness?"

Her servants reminded her that she could have any man she wanted and should not pine for a foreigner who looked so old and therefore so odd.

Zal's oddness was one of his attractions for me and it raised Rudabeh in my esteem that she would choose such a man. I should perhaps say that Father's way of telling the story was also what made me like her. By the time I read the story myself, I was hooked. Father said, "It was hard for a girl to disobey her parents. Don't you go getting ideas. If you disagree with your parents, you must have very good reason to do so."

But Rudabeh had made up her mind and would not be discouraged by prejudice or entreaties. "It's pointless to listen to such foolish talk. I don't want the Chinese emperor, nor the king of the West, nor the king of Persia. Sam's son, Zal, is the man I want. With his lion-like strength and stature, he is my equal. Call him old or young, he will be body and soul to me."

I knew by heart the scene when Zal first came to visit Rudabeh at her palace. I had imagined that scene so concretely that I was a little disappointed when I was first able to read it myself in Ferdowsi's actual words. From her high palace window, Rudabeh heard Zal outside, and she loosened her hair, "which cascaded down, tumbling like snakes, loop upon loop." She said, "Come, take these black locks which I have let down for you, and use them to climb up to me." Zal gazed in astonishment at her face and hair but refused to do as she asked. Instead, he took a lasso from his page, looped it, and hurled it upward without saying another word. The lasso caught on the battlements, and Zal quickly climbed up its sixty cubits. They embraced, kissed, and drank wine.

> *From moment then to moment their desire*
> *Gained strength, and wisdom fled before love's fire;*
> *Passion engulfed them, and these lovers lay*
> *Entwined together till the break of day.*
> *So tightly they embraced, before Zal left,*
> *Zal was the warp, and Rudabeh the weft*
> *Of one cloth . . .*

Their union was opposed by both sides. Although Rudabeh's father's kingdom was now under Iran's rule, he was a descendant of Iran's most hated enemy, the devil-king Zahak, and neither side trusted the other completely. King Manuchehr and Zal's father, Sam, admonished Zal for wanting to wed someone from Zahak's lineage. The lovers had to overcome great obstacles, connive, and pass trials before they could finally marry.

Soon after their marriage, Rudabeh became pregnant. Hers was a very painful pregnancy, making her face as sallow as saffron. She complained to her mother that she seemed unable to carry the heavy burden inside her, and that she felt she was dying. One day she fainted and none of the physicians could revive her. Zal, distressed, remembered the feathers Simorgh had given him to summon her in times of trouble. He lit a feather; Simorgh appeared. She told him he must celebrate because he would soon have a son who would be unique in the whole world for his courage and goodness.

Rostam had to be fed by ten wet nurses, and when he was weaned, he ate enough for ten grown-up men. He was handsome and strong, like his heroic grandfather, and with the same warrior-like qualities. And for over four hundred years, Rostam was the champion and protector of Persia, without whom no king could have ruled in safety. His courage was unequaled in the whole wide world and so was his cunning.

Later, when I read the *Shahnameh* I thought of how Father had presented Rostam as almost flawless, but he had one fatal weakness: he was too involved with affairs of state to make room for the more enduring affairs of the heart. Rostam mistakenly killed his son Sohrab in a battle. I would like to think that this refusal to allow a space for the heart cost him dearly. But that is another story.

The men in the *Shahnameh* were first and foremost identified by their show of physical courage; they were warriors, although the most sympathetic ones, like Iraj, were complicated and tender, with moral courage and integrity. But the women, like Rudabeh, possessed a different kind of courage, more private but no less essential. Rudabeh brought to the story the personal feelings and emotions that men like

Rostam shunned or ignored. How shabby all the glories the magnificent warriors gained when devoid of the love for which Rudabeh was ready to give her life!

Rudabeh is one of the many important women in the *Shahnameh* who are of foreign origin. She is mainly remembered as Rostam's mother. Her father-in-law, her husband, and, later, her son are the ones who perform feats of valor, go to war, and win glory for their land. Ferdowsi's women's claim to immortality is their role as mothers, wives, or mistresses. They display a different kind of courage, asserting themselves against all odds and choosing the men they love. In the parallel world of fiction Ferdowsi created characters who defied the norms of his own society and broke its taboos. These women, without any public pretenses, with their open and unabandoned sensuality, their firm persistence, were far more romantic and appealing to me than any male hero.

There are women in the *Shahnameh*, like the beautiful Gurd Afrid, who showed courage, such as donning men's clothing and fighting on the battlefield. But it was women like Rudabeh who planted in my mind the idea of a different kind of woman whose courage is private and personal. Without making any grand claims, without aiming to save humanity or defeat the forces of Satan, these women were engaged in a quiet rebellion, courageous not because it would get them accolades, but because they could not be otherwise. If they were limited and vulnerable, it was an audacious vulnerability, transcending the misogyny of their creator and his times.

My role models as I grew up were the imaginary women of my father's stories—not the passive heroines of fairy tales, the "good" girls handsomely rewarded for their goodness, but rather the erotic and sensual women of Ferdowsi. Later, when I finally read *Vis and Ramin*, the book Amoo Said had given me before my departure for England, I found there another extraordinary tale that affected me deeply. In all of these works, I could detect the faint scent of a repressed sensuality coming through women's idealized figures. The story of *Vis and Ramin*, written forty years after Ferdowsi's *Shahnameh*, also dates back to the pre-Islamic Zoroastrian Iran and appears to be another attempt to celebrate and retrieve Iran's past culture. It is told mainly from the viewpoint of its beautiful and daring heroine, Vis. There was an eloquent earthiness, a healthy sexuality in Vis that gave flesh and blood to the poetry's abstractions. Look at these magnificent women, I thought, created in such misogynistic and hierarchical societies, yet they are the subversive centers around which the plot is shaped. Everything is supposed to revolve around the male hero. But it is the active presence of these women that changes events and diverts the man's life from its traditional course, that shocks him into changing his very mode of existence. In the classical Iranian narrative, active women dominate the scene; they make things happen. As I continued to read Iranian poetry, I was not surprised that almost a thousand years after Gorgani immortalized Vis in his poem, we have a woman called Forough Farrokhzad who celebrates her lover in poems of unabashed sensuality and honesty. Our best poetry has always been rulebreaking and subversive, always redefining and reshaping reality and our perception of it. I would find traces of these insubordinate women in the modern female poets. Not just Forough Farrokhzad but Alam Taj and Simin Behbahani, and in the works of Western fiction, in Emily Brontë's Catherine Earnshaw, Jane Austen's Elizabeth Bennet, George Eliot's Dorothea Brooke, Charlotte Brontë's Jane Eyre, Stendhal's Madame de La Mole and Mathilde. Even the mild-mannered Sophia Western of *Tom Jones* and Richardson's annoyingly pious Clarissa Harlow distinguished themselves by saying no to the authority of their parents, their societies, and norms and demanding to marry the man they chose. Perhaps it was exactly because women were deprived of so much in their real lives that they became so subversive in the realm of fiction, refusing the authority imposed on them, breaking out of old structures, not submitting.

THE WEEKS BEFORE my departure for England went by quickly. There was a popular song at the time by a famous singer about his beloved's departure. Calling her "my newly arrived spring," he laments her departure and hopes that she will remain faithful to him. Every time she heard it, my mother would turn to look at me, her eyes glittering with tears. By now she was too busy preparing for our trip to wrangle with me, although we had our moments, fighting over what clothes to take, how long I could stay out with my friends. She and Monir joon had been busy knitting scarves and sweaters that would last me many, many years. England was cold, she said, and I would need them all. My brother had announced a ceasefire in our regular fights, and he even stopped eavesdropping on my conversations with friends. There was always some sibling rivalry between Mohammad and me, despite our great affection for each other. On my part it was tinged with jealousy because of the attention my mother paid him. But his was more tender: although I sometimes hurt him and my mother encouraged him to complain about me, he never told on me. Perhaps he did not so much want to compete with me but to share my activities—after all I was his big sister. He eavesdropped on my conversations with my friends and imitated me by writing his own memoirs in my diary—I still have the pages written in his childish hand: "Dear diary, I am a nine years old boy and I am writing in my sister's notebook . . ." But he was also very innovative, trying to set up a chemistry lab or a library with the help of our uncle. In time the rivalry faded into a genuine sharing of common interests.

What I remember from the day of my departure is a series of very noisy good-byes, mingled with shameless tears, hysterical protests, and the sudden silence of the airplane announcing the irrevocable fact that no amount of self-pity could reverse the turn of events. I tamely sat by the window and suddenly felt as if Mother and I were the only two people in the world. She showed me how to buckle my seat belt and held my hand in hers while I tried to fight back the tears. After a while she started to talk to me very softly. I was lucky, she said, I had parents who cared for me, who loved me enough to accept this separation, but she had never had the joy and comfort of having a mother. "I want for you what I never had," she said. After a while her voice became dreamy and took on a singsong tone as she told me a story she would repeat many times in the years to come.

"I was four years old," she said, holding onto my hand as if to prevent me from slipping away. "We were living in a house in the middle of a very large garden in Kerman—that's where we lived then—there are so few of them left now, those old Persian gardens with tall trees and running streams and miniature wildflowers growing on their banks. I was woken up in the middle of the night by the sounds of women crying. I ran into the living room and found my aunt, my Naneh, the servants, all gathered in the room. My father was also there. Nobody paid any attention to me. Father walked out onto the verandah and I followed him. I think the moon was out although it was still very dark out there. I was afraid of the trees and their shadows and had almost to run to keep pace with him as he walked along the large stream that ran the length of the garden. Then, suddenly, he stopped. I stopped with him. There, on the ground by the stream, was my mother's body."

And this was my mother's only memory of her own mother. Later, in telling the story again, she decreased her age from four to three and finally to two. My step-grandmother would tell me that Mother was a grown girl when my grandmother died, at least seven or eight, but her account was contradicted by my mother's paternal aunt—an ally against my step-grandmother—who said my mother was very young when her mother died. Her mother's age was equally variable: in the early accounts my grandmother was eighteen when she died, and later Mother settled on sixteen. But this really did not matter, what mattered was that she died very young, when my mother was a small child.

I am struck now by the fact that each time my mother told this story over the years she told it in the same order. She always veered into the dreamy and mechanical tone her voice took on whenever she was excavating memories in which we had no share. Oddly enough, this made her account even more poignant. While the woman who danced with Saifi was unknown to me, this one, frozen with fear, looking at her mother's corpse, was all too familiar.

She always stopped her story right at the point of discovery. In those days, the wealthy washed their dead in the streams running through their gardens before taking them to the morgue. I often tried to picture the scene, following my mother along the stream and coming to a standstill by my grandmother's corpse. I tried to imagine what happened next. Did she understand what it meant? Did her father finally notice her and take her away with him? Did he hold her in his arms?

The dead become frozen in the fixed caskets we create for them. They change as we change, especially those who die young like Saifi or my grandmother. That is what makes it so strange now, not that my grandmother died, but that no one had any memories of her, no one would say, this was your grandmother's favorite dish, or this reminds me of Shamoluk Khanoom. Not once did my grandfather talk of her. We did not even know where she was buried. I doubt my mother ever visited her grave or knew where it was. It pained me enormously and made me feel sympathy for Mother, even when I was angry with her, because the only thing she could remember of her mother was her death, and she never, not once, recalled anything about her mother alive.

That flight to London was memorable for many reasons, but the few minutes it took my mother to tell me that story, the pressure of her hand holding mine, and the silence that followed have always remained with me. I had little feeling then for the dead grandmother I knew nothing of. It was only with time that I would come to focus on her. But the story of her death had a miraculous effect on my feelings and attitude toward my mother. It made me empathize with her, and somehow it explained her anger. I wished I could resurrect my grandmother, to relieve her and my mother from that one scene, that one night, when she died. It made me want to console my mother. I regret now that I never did. Instead, I nonchalantly asked, "And then what?" She didn't answer. Unlike Father, who told us long stories about himself and always analyzed them, my mother constructed her stories in such a way that they had no beginning or end. They were usually composed of a single event, a momentous occasion offered as a puzzle, insinuating all manner of significance.

Like Saifi's, my grandmother's absence made her more present in our lives. As time went by we became increasingly aware of how her death had defined everything my mother had become. In *Cinderella*, as in *Snow White*, the dead mother is an excuse, her absence more important than her presence. Stories need conflict and sorrow, they need fear of loss and hope of retrieval. Had my grandmother lived, there would have been no need for a stepmother. It is the wicked stepmother who is so colorful, so beguilingly alive—her wickedness sets off a whole series of actions and reactions. My mother was also acting out a version of a fairy tale, only her Prince Charming had died on her. Nor were the rewards for her patience eternal peace and happiness.

Even Cinderella must act in a certain way to attract her prince, and my mother did not have such talents. As time went by her bitterness about the past faded into a more general dissatisfaction with the present. Somehow we had failed her. Her ghosts would become more real with time and we, her family, would become more inaccessible and remote.

I am not sure what would have happened if I had not spent those three months in Lancaster with my mother. I did not realize it then, but the experience would remain with me, opening up a new feeling, a soft spot, if you will, that would later on shape my whole assessment of her. It was like a tiny rivulet, promising a large and bountiful river whose potential, once revealed, could never be forgotten.

at scotforth house

W E ARRIVED AT THE LANCASTER train station on a deceptively sunny day. I was soon to discover that what would keep me forever homesick in England, the constant rain and gray skies, was also responsible for the dazzling green meadows and magical bluebells. We were greeted at the station by a large round man on crutches, accompanied by his housekeeper, Ethel.

It was said that Mr. Cumpsty, who was known as Skipper, had been injured in an accident as the captain of a ship, possibly during the war. But the more interesting story was that of his romance with the original owner of Scotforth House, a wealthy woman who fell in love with him and he with her, leading him to abandon his wife and family. When she died, she left him the house and her money. The only time I saw Skipper's previous family was when he died, three years later, and left everything he had to Ethel. His rather questionable moral rectitude might have aroused a few doubts as to his suitability as a guardian for me were it not for the fact that he had been recommended by Amoo Said's sister, the impeccable Ameh Hamdam.

Mother had come to help me settle down, but from the moment we arrived she wreaked havoc in that house in order to provide me with the kind of comfort she imagined I needed. She was as scandalized by conditions in Scotforth House as its inhabitants were by her behavior. Mother had a criticism for everything: the bath had no shower, the dishes were never washed properly. She followed Christine, the timid maid, into the kitchen, taking the dishes from Christine's almost trembling hands and forcing the poor woman to rinse and re-rinse every one without letting them once come into contact with the sink. Skipper kept promising to do something about the bathtub but clearly he had no intention of installing a shower for his temporary tenant, so in the end Mother bought a plastic hand shower that she made me use, forbidding me to take a bath.

Mr. Cumpsty, "Skipper."
Mother entrusted me to his
care while I was at school
in England.

Ethel brings our breakfast and afterward Christine clears the table. Cereal, two eggs sunny-side up that I immediately squash on the toast, plus butter, marmalade, and tea. On the first day of school, as we settle into our chairs for breakfast, my mother looks at me and breaks into a laugh. I am wearing my uniform: navy skirt, white shirt, navy sweater and blazer with the school insignia on the pocket, and a navy beret that I hate. She takes the beret, which keeps sliding off my head, and puts it on the chair beside my schoolbag. You really don't need that at the breakfast table, she says, but you might as well get used to this. She puts on my school tie, takes one look at me, and again bursts into laughter. Poor Azi, she says with uncommon sympathy. She so seldom laughed or smiled—we knew mainly bitter smiles, reminders of our wrongdoings—that I am caught off guard. What? I say a little crossly. Tears well up in my eyes and she pats my hand. There, there, she says, still laughing. Later I learn how to take advantage of my "foreignness," forgetting my beret one day, misplacing my tie, or accidentally coming to school without the blazer.

My mother was an avid believer in exercise. Ever since I can remember, she skipped an imaginary rope in the mornings. In Lancaster the only place she could perform this ritual was on a small paved space in the garden below my second-story bedroom window. Every morning before breakfast she would go down and start skipping on her imaginary rope—a thousand skips a day, she would boast. I sometimes stood by the window watching her and she would look up at me and smile, happy to perform to an audience. This image overlaps with another, when I was about three or four years old, sitting by the French window of my parents' bedroom, watching my mother skip rope on a sunny wintry morning on the terrace. For a moment her eyes caught mine and she smiled. I can still see her smile as my eyes follow the imaginary rope going up and down, up and down.

In the evening I returned to my immense room where, without fail, Mother would offer me a plate of peeled oranges, chocolates, and pistachio nuts, her face glowing with purposeful determination. At night I left her a list of English words and by the next day she would have their meanings, which she looked up in the dictionary, ready for me at my desk. She helped me memorize words for one or two hours

after dinner. In later years, she would bitterly remind me that if it weren't for her I would never have learned English. And it was probably true. When I first started to learn English, in first grade, she didn't know a word (her second language was French). Yet every day she would study the assigned pages in my English textbook

Scotforth House, in Lancaster.

with Aunt Nafiseh, and she would test me every night. When she wanted something for us, she went after it with amazing energy and focus.

Her fixations, her energetic drivenness, was not directed toward any specific goal—although it might have appeared purposeful to the untrained eye. She seemed always compulsively motivated by a firm sense of who or what she did not want to be. She loved smoking but never smoked; she loved playing cards but almost never played; she was a talented dancer but never danced. She made us feel that no one did their jobs as well as they should.

This negative urge at times pushed her to take up projects, none of which bore any relation to the other. To each task, however trivial or important, she devoted herself wholeheartedly. For a few years when I was young her principal goal was to become fluent in English. She even went to London for five months, staying at a bed-and-breakfast and spending almost all her waking hours in language classes and studying at home. For a while after that she went to flower-arrangement classes and filled the house with her precarious creations—until one day she grew tired of this activity and we never heard of it again. She applied the same energy to getting a driver's license, which, for some now-forgotten reason, my father was opposed to. (She was not hallucinating when she claimed that he tried to use his influence to prevent the issuing officer from giving her a permit.)

Of all her projects, perhaps her main ambition was to create a model family. No one had paid attention to her well-being as a child: to what she ate, whether she exercised, what she wore. All of this now she wanted for us. Mother was in the perfection business: perfect family, perfect friends, perfect country. A totalitarian mind-set destroys you not just with its impositions, but with its unexpected acts of kindness. Had she been persistent in her cruelties it would have been easy to cut the relationship. But we felt trapped because, although she ruled our lives, she was also terribly vulnerable, and although she hated me at times, she also sacrificed so much for me. She wanted me to be beautiful, polished, sophisticated, intelligent, an obedient daughter, a successful and educated career woman. I was perhaps her greatest disappointment.

It pains me now to realize that when she looked at me, she might have seen the young woman she had been—neglected and unwanted. This may explain why in some rare moments she would glance at me, her eyes almost brimming with tears, and say, with a shake of her head, Poor Azi, poor, poor Azi!

—

N THE THIRD DAY OF SCHOOL, when I got back to my room and saw the plateful of oranges and pistachios, I started crying. I felt helpless. The first class of the day was English literature and the book we were to read was Shakespeare's *Much Ado About Nothing*. I could not follow the husky Mrs. Weaver's lecture. And it wasn't just Shakespeare. The lovely biology teacher, the ill-tempered music teacher, and the bus conductor, all were equally incomprehensible. Did I not have the highest grade in English back home? Why couldn't I understand these people? My mother sat me down and murmured soothing words. She smoothed my hair, helped me take off my clothes and put on new ones, and as she placed the peeled oranges in my mouth, she said, "You know, you really don't have to do this if you don't want to. I can let your father know and you'll be back in Tehran next week."

"I thought you wanted me to come here, to make something of myself," I said. Her eyes were soft as she continued, almost mechanically, to put oranges and pistachios into my mouth. "I wanted for you what I couldn't have," she said. "You know I was first in my class. My teacher Ozra Khanoom loved me more than any of her other students. She expected me to continue my education, like some of the other women in our family, like Ameh Hamdam or Mah Monir . . ."

She talked mainly to calm me down but then, I think, she talked also to revisit the ghosts of her own past. Ameh Hamdam was one of my mother's heroines. She was among the first Iranian women to be sent to Europe for an education in the 1920s. After her return she did not marry but went to work right away, first as a teacher and later as provost at a well-known girls' high school in Tehran. I remember her well, because she looked so different from the other women who came to our house. She wore little makeup and always dressed in soft browns. Sometimes, when we visited her house, as I sank into her soft, light-brown armchair and listened to the soothing drone of her calm and authoritative voice offset by my mother's harried interjections, I wondered what it was that excited me about her. Was it her stories about the women my grandmother's age who had carried guns

Ameh Hamdam's wedding. The bride, who did not get married until she was in her forties, is standing in the center in the white dress, with my mother's father, Loghman Nafisi, to her right. Mother and I are in the front row.

under their black chadors to help the constitutionalists? She told me I owed a lot to these women because they were the ones who had built the first public schools for girls in Iran. They were beaten, ostracized, and sometimes even banished from their hometowns for their efforts. "Women," she would say in her quiet drone, "have to fight for what they want, always. And not just in this country. It wasn't so long ago that British women had to hand over all their money and property to their husbands." She kept telling Mother, "This child has to appreciate the opportunities she has, she can't take them for granted."

It was only later that I came to understand what was genuinely romantic about her: in a society where "femininity" was so overdefined, her refusal to comply with conventional notions of womanhood was both courageous and exceptional. Women like her were pioneers—highly educated, usually unmarried—who dedicated themselves to their work and developed a style that was deliberately unfeminine.

And yet, Ameh Hamdam was pitied. Some felt she belonged to the category of women who had gone to waste, because they were unwomanly. Although her achievements were duly noted, she was not considered physically attractive. As in any puritanical culture, in the case of women, sex and respect did not mix well. When there was talk of sending me abroad for schooling, some of my mother's friends reminded her that she should not encourage me to become like Ameh Hamdam, who finally, in her early forties, married a pharmacist with four children. This was the fate of overeducated women, we were told: to have to look after someone else's children. I could never find much to pity in her condition. Her husband loved and respected her and she was devoted to her stepchildren, who in turn were devoted to her. It was not until much later that I realized how much better off she must have been than all those wagging tongues and nagging bores.

Allow me to return to that day in Lancaster, when my mother and I sat in the enormous room with its cheerful floral wallpaper, faded carpet, stately bed, and colorful duvet. She told me that her most ardent desire in life had been to become a doctor—like her brother, like her uncles, like so many in our family. But her father did not let her complete her studies after high school. I have often thought that I owe my education to my father, to his storytelling and to the intellectual space he and his family created for us. But that day, if it weren't for my mother, for her understanding and the stories she told me, I would not have been able to continue. I began to believe that becoming an educated woman had little to do with being a good Iranian or making your family proud. Instead, here was a gift I could offer her. I wanted to become the woman she claimed she had wanted to be.

The trip to England and our shared three months became for me the embodiment of all that I loved and came to grieve for in my mother. When Mohammad and I needed her she turned soft and caring, as if her good genie had suddenly woken from a long sleep. In so many ways my mother saw and treated me as she herself had never been treated as a child and a young woman. She paid me all the attention that had been denied her. The irony is that, in order to become what she wanted me to be, I had to distance myself from her. I could not be her puppet. She never realized when I later learned to fend for myself how much she had accomplished.

Mother and me, saying good-bye in the Lancaster train station,
that first December.

She left Lancaster early one afternoon in late December. It was a
cold and cloudy day, a fact of which I am reminded by a picture of the
two of us at the train station. I am wearing the brown raincoat she
bought me, which we were both very proud of, and she a black-and-
red overcoat. She is leaning toward me, smiling. Although neither one
of us is looking at the camera, it is obvious that we are both very conscious of it. She is looking at me, with her hand on my back, as if for
protection. Both her gesture and her expression are typical of how she
appears in photos when she is expected to radiate family love and intimacy.

"I don't want you to feel sad," she said. She looked at me in such a
piteous way, as if I had a terminal illness. "Before you know it, you
will be back home for the summer. There, there," she said with a
smile. What would you have done had you been in my place?

politics and intrigue

FOR A LONG TIME AFTER Mother left, I felt so displaced. It was not just the differences in language, culture, and environment that separated Lancaster from Tehran, or homesickness for family and friends, it was the shock of a sudden change in lifestyle, as different as the constant gray skies and rain in Lancaster were from the blue sunny skies of Tehran and its snowcapped mountains. My life in Tehran had been framed and protected; almost every move was accounted for: my mother monitored what I ate, and I was always driven to and from school and attended no outings without my parents or their consent. Now I was all alone, with a guardian who did not know or care what I did. I was left pretty much to my own devices.

Most other young Iranians who were sent abroad went to boarding schools, but I was sent to an ordinary day school in a small town where most people had never heard the name Iran. I was the only foreigner in my school. The teachers were patient and cautious with me, and my classmates' attitude was mainly one of amusement. They asked me questions tinged with some curiosity, in a tone that was both indulgent and mocking: How many camels do your parents own? Ever been kissed? It amused them to no end that I did not know what a hickey was or that I had once seriously asked a girl what a kiss tasted like. But soon I became one of them—almost. There were many eccentrics in the class and I was simply one of them. I had a number of friends: Sheila the sensitive artist and Elizabeth the joker, Dianna the

studious one, and my best friend, Barbara. I believe Barbara and I
became so close not just because of what we shared but because of
our differences. Barbara: blue-eyed, short brown hair, always on the
verge of a smile. Her friendship was soothing, because on the
surface—and I believe to a great extent in reality—her life was so
much less complicated than mine. She knew what she wanted. She had
kind parents who lived modestly, enjoyed each other's company, and
seemed to be on the best terms with themselves and with their children. She was very intelligent but at fourteen had already found a
steady boyfriend who proposed to her; he was kicked out by her father. With no forced sense of obligation to her family and country, she
was happy in a carefree manner that I never was. I always felt a little
guilty about being happy, a little anxious. There was an uncompli-
cated straightforwardness about Barbara that I loved. Of course no
life is straightforward, but that is how she appeared to me then.

During the daytime, I was busy with school and my friends, but
the nights were so lonely. I would usually retire to my room after dinner, around six thirty. The room was huge. I drew the curtains and left
the light on even when I went to sleep. I often felt terribly alone, sad,
and somewhat scared. So I read, I read every single book that I could
get my hands on. The room was very cold and in order to heat it I had
to drop shillings into the heater, which burnt you if you sat too close
to it and never warmed you if you sat at a distance. So I started reading in bed, feeling secure and warm under the duvet with the hot
water bottle next to me (around that time I read a book called *How to
Be an Alien*. I still remember the line where it said that the Continen-
tal people have sex lives, the British have the hot water bottle). Two
books were always by my bedside—the poems of Hafez and the
poems of Forough Farrokhzad, the contemporary feminist poet. But
mostly I read novels. That was how I made my home in this beautiful,
gray, and damp place, populating my empty room by reading Dickens
and Dostoevsky, Austen and Stendhal.

I was not prepared for the scene I would encounter at the airport
that summer, when I finally went home on vacation. Among the sea of

faces were a number of eerily welcoming strangers. At last I spotted my mother and Aunt Nafiseh standing by a shabby, cheerful-looking middle-aged man holding a huge bouquet of shocking-pink gladiolus. Mother's hairdresser, Goli, was standing a little behind this man, waving and smiling, but my gaze kept returning to that man with the gladiolus, who beamed in the manner of a stranger who so badly wants to be your best friend. "Let me introduce you to Mr. Zia," Mother said as she kissed me on both cheeks. "He works with your father." Aunt Mina and her daughter Layla stood by my father and brother and I spotted Uncle Reza, one of my father's younger brothers, who had recently enrolled at the University of Tehran and was staying with us, but there were many others I didn't recognize, all of whom appeared to share some sort of secret. You could see it as much in my mother's gestures as in the sycophantic smile of Mr. Zia, who was, it turned out, my father's chief of staff. This was to be our life, infected by my father's new position as the youngest mayor of Tehran. From then on, everywhere I went, I would be surrounded by strangers acting as if they were close friends, up until my father was jailed, in the winter of 1963, when the process would be almost exactly reversed. "Welcome to your father's Tehran!" my uncle Reza whispered sarcastically in my ear.

"Your mother," Father had written me, "misses you so terribly that she constantly accuses us of callous indifference to your plight. She objects to keeping the house warm because 'Poor Azi' is there in England, shivering in that big house from cold, day after day." My mother had written me commiserating letters, full of anxious questions about my health and happiness, and she had pressed Father to send me cuttings from women's magazines about the benefits of grape juice and of cleaning the soles of your feet with pumice stone. She had sent dried cherries, plums, and apricots, along with hand-knit woolen socks, mittens, and sweaters that were usually either too small or too big. This set a pattern for the years ahead: while we were separated my mother and I pined for each other, and after a few days or at most a week together, we reverted to our old habits.

—

*F*iroo*z*eh-e Bu-eshaghi Khosh Derakhshid vali dowlatash mosta-jaal bud. When I entered the living room on that first Friday after my return from England, I heard a familiar voice uttering this line from our classical poet Hafez, a reference to Eshagh, a king whose reign was brief, thanks to the machinations of his enemies. Hafez laments Eshagh's bright but short-lived star.

Many of the old regulars were there that morning: my father's old friend Mr. Khalighi; mother's hairdresser, Goli; the well-heeled colonel; as well as Uncle Reza, who whispered that he was so ashamed of my father's new job he denied being related to him. For many Iranians, having a high position in the government meant selling your soul to the devil. Aunt Mina was there too, and, when I entered the room, she gestured for me to sit by her side.

There were a few new faces: Mr. Zia, he of the shocking-pink gladiolus, sat on an upright chair, which did not prevent him from managing to slump. Next to him was a young, thin, dark man whom I later discovered to be Mr. Meshgin, a reporter; and an unassuming man with a submissive smile whom my father introduced as Mr. Es-maili, one of his deputies in charge of the parks and green spaces.

The voice I had heard quoting Hafez belonged to Mr. Khalighi, who, after greeting me warmly, went on to say, "Hafez lived over seven hundred years ago, but what he says about Eshagh, the star-crossed king, still applies. Our dear Ahmad is young and ambitious. His aspirations are all very good and well-intentioned. But he doesn't know that in this government good intentions have no place. You can't survive on goodwill."

"You give me too much credit," my father said, laughing. "My ambitions are modest and I pose no threat to those gentlemen surrounding the Shah. Nor am I answerable to them." I listened with mixed feelings, mulling over my uncle's hushed aside. "What's more," Father continued, "the Shah knows it. He has no reason to feel threatened by me."

"The Shah, my dear man," Mr. Khalighi shot back, "feels threatened by everyone. And perhaps with good reason. After Mossadegh, the Shah lost what little trust he had in others' loyalties. Now he's convinced that anyone articulate and popular is out to get him. So you see," he said, leaning toward my father, "you cannot put your fate in the hands of a man who has no confidence in himself."

This was a reference to Mossadegh, Iran's stubborn prime minister in the early fifties, who was best known for resisting the Shah and pushing for the nationalization of Iran's oil industry, which was then controlled by the British. This led to a hysterical and tension-filled international confrontation, mainly between Iran and Great Britain, and to a boycott of Iranian oil instigated by Britain that exacerbated Iran's troubled economy. The Shah was forced to leave the country for a brief period. The Soviet-backed communist Tudeh Party, which had representatives in Parliament and had infiltrated the army ranks, took advantage of the crisis to foment unrest. One of Ayatollah Khomeini's mentors, Ayatollah Kashani, initially backed Prime Minister Mossadegh, but then turned against him and made peace with the royalists who backed the Shah. All this culminated in the 1953 military coup against Mossadegh, supported by the Americans and the British, and the Shah's return. Mossadegh and the coup that overthrew him remains ever raw, a topic of endless debate—who was wrong and who was right, who betrayed whom and what price did we pay for these betrayals?

Mossadegh was, and by most accounts still is, Iran's most popular political figure. My parents sympathized with him and Mother loved telling the story of the day of the coup leading to his controversial trial and exile to Ahmad Abad, a village he owned. His aborted premiership came to embody Iran's as-yet-unrealized democratic aspirations. He carried with him the corrosive charm of unfulfilled dreams. And yet, years later, in 1978, when we had the chance to choose a follower of Mossadegh, Shahpoor Bakhtiar, a well-known liberal nationalist figure, as the Shah's last appointed prime minister, the majority of people opted not for Bakhtiar but for Ayatollah Khomeini, a figure far more despotic than the Shah. One can ask, at least in hindsight: how far should we trust people who would lament Mossadegh but vote for Khomeini?

Mossadegh at his trial.

Much speculation followed on that first morning of my return about the fate of the Iranian people. It was suggested that all of our misfortunes were due to our stubborn attachment to a cult of personality, created around the Shah. No one can drink a glass of water without the Shah's approval, someone said. "It isn't his fault," objected Mr. Meshgin, the dark-featured reporter. "It's in our blood; this is how we respond to our leaders. We call them King of Kings, Shadow of God on Earth. How long before even the most mild-mannered of men starts believing what he hears? Mossadegh himself had many autocratic tendencies." He turned to my father. "You, my friend, are building castles in the sky if you rely on the Shah. You know your Ferdowsi. Keep in mind how often his kings betray their advisors." Before Father had a chance to reply, Mr. Khalighi said to my mother, "Nezhat Khanoom, I hope you agree with me. Many good men in your family have already paid dearly for their services to the Shah."

Mother, who had been oddly silent throughout this conversation, nodded and glanced up with a bitter grin. "I am not listened to," she said. "I only pay the price. Amoo Said has been trying to tell him the same thing." No matter how much my mother enjoyed her new status as the mayor's wife, at no time did she forget the injustices against a whole host of other Nafisis, known for their stubbornness, who had at one time or another fallen out of favor, either going to jail for a short time or being forced out of government jobs and sent into exile. These incidents were alluded to with pride, despite the hardships they brought to our lives, so that a stranger overhearing our discussions would have been forgiven for believing that we were talking about honors and promotions.

"Things are more complicated than that," my father said defensively. "I'm not Mossadegh, times have changed, we have to do what we can."

IN MY FATHER'S PRIVATE DIARIES from that period I find the same muted excitement that I sensed in him at the time. As I discovered later, this excitement came not from the fact that everything was going well, but that so many things could be done so much better and he had been entrusted with the power and responsibility to fix them. In such a situation, I would in time learn, you feel needed, and elated, as if your own possibilities are endless, like a child with an infinite number of LEGOs, gratefully overwhelmed by the promise of all of the castles needing to be built. That, of course, is a mirage. And responsibility for the disillusionment that followed cannot solely be blamed on the Shah, or on Khomeini.

Father's diaries abound with breathless descriptions of the plans he set in motion for the city of Tehran—building parks and creating the first comprehensive map of the city, initiating local city councils, fighting corruption—and of his countless conversations with the Shah, who sounds attentive and charming. The text brims with activity: the verbs are positive and the prose energetic and concrete. This is how I remember him in those years. He was filled with an energy that I would glimpse only occasionally in later years when he puttered around in the garden with his plants. He put his trust in the Shah's trust in him. With each gesture of intimacy from the Shah he seemed to gain confidence, priding himself on being frank in what he dismissed as a sycophantic court. I remember his boasting about how he had refused a favor from the Shah, the offer of a piece of land near the Caspian Sea, for example. "I don't shirk from voicing criticism," he said. "I'm open in my disagreements."

From the very start there was discord between Father and other high officials, especially the prime minister, Assadollah Alam, and the minister of the interior, Seyyed Mehdi Pirasteh. "Sly as a fox," my mother said of Alam; "I could never trust that man." He had a reputation for ruthlessness. Many dark stories circulated about the way he disposed of his enemies and the favors he bestowed on those who toed the line.

Although Father was sincere in his insistence that he was not ambitious in the usual sense, he was in fact far more so than the prime minister or the prime minister's cronies. I think on some level he wanted to prove to them how insubstantial they were, that what they craved—position, wealth—meant nothing to him. Every time he refused a favor from the Shah, he undermined their status in the Shah's eyes. Yet he was also undermining his own position, which he both loved and despised. My mother also boasted of the way she snubbed some members of the royal family and hostile officials. And that was the problem with my family: they wanted the power to fulfill their ideals but they didn't want to be stained by politics. This partly explains my parents' obsessive affection for those who were out of favor with the ruling elite, even when they themselves were part of that elite.

Despite my father's confidence, throughout this euphoric phase I detected an undercurrent of deep anxiety, which extended into my dreams. Every once in a while, when political disagreements became particularly confrontational, he would tell us, "I handed in my resignation, but the Shah refused it." Although Mother would later claim time and time again that she had foreseen the disastrous turn my father's career would take, he kept her in the dark about his problems and she was in fact too wrapped up in a general state of apprehension to be able to predict any real threat. My father's arriving home ten minutes late, an unexpected phone call, a certain expression of concern, and she would immediately ask *What? What has happened?* with such intensity that her anxiety seemed to be almost a matter of pride.

Her old rivalry with my father and her basic dissatisfaction with life did not allow her to fully appreciate her new circumstances, but she did enjoy the power that came with them. Even during this time she did not forget to remind us of her charmed life with Saifi in his father's house— as if any admittance of satisfaction in her life with Father would be a sign of disloyalty to Saifi. "In Saham Soltan's house there was always some hustle and bustle," she would say. "Politicians were different back then, they had *backbone*." Once Father, in a good mood, said lightly, but with unmistakable bitterness, "Have you noticed that every time your mother talks of her past glories, Saifi is absent? What exactly were his accomplishments? Except for being his father's son, did he ever achieve anything? To hear her talk it would seem my greatest fault has been not being at death's door!"

I sometimes think we become so dependent on the images we create of ourselves that we can never discard them. My mother from the start had decided that her marriage to my father had been a mistake, a poor second to her life with Saifi, and despite all evidence to the contrary she would never revise that first assumption. Aunt Mina claimed that Mother really did love my father but didn't know how to demonstrate her love and so it manifested itself in anxiety for his safety, a distemperate defense of his political actions, and constant concern about his health. Only her anger was deep and incontrovertible.

mayor of tehran

ALMOST EVERY MORNING my father left home around five. Before going to his office he liked to tour the city, paying occasional visits to the fire stations and sanitation crews and checking in more regularly on Tehran's large fruit and vegetable market and on its unofficial boss, Haji Tayeb, who had a reputation for fixing prices through a combination of bullying and intimidation. My father was proud of the way he handled Tayeb, making him work within the municipal rules and regulations.

Mother had her own set of spies with whose help she managed to meddle in the affairs of a city that, in many ways, she knew more intimately than my father did. Throughout her adult life she had stalked the streets of Tehran, finding the best quality material, the fairest prices, bargaining, cajoling, quarreling, and making friends with shopkeepers. She knew how the fruit vendors would hide their best fruit to sell at inflated prices to their wealthier customers and she would field calls from friends and acquaintances reporting on such and such a butcher or baker. What sensuality she lacked in her personal relations came out in her daily forays to the market, where she would create a row one moment and flirt and coax the next. It was not unusual for her to spend half an hour at a time talking to the fruit vendor, with an orange or apple in hand, smelling it, inspecting the skin, guessing at its taste. Accompanying her on these adventures, I felt somehow closer to her, as I had as a young child when, absentmindedly holding my hand, she would walk from shop to shop seeming so much at home in this world of chocolates, leather, and spices.

So much of my parents' idea of Iran was encapsulated by their differing visions of Tehran. My father loved the city and was curious about its past, but he was also eager to push it forward and to leave his mark. Mother loved the idea of Tehran, its customs and rituals and dusty alleys, all pregnant with traditions that she felt compelled to preserve at all cost. Sometimes, when she went from shop to shop, eyeing and touching the merchandise, I felt she was in some way making sure things were as she imagined them to be. Sure, she made enemies and people talked behind her back, but here at least, unlike at home, she was obeyed and respected.

She enjoyed undermining Father's rules and regulations, and often invited her favorite shopkeepers to our house. On Friday mornings, alongside reporters, one might find the grocer or the Armenian baker, sitting politely on the edge of his chair. My father, exasperated, would remind her that this might be taken as a sign of favoritism. "They will accuse me of bribing and being bribed," he would say. "You cannot do this." It got to the point where he had to ask them without her knowledge not to come to our house, much as he would bribe the servants to stay on and not mind the mistress's temper tantrums.

ABOUT THREE WEEKS AFTER my return from Lancaster my parents and I went to visit Amoo Said. Mohammad insisted on coming along. His passion for chemistry was over and he had a more ambitious project in mind: he had begun to set up a library. He already had a seal and a name for it, Prosperous Iran, after a magazine founded and edited by my father when he was working in the Planning and Budget Organization. Mohammad, shamelessly from my point of view, solicited contributions from relatives and friends. In this he was generally encouraged. Mother, who constantly nagged us both for reading too much, had concluded that his project was very clever and boasted about it everywhere she went. It is one thing to sprawl across the floor engrossed in a book and quite another to build a library, where books are organized and categorized. Mohammad had decided to come with us to solicit Amoo Said's support—and from Amoo Said he would receive two novels and a book on Persian mysticism for his effort, plus a great deal of attention and encouragement.

That day, not even the magic of Amoo Said's house could deflect my bitter and self-pitying mood. I had quarreled with my mother over something all morning. I wanted to go to a close friend's house that night. The friend was leaving in a week and had invited me and two other friends to spend the night with her. "It's not a party," I told my mother, "just girls." But suddenly she wanted me home. She missed me. It was not right, children neglecting their family, returning home on vacation and never spending a moment with them. "Please, Mom, please," I had begged. "I said no," she shot back, "that's final. Not another word." It ended as it so often did: with cries, recriminations, and a long, brooding silence.

No sooner had we had taken our seats in the living room than Amoo Said started teasing me about my recent appearance on television. A few days earlier I had accompanied my father on a tour of Tehran with some Americans who were visiting the city with USAID. It was reported in the news and I was picked up on camera. "Usually when foreigners visit they are shown the best parts of the city," Father said, "but we started with the poorest areas, to give these Americans something to think about. They were a little surprised to see how young a city Tehran was. My own daughter," he said, "also did not appreciate this, so I think she needs a history lesson as well."

"Is that right?" Amoo Said asked me lightly. "One would not expect it of such a cultivated young lady." At this my mother made an almost imperceptible grunt. He went on to tell us how before the Qajar kings chose it as their capital in the eighteenth century, Tehran had been a small village full of beautiful gardens, whose inhabitants lived in underground caves to protect themselves from invaders.

"Not much of that old city remains," Father said dryly, choosing to ignore the silent anger seething between my mother and me. "True enough," Amoo Said rejoined. "It's easier to boast of our glorious past than it is to preserve it. Not a century since the Qajars abdicated and most of the buildings from their time have already gone, part of the modernization project." Father explained that until then there had been no real comprehensive plan for the city. It just grew haphazardly. He boasted that he had employed a conscientious German engineer to draw up a plan with a five-year target as well as a longer, twenty-five-year plan.

As Father and Amoo Said went on talking, occasionally addressing their comments directly to Mother, who nodded without evincing much interest, I drifted in and out of their conversation. At one point it turned to Tehran during the Constitutional Revolution of 1905 through 1911. "Every garden and park in this city carries mementos of that revolution," Amoo Said told us. "Let's hope the ghosts of our fathers have not abandoned this city."

They talked a great deal that day about the gardens of Tehran—which had become places of both refuge and graves for the constitutionalists—but I was more focused on what I would be missing that night by not going to my friend's house. By the time we were ready to leave, I had decided that I should leave Tehran at once, as soon as we were back home.

We ARE ON THE TERRACE of one of Tehran's more trendy restaurants, my father, Aunt Nafiseh, and I. Like most fashionable spots in Tehran the restaurant has a foreign name, Sorento. I don't know where my mother is. These days Father and Aunt Nafiseh have become very chummy. Since he has taken on his position as mayor, they have developed a new and more intimate relationship. She enjoys parties and the admiration of powerful men, and is a great flirt.

Trapped between his desire to understand and help my mother and his resentment of her behavior toward him, my father confided his frustration to others. I believe that it was not deliberate on his part, but in this way he did get sympathy. He was charming and sociable and was more fun than my mother, who seemed to have made a pact never to enjoy herself. Aunt Nafiseh liked to laugh and drink and gamble and go to the movies and the theater. She enjoyed the good life that my father had hoped for when he married my mother, the good life that his austere family in Esfahan so vehemently denied. So while he empathized with my mother, telling us stories of how she had been robbed of her inheritance by her wicked stepmother, he also flattered my aunt and was in turn flattered by her attentions.

They sit opposite me. I feel honored to be spending the evening with two of my favorite people. I never warmed up to my step-grandmother, who was cold and mean by nature, but I loved going to Aunt Nafiseh's house and I desperately wanted to please her. Their eyes are shining and focused on me as I bask in the light of their compliments. But in that repartee, something else is happening that has nothing to do with me. It implies a mute excitement that only relates to the two of them: a young, attractive and successful man and woman, having fun, admiring one another.

Although I do not think we are doing anything wrong, a sense of guilt clings to me afterward. Their relation did not go beyond a certain flirtatious camaraderie; what made it suspect was the deliberate omission of my mother from the occasion. Long before my father was unfaithful to her, my parents had already paved the path with emotional

Father, Aunt Nafiseh, and me.

betrayal. Aunt Nafiseh would be replaced by faces of other women— my father's secretary, a friend of the family— who would smile at me across the table, complimenting me on something or other. It is eerie how, in my memory, they all look alike, sitting opposite me, close to Father, smiling and talking about me in the third person, using my nickname, Azi. During these moments, although I tried to please my father and the woman beside him, I always felt the weight of my mother's absence.

—

A FEW DAYS AFTER the dinner at Sorento, my mother, Aunt Mina, and skinny Monir joon gather in our living room. Mother is holding her small percolator over the gas fire and they are talking about Aunt Nafiseh. Aunt Mina is saying, "Nezhat, you never confronted Nafiseh about family matters, about the way she or her mother mistreated you. But now it is different. This is your husband and you should not remain silent."

"It is beneath me even to acknowledge it," Mother says. "The best response is to pretend not to notice."

"Okay, okay," Aunt Mina says impatiently, "but there's no need to boast about your stubborn silence."

Mother dismisses Aunt Mina's comment with a wave of her hand and embarks on a story she has told us several times before. It is about her stepmother's involvement in an alleged affair. Apparently her stepmother, Ferdows, was indiscreet in front of my mother and my grandfather's youngest brother, who threatened to inform her husband. According to my mother, her stepmother turned the tables on her brother-in-law and claimed that he was spreading rumors because she had refused his advances. This accusation led to an estrangement between her husband and his younger brother.

Mother pours the coffee into three small cups and, as she hands one to Aunt Mina and the other to Monir joon, relates how, for a whole afternoon, her father walked up and down the garden with her asking her to tell him what she knew of these allegations, but she refused to say a word. She was so proud of this fact. I was silent, she says. I divulged nothing. She says this with the same boasting tone with which she would later claim to love the smell of smoke but never to have smoked a cigarette. Why? Why did she say nothing? If she kept it a secret from her father, why would she talk about it to others? Her pride was at times indistinguishable from her bitterness.

I wonder if, by writing about her now, by breaking this cherished silence, I am indulging in one last form of resistance to her. I now believe that we cannot keep silent about the truths we know. She did not really keep silent; in her own way she revealed their secret, by repeating time and again how she had kept silent about it. But what would have happened if she had confronted her stepmother and not felt the need to keep up appearances? What would have happened, for that matter, if I had confronted my father?

ONE PLACE SEEMED not to have been much affected by my father's job: Esfahan. When we visited our relatives for a few days nothing seemed to have changed. Mohammad and I were feted and dined as we moved from one relative's house to another. My cousins and younger uncles published their own magazines, which they wrote and illustrated by hand. They had established a sophisticated library system that had branches in our grandmother's and two older uncles' houses, and held weekly meetings at which literature and philosophy were discussed with great intensity. When we visited Esfahan, these meetings were convened almost daily. Over breakfast and lunch, in the streets going from one historical site to another, in the evenings on the cool terrace, at nights on the upstairs balcony under the stars, we talked, exchanged poetry, and debated. These are my memories of Esfahan: standing on the lower steps of the terrace that led to the garden with Cousin Mehdi; loudly reciting poems by Forough Farrokhzad; walking on the wide avenue along the river with Cousin Majid, talking about his poetry; standing by the breakfast table with Cousin Nassrin and, while her mother shuffles to and from the kitchen, talking of Sartre, Camus, and Dostoevsky, while I try to ignore a slight nagging guilt at not helping with the breakfast arrangements.

Two years later, on that same terrace, my uncle would summon a family meeting to address an article by Mehdi in their homemade journal. "In order to live, one must have hope," Mehdi had written. "We have no hope . . ." He went on to complain about the stifling atmosphere in Esfahan, one that stunted the growth of young people and deprived them of the joy of being young and the possibility of living differently. My uncle turned to me, and said with a hint of sarcasm, Let's start with our modern lady from Tehran. Can a place where such writing is freely published and debated be suffocating?

My mother is mostly absent from these memories. She found it outrageous, my obsession with my father's family. In a way she saw it as an affront to herself. Later she would complain that my brother and I never accorded her family the same kind of respect and love we showed our father's family. But one scene in particular has remained with me. It was during a short visit to Esfahan that summer. After dinner my mother followed me from the dining room to the terrace, with a small plate full of sliced pears, stopping at intervals to push her fork with a pear at its tip into my mouth. I am aware of sideways looks by my uncles and my cousins. Finally, with a theatrical gesture, proclaiming, Please observe my predicament and sympathize! I surrendered and sat opposite her, as if in a staged play, while she forced slices of pear into my mouth. I remember her smile of triumph, and the small fork moving to and fro. In a diary that has miraculously survived over three decades, I have written for half a page:

I hate pears
I hate pears
I hate pears
I hate pears
I hate pears . . .

And for another half page:

I eat pears
I eat pears
I eat pears
I eat pears
I eat pears . . .

This memory is washed over with other memories: waves of sympathy and understanding from my uncles and cousins. We argue—about the veil, relations between men and women, love . . .

———

A WEEK OR SO BEFORE I leave to return to school in England my family pays a visit to a psychiatrist's office. He is not really a psychiatrist, he's a neurologist with knowledge of psychiatry—one of the best in the country, by all accounts, and a friend of my mother's half brother, Uncle Ali. We chose him out of a need for discretion— first of all there is nothing wrong with anyone, and second, it is useless anyway, and third, why should one air one's dirty laundry in public?

We are all at the office with Uncle Ali. It is after office hours and we're in a bit of a hurry (my parents have to attend an official function that evening). After desperate consultations, Father had reached the conclusion that medical advice might help my mother. I think his new position as mayor, his certainty that he could make a difference in the political arena, has given him the power to believe he can also change his domestic life. We are all four there because there is no way my mother would agree to see a psychiatrist on her own, and my uncle is there because he is the psychiatrist's friend and my mother has asked him to be there. We have persuaded her to come along by putting forward the theory that talking to him might help solve our collective problems.

You know how teenage children are, my uncle says, awkwardly, leaving the rest to our imagination. In my time, teenagers did not exist, she says impatiently, taking a cursory look at the indifferent landscape paintings on the walls of the waiting room. We obeyed our elders no matter how old we were. And what with your husband so busy . . . You think *he* is busy? she says. What about me? He enjoys the fame and I get the criticism. Add to that the management of the house, and the children. All of this takes its toll, my kind uncle says in his calm, Zen-like manner; that's why we are here. He calls her Nessi, the nickname he and Aunt Nafiseh use for her. My mother adores her half brother and he is very sweet. His attitude toward everyone is much the same: detached and sympathetic.

One by one we are called in by the doctor. Father goes in first. As soon as he comes out, she pulls him to a corner and I am called in. Like my father and my brother, I am there to enlighten the already enlightened doctor about our relations with my mother. It takes about ten minutes. I am immersed in the excitement of conspiracy. The secretive mission we have all embarked on makes me foolishly open with the doctor, counting all my grievances, sympathizing with Father. God knows what kind of marriage he himself has. Two illusions: that he could make a difference and that our trick would bear fruit.

When my brother emerges and the doctor calls Mother in, she asks the doctor to come out of his room. She says she has nothing to hide; unlike the rest of us, she has no secret. Now, she says, they may have problems they want to discuss, but not me. Well, Ahmad Khan is a very important public personage, she says with a sarcastic smile. After all, he has so much responsibility. Now this lady—meaning me—and her brother are at the start of their life. They have anxieties about their studies, their future, and they also have to think of their very important father—he has always been the center of their lives. But I, she says, I am a poor housewife. I am a nobody. I have no anxieties, nothing to worry about. And I never felt I had to complain to doctors about my problems. She extends her hand, thanks the doctor with a poisonously sweet smile, and goes out; we sheepishly follow her.

In the car my father seeks to justify his action in going to the doctor. He offers up all the usual reasons and excuses and tries to convince her she is wrong, that it would be good for the family to go. Every once in a while he turns to us for confirmation and we mumble something in assent. They have to drop us off at home before heading on to the reception. I expect her to make trouble but, unexpectedly, there is no fuss. She responds icily to our anxious, barely audible good-byes and they go on their way.

As a defense against Mother, Mohammad and I had developed a bantering tone, turning our frustrations into games, little jokes. Feeling close to Father made us feel closer to each other. That night during dinner we go over the visit to the doctor's. That worked well, he says, as he fills his plate with as much crust from the rice as possible. I pull the plate out from under him. Hey, leave some for me! What now? he says. What now what? I snap back. What will we do about her now? he asks. That night we hatch several plans: we could drug her by dropping Valium into her coffee, invite the doctor to come for a social visit and have him diagnose her on the sly. He could hypnotize her. . . . Poison, what about poison? I say. You want to kill her? No, we give her a little poison and then rescue her; that way she will appreciate life. Ah, she will say. I never knew how precious life was. Or what if the three of us, Father, you, and I, committed suicide. That would teach her a lesson, I say excitedly. Yes, that might be the best solution.

rehearsal for a revolution

By the end of that summer, I had vowed never to return home for another vacation. In my last week, my mother and I fought almost every day, about my going out with friends or their visiting me, about trips to Esfahan, about my lack of respect at all times. But after a week back in Lancaster I was already planning my next trip home. Mother informed me in a loving letter that she had sent me a package with dried cherries, walnuts, wool socks (for those awful English winters), and a sweater (blue, my favorite color). Did I want anything else? A friend would be visiting England and she would send along a gold chain for my birthday.

The next summer I found myself in Tehran a little before the end of the school term. I don't remember exactly why, but it must have had something to do with the turmoil raging across Iran throughout that winter and spring of 1962 and 1963, escalating in the holy month of Muharram, which started that year in mid-May. The unrest was triggered by the passage of a new council election bill allowing women to vote for the first time and revoking the condition that all parliamentary candidates must be Muslim. The bill, announced on October 8, 1962, engendered a great deal of furor in the religious establishment, mainly instigated by Ayatollah Ruholla Khomeini.

Looking back at our history, what seems surprising to me now is not how powerful religious authorities have been in Iran but how quickly modern secular ways took over a society so deeply dominated by religious orthodoxy and political absolutism. The Pahlavis replaced the religious law with a modern judicial system, but the damage done to the religious establishment was far more substantial than this act alone would suggest. Before the Constitutional Revolution, the clerics had not only controlled the legal system, they had dictated the way of perceiving the universe. While some clerics wanted to preserve the old system and perhaps saw correctly in its demise their own dwindling influence, others among them opted for change and actively participated in the struggle.

From the time of the Constitutional Revolution to the days of upheaval in 1963 to the Islamic Revolution of 1979, the bloody and violent struggle that divided Iran was not just political but also cultural and ideological. In a sense it was existential. Opposition by the traditionalists stemmed from a revulsion, at once institutional and personal, at the modernizing moves that they perceived the Shah, Mohammad Reza Pahlavi, and his father, Reza Shah, had set in motion. Now the truth of the matter was that the movement for modernization had been under way before the Pahlavis and never stopped after them. Women's rights, minority rights, and culture became the main arenas of contention. Time and again in that fateful summer of 1963, Ayatollah Khomeini and his supporters linked political oppression and foreign domination to the Shah's lifestyle, his father's mandatory unveiling of women, the Shah's love of nightclubs, his keeping dogs (considered unclean in Islam) as house pets. They railed against films, music, and novels and lampooned the idea of individual rights.

The government retreated in the face of the unrest and it repealed the bill that had passed in October. But the Shah was not about to give in. He soon came up with a new and more comprehensive proposal, called the White Revolution, which he decided to put to the test of a popular referendum.

The White Revolution involved a host of modernizing measures: redistributing the land among peasants; giving women the right to vote and to stand as candidates for Parliament and local government; nationalizing natural resources; establishing a literacy corps for remote towns and villages; and an industrial profit-sharing scheme by which workers could benefit from factories' profits. Much was made by some of the Shah's opponents of the fact that the plan had the blessing and strong support of President Kennedy. Some supported the White Revolution, feeling that its basic tenets were progressive, while others believed that revolution from above would not solve the country's many problems.

A date, January 26, 1963, was set for the referendum. While the nationalists and leftists had been weakened by the 1953 coup that had toppled Mossadegh and reinstated the Shah, the clerics had been quietly mustering support among the influential *baẓaaris* (the traditional businessmen) and in religious seminaries. On January 23, Khomeini's followers closed down the shops in the bazaar as an act of protest. This was followed by marches and provocative preaching from the pulpits. Confrontations ensued between the police and the crowds, leading to more violent protests in the religious city of Qom. These protests resulted, in turn, in the shutting down of the seminaries.

IT IS STRANGE, the difference between living through a historic moment and reflecting on its aftermath. In my memory the many events of that spring and summer seem to be crammed into the first few days of June, culminating in what was later known as the June 5th uprising. Those of us who lived through this period could not of course wholly comprehend what it would come to signify. The days come to me as frantic moments, haphazard freeze-frames that need to be edited and organized for them to make sense. Even then it was clear that something significant was happening. For the first time I could detect the rifts between traditional and modern worlds whose side-by-side existence I had taken so much for granted. It appears now as if all the events of the Islamic Revolution of 1979 were playing themselves out in advance on a miniature scale.

My concept of traditional Muslims came from my father's family, strict and firm in their religious practices but flexible enough to tolerate the intellectual experimentation of their children. My paternal grandmother enveloped her children, believer and nonbeliever alike, with love and compassion. My cousins in Esfahan did not object to giving women the right to vote. They confronted on a daily basis the paradoxes of their lives as modern, educated women who had chosen to be bound by a traditional lifestyle. Who were these people using such strong rhetoric, calling women like my mother prostitutes?

Gatherings at our home in Tehran took on the frenzied atmosphere prevailing through the whole country. My father was busier than usual. In addition to his responsibilities as mayor he had been appointed head of the Congress for Free Men and Free Women, a group that was tasked with garnering popular support for the Shah's reforms and drawing up a list of candidates for the new government. This further alienated my young uncles and cousins who, if not actively rebellious, still disapproved of the Shah's government. Mother's coffee sessions were haunted by the alien and persistent beat outside our doors.

The question of the *real* Iran kept coming up in discussions between my parents and their friends. Which was more legitimate: the ancient traditions with which the Shah propped up his power, or the strict Islamic principle of Ayatollah Khomeini? As I write about those questions that I heard my parents and their friends repeat at so many different times in my life, I would like to add a few of my own: What of Ferdowsi with his sensual women and his pre-Islamic heroes and kings? Or of the satirical turn-of-the-century poet Iraj Mirza, with his erotic satires of clerics and religious hypocrisy? What of Omar Khayyam, the agnostic poet-astrologer who urged us to defy life's transience by drinking wine and making love, or the great mystic poets Rumi and Hafez, who rebelled in their miraculous poetry against religious orthodoxy?

"Don't ever trust the wily clerics, their livelihood depends on deceit." I could hear voices crisscrossing our living room. "How can you believe the Shah when he says he wants to give women the freedom to vote? Do men in this country have the freedom to vote? How many free elections have we had in the last decade?" So went the arguments, round and round, back and forth, returning to the question of trust and the fickleness of the Iranian people, who would one moment ardently support one leader, only to support his worst enemy the next. Many were surprised by the violence of Ayatollah Khomeini's supporters; they appeared to have organized their own vigilante groups who beat unveiled women and set fire to various government institutions.

What I remember most vividly from that summer—perhaps because its truth came to me only many years later—was a comment by Mr. Meshgin, the reporter. "What is amazing," he said, "is not how strong the clerics are, but how, in such a short period of time, the seculars have managed to take over our imagination." Mr. Meshgin did not live to see the truth of his words—he died of cancer a few years later—but even after the Islamic Revolution, the academic and cultural realms were fiercely dominated by the secular and nonreligious elite. It was in these areas that the clerics remained vulnerable, and gradually it was through them that secularism made its comeback, often by way of the very Islamists who had so persistently fought against them.

It was during one such meeting and heated discussion that I first met a new addition to my parents' circle, a striking man with a receding hairline and a low, booming voice that preceded his entrance into the room. I took an instant dislike to him. He was obese. His stomach burst out of his crumpled white shirt and his tie seemed to be tied too tightly around his neck. What I remember most clearly about him are his eyes, jumping out of their sockets, peering at me with lascivious greed. Everything about him seemed charged with a demonic energy, as if some evil genie were trying to release itself from within. He was introduced as Mr. Rahman.

He was a carpet merchant who claimed to have spiritual powers: he summoned ghosts, could tell the future with the help of the Koran, and, as I soon discovered, he had become my mother's number one confidant. My parents met him through one of my mother's relatives. Upon seeing him, Mother blossomed into a welcoming smile. Father's expression was more sardonic. When Mr. Rahman came to greet me, he held my hand in both of his for an uncomfortably long time. "So this is the little lady," he said. "Remarkable, remarkable indeed." His hands felt clammy. He didn't so much scare as repulse me.

Mr. Rahman would appear and disappear like the Cheshire cat throughout the next decade of our lives. He surfaces several times in my father's memoirs: "Rahman looked into my eyes and gazed at them for a while, then he gazed at the palm of my hand," Father writes at one point. "He said a few things about my personal characteristics and then he started to tell me about problems at work. He named those who were my sworn enemies and went on to claim that the Shah was still very much on my side and had not given in to the slanders and lies and false reports against me. But this struggle would end with my enemies' victories and he advised me to resign." Father was wary of Mr. Rahman and suspected that his information was not the result of his prophetic powers but because he was an agent of SAVAK, the intelligence service. He pointed out in his memoir that he had already offered to resign twice over his differences with the prime minister and Pirasteh, the minister of the interior, who among other things accused him of appeasing the mullahs. But the Shah had firmly refused his offer to resign and forced Pirasteh, who was Father's main rival, to apologize to my father in front of the minister of court.

I don't remember when exactly the big flare-up happened between my mother and Mr. Khalighi, of all people. There had been talk of including her among the first female candidates for Parliament in the next election, scheduled for the fall. She would run from the Kerman province, where she was born and where the Nafisis had originated. Suddenly she had become enamored of the Shah and would not tolerate all the rubbish being said about him. "You, my dear Nezhat Khanoom," Mr. Khalighi said, "are even less equipped than your husband here to enter this arena."

Mother missed the goodwill behind those words and took them as a clear sign of contempt. No entreaty would rectify the situation. Later that evening, my father's attempts to mollify her fell on deaf ears. From that day on until my father's imprisonment several months later, we didn't see Mr. Khalighi again—on Fridays or at any other time. Although, as he did with other banished friends and acquaintances, Father continued to see him on the sly.

Father was on good terms with many of the clerics, especially those he considered progressive. He ignored the prime minister's "recommendation" that he keep his distance and participated in a mourning ceremony at the house of the respected Ayatollah Behbehani, where disparaging remarks against the Shah and the government were made by a young cleric. The prime minister told Father that the government had decided to take strong measures against the protestors and advised my father not to meddle. He suggested it would be to

Father can be seen standing behind the Shah, as he meets with a cleric.

his advantage to keep a low profile, and ordered him to close the shops on June 5th, the day Khomeini and his supporters had chosen for widespread protests and demonstrations. My father disobeyed this order. Instead he decided to let the stores open earlier than usual that day, so that people could stock up on necessities. He created emergency centers in different parts of the city, and alerted the hospitals to be prepared to receive any protestors who were wounded.

ON THE MORNING OF JUNE 5TH we were all up very early. Father had left at dawn and Mother was growing increasingly agitated because she could not locate him on the phone. Sometime early in the morning a chauffeur from the municipality came to let her know that Father was okay but that he was moving around so much it was difficult for him to call home. He was on his way to the fire station, which he had turned into one of his headquarters.

Mother had her own headquarters, in our living room, where throughout the day different people rushed in and out, breathlessly offering the latest news. The coffeepot was on constant duty. My brother and Uncle Reza had left early in the morning, to see what was happening around town. I stayed home. With a book in hand, I drifted in and out of the living room, where Mother presided with calm while managing to convey the impression that underneath she was all nerves, worried about my father, the city, the people. What could she do under the circumstances but hold the fort and be prepared in case of emergency? And in truth she was worried about him. As my observant aunt Mina had said, she had seen women pretend to love their husbands when they did not, but she had never seen a case like that of Nezhat, who adamantly insisted she didn't care for her husband while in fact she cared about him a great deal.

Thinking of the people who came by that day, I marvel at how dissimilar they were. All were there because of her. This was a peculiarity of hers: no number of recommendations would persuade her to hire a person, or go to a doctor or hairdresser, unless she liked him or her. She liked these people partly because they agreed with her, and partly, I think, because they knew how to manipulate her and make her believe that they were on her side. This was true not just of people she knew; there were many strangers who knocked on our door saying that they had met Mrs. Nafisi at a shop, in a taxi, on the bus, and she had asked them to come over and have coffee with her.

Although most were not politically minded, in our living room they became passionately involved in political discussions. We were disastrous as politicians in our family, but avidly civic-minded. I could perhaps generalize and say that this was true of almost every Iranian family—the state has had such an intrusive presence in our lives that no Iranian citizen can choose to ignore it. But my parents liked to ponder and analyze events in a way that others did not. Aunt Mina's loyalties and preoccupations were private and personal; her allegiances were to her family and her small group of friends. Mother, on the other hand, was at heart a public person and a political meddler. She was not interested in exchanging recipes.

Around mid-morning we had an unexpected visit. Ameh Hamdam, who never visited unannounced, suddenly dropped in. She said she couldn't stay long, but she needed to talk to Mother. Her presence always intrigued me. I tried to make myself invisible and remained within earshot. They talked quietly and I could hear snatches of conversation. "But it isn't because of him," Ameh Hamdam said. "Oh yes, it is," Mother said, shaking her head knowingly. "He never wanted me to amount to anything. Remember when I wanted to get my driver's license? Even then he interfered."

I began to suspect that Father had sent Ameh Hamdam to dissuade Mother from running for Parliament. He knew there was no way he could control her and her wayward tongue. "You know better than anyone," she insisted. "I was cut out to be a career woman. I wanted to become a doctor." "This is different," Ameh Hamdam said quietly. "They are like wolves. They will not have pity."

Mother was pursuing her own train of thought. She said that her brother, Ali, had become a doctor and that medicine was in her blood. "I was so good at it," she said wistfully, "but I was not allowed to pursue it. You see, Saifi was so sick. I couldn't leave him. And then," she sighed, "it became too late. Now that I can do what I want *he* doesn't let me." All the time she was saying this, her eyes were focused on the coffee percolator, avoiding the eyes of Ameh Hamdam.

"You know I've never wanted anything but your own good," Ameh Hamdam said, accepting a cup of coffee. "But this job will bring you nothing but grief." "How can you say that?" Mother shot back, turning to look at her. "You have been a model to me." Ameh Hamdam protested that she was a teacher and had nothing to do with government. The other women candidates had all been in one way or another public figures. "Believe me, Nezhat jan, I would not be here if I did not believe this job would bring you grief."

Mother stiffened. "I should have been a man," she said, shaking her head knowingly. "Then I would be free to do what I want. Will there ever be a time when I can do what I was born to do?" "This has nothing to do with your being a woman," Ameh Hamad said patiently. "Our family is not good at politics. I wish Ahmad were out of it. Look at my own brother, Said. He is out of favor and out of a job. His poor family has to suffer. Politics brings us bad luck."

I was by this point firmly on Ameh Hamdam's side. My father had told me in confidence, with some exasperation, that it was impossible to persuade my mother not to run. By now her name had been put forward and approved by the Shah among the list of suggested candidates for Senate and Parliament—no candidate could run without this process. In his memoir, Father explains that his opposition was based on my mother's lack of political experience and her unpredictable temper. Mother, however, saw things differently: this was her only chance to prove herself in the public arena. Later she forgot her eagerness to run for Parliament and would claim that she had been forced by my father into accepting the nomination. She even told the story of how she had gone to see the Shah and pleaded with him to release her, but the Shah, although very kind to her, had pointed out that this was her husband's wish. When we lied to her we knew that we were lying, but she seldom lied knowingly. In this sense she was telling the truth when she boasted of her insistence on honesty at all costs.

Their conversation was interrupted by the arrival of a messenger from my father, this time from the fire station. Mother invited him in excitedly, made him coffee, and peppered him with questions. Ameh Hamdam made her excuse and left. Around three our dentist showed up. He had been forced to close shop early. "All hell will break loose now!" he said excitedly. "They've arrested Haji Tayeb!" The boss of Tehran's vegetable market had been an active organizer of the protests. As it turned out, hell would take sixteen more years to fully break loose, but that day we got a taste of what was to come.

Around lunchtime Goli arrived, then Shirin Khanoom. At some point they both left. The day seemed interminable. I moved in and out of the living room and with each ring of the bell some new person barged in with news. The protestors had attacked the ministries of justice and the interior and were making their way to the radio station. The prime minister's house had been surrounded by over two hundred men wielding clubs. The protestors had set fire to the Zoorkhaneh, where traditional sports were performed. They were beating women without veils and had attacked the fire station before my father got there. The government had opened fire on the protestors and the hospitals were filled with those who were killed or wounded, and their relatives.

Sometime in the afternoon Aunt Mina came in, looking (unusually for her) ruffled and excited. "It took me an hour just to get here from outside the Parliament," she told my mother, accepting a cup of coffee. "You won't believe the commotion outside." She took a look around the room. "Do you know where Ahmad Khan is?" she asked. "I am concerned for him. People are saying in the streets that the clerics' supporters, protesting against the government, are all armed. The wildest rumors are circulating—I heard that the British have secretly armed a group of fake mullahs to assassinate the prominent politicians."

Mother was patience personified. She pursed her lips and said, "Well, I am sure that is a rumor, but yes, I am worried. Only, do you think anyone listens to me?" After a while, despite the urgency of the moment, they did not forget to gossip about mutual acquaintances. *She* had been seen with the colonel in a compromising situation. "Her husband is so blind." "*Some men,* how foolish they can be." "Yes," Mother almost sighed.

In between chats about politics and sex, my mother would pick up the phone and dial a few numbers in an effort to locate my father. She returned every time with the same expression of patient suffering. At one point she was very agitated because she had been told that Father had gone visiting the hospitals and that the areas surrounding the hospitals and the fire station were very dangerous. She'd mumble something about how she had pleaded with him not to take this job, if not for her at least for her children's sake. "He does love them, we know that," she sighed. "Whatever else we might say about him, we know he loves his children."

By evening Mother was becoming visibly nervous. She had received no call from my father, and this was not in character. The doorbell rang and a few minutes later Mr. Rahman came in, pushing the servant aside, eyes bulging, his eternal gray suit crumpled. He caught me in the hall with a book in my hand, walking lazily to my room. "Stop!" he said, hurrying forward and holding my hand in both of his. His attention always made me panic. Mohammad he ignored, but he always managed to trap me. "I have to work," I said. "You have no work," he said. "You are reading some mumbo jumbo, I can tell. But I need your help," he confided in my ear. "Your father sent me here to reason with your mother and I need you." I said, not untruthfully, "She never listens to me." "It isn't for her sake but for mine," he said. "Your presence brings me luck. It will help me with my powers."

At this point my mother opened the living-room door. "Oh, Rahman," she said, looking pleased, "what are you doing here?" "Ahmad Khan sent me," he said. "I come from him. How lucky you are not to have seen the goings-on today!" Mother was now smiling and Rahman, without relinquishing my resistant hand, followed her to the drawing room. "Nothing a good coffee won't take care of," she said with a smile.

"My dear Nezhat Khanoom," he began, once he had settled in his chair, "dark days are ahead. You have a brave husband . . ." Seeing my mother's disapproving expression, he added, "but a foolish husband. My heart goes out to you. Your mother," he said, turning to me, "is the backbone of this family. What would you do without her?"

Head down, frantically focused on my book, I did my best to ignore him. He turned toward Aunt Mina with the same question, but she was in no mood for this and, mumbling something about it getting late, she swiftly said good-bye and left.

"He can't call," Rahman explained, "because the phones aren't safe. So many wounded. The clerics came prepared. This protest, my dear Nezhat Khanoom, was a calculated and carefully orchestrated event. The clerics had their own group of vigilantes with clubs and knives. They set fire to so many places. They have allies in the bazaar and among the people. Hundreds of men in white shrouds have started to walk from Varamin village toward the city. They've already attacked the police station there, and the military is preparing to receive them with guns. I want you to know he's safe—for the time being," he added cryptically. "How many times have you and I asked him to resign his post?"

Mother murmured that she had never wanted him to take the job in the first place. "Yes, that's what I told him today. Danger everywhere, I see danger."

Mother handed me a cup of coffee and shook her head. "Have you seen it in the Book?" she asked, referring to the Koran, from which Rahman ostensibly received his messages from beyond.

"I have seen it in the Book, yes, but I have also talked with people in the know. Thank God one person in this family has her head in the right place. I told your husband today that you, at least, have the good sense not to run for Parliament."

My mother gave him a bitter look, and I at this point became more interested. "This has nothing to do with me," she said coldly. "I was born into a political family. My father ran for Parliament and was defeated because his so-called friends betrayed him. My husband . . . my husband, Saifi," she stammered, "was the son of the prime minister. I was in the company of people like Doctor Millspaugh since I was . . ." there was a pause, and then she continued, "since I was a mere nineteen-year-old girl. I could have become a doctor, but that's now impossible."

"I know," he said, "I know. But these are dangerous times. We need you, believe me, we need you. Your husband belongs to no group. He is alone."

"Should I always pay for his mistakes?" she said indignantly. Then she added more quietly, "Did you find out about what I asked you?" They both turned to me, and I, by now very interested in hearing what would come next, pretended to read my book. "Azi," my mother said, "I need to talk to Mr. Rahman alone." "I'm not bothering anyone," I said. But I knew I had no choice but to leave. I picked up my book, dragged my feet slowly, dodged Mr. Rahman, and left the door open behind me.

By the time Father returned home, around ten that night, we were all so exhausted that one might have been forgiven for imagining that we had been participating ourselves in the events of the day. I had been worried sick, but I went out of my way to make sure Mother didn't know it. Every once in a while I would go to the door and look out. I drank coffee with every new person who came in. When Father finally entered the drawing room, Mr. Rahman said reproachfully, "Well, Ahmad Khan, it's about time. This poor woman has almost gone out of her mind with worry." The poor woman looked at my father with a stony glare, as if he had just returned from an all-day assignation without bothering to call and say he would be late for dinner.

That summer it was agreed that Mother would run for Parliament along with five other women. She took office in the fall of 1963. My parents decided to send me to the posh and trendy Ecole Internationale in Geneva, a decision that made me long for shabby, gray Lancaster and my mocking British friends. On that day, June 5, 1963, the first page of my father's secret-service file was written. In the file, it was claimed by anonymous agents that my father had collaborated with the opposition to the Shah and with the clerics. At the time, none of us would have been able to predict what effect those few pages would have on our lives, transforming them in ways we never could have dreamed of.

PART THREE | MY FATHER'S JAIL

There is a pain—so utter
It swallows substance up—
Then covers the Abyss with Trance
So Memory can step
Around—across

—EMILY DICKINSON

a common criminal

I<small>N DECEMBER OF</small> 1963, I was pulled out of my history class and taken to the principal's office, where I was told in solemn tones that a Swiss radio station had just reported that my father was in jail. "Has there been a revolution?" I asked. There seemed to be no reason, despite our habitual anxiety, for him to be imprisoned under any other circumstance.

Everything seemed to be going well for him. That whole fall I heard glowing reports about Father hosting different heads of state. Three weeks earlier I'd seen a two-page spread of my father standing alongside General de Gaulle in *Paris Match*. No other dignitaries were in the photo, not even the Shah. De Gaulle had taken a liking to him, perhaps on account of Father's welcoming speech, which he delivered in French with various allusions to French literature. De Gaulle rewarded him with the medal of the Legion of Honor. When I excitedly mentioned the photograph to Father on the phone, he said, "Well, that will cost me, so let's not be too quick to celebrate."

At my school in Geneva we lived a secluded life. I had no access to Persian newspapers, and contact with the outside world was limited to monitored visits from relatives and friends. When I called home to ask Mother about the arrest, I was assured it was just a rumor, that Father was in between jobs and was at our place by the Caspian Sea for a much-needed rest. Aunt Mina wrote to say that he had been offered the job of interior minister and she looked forward to seeing me back home for the holidays. I was supposed to spend my Christmas vaca-

Father meets with French president Charles de Gaulle.

tion in France but I was told that plans had changed and I would be going home. Otherwise all seemed much the same.

My cousin Reza (Aunt Nafiseh's son), who was enrolled at the Le Rosey school in Switzerland, was on the same flight back to Tehran.

As soon as we settled into our seats, I told him I wasn't sure why I'd been summoned home (sudden changes had been made to his plans as well), and suggested it might have something to do with my father. Indeed, he said, casually waving his newspaper in my direction. On the front page was a picture of Father under a big headline about his arrest.

The article enumerated a list of charges, including bribery and mishandling of funds. Some forty other people—mainly contractors—had been arrested with him. In reports filed by SAVAK, the secret police, my father was reported to be consorting with the opposition, and was accused of being on good terms with the clerics and of "insubordination." Two prime ministers, Assadollah Alam and his soon-to-be-successor, Hassan Ali Mansour, who was the same age as my father and ostensibly his friend, had considered him a "problem." One could not forgive my father's arrogance and the other, young and very ambitious, saw him as a serious rival.

The morning after my arrival the familiar sounds and the smell of coffee made me feel for a moment that nothing had changed, that walking into the living room I would find Father smiling indulgently at our guests. Aunt Mina was there and Mr. Khalighi, who had brought a poem to welcome me back, in which he lamented the fact that Father could not greet his beloved daughter at the airport. Mr. Meshgin's gloomy expression was offset by a rare and forced smile. Goli gave me a warm smile as Shirin Khanoom freely vented her anger at the decadent Pahlavis and their godless ways.

Mr. Rahman sat close to Mother, fixing his eyes on me. I was sure he did it just to make me feel uncomfortable. He was now officially part of Mother's entourage, a fixture both at home and in my father's diaries. Rahman warned that Mansour seemed all-powerful now, but who could say what fate might have in store for him? Mother was less charitable. How could one forget, she said, that his father, the Shah's father's last prime minister, had handed Reza Shah over to the British? "His son has a less reliable protector in the Americans, and we see how he chooses to betray his country."

Mr. Behdad, a prominent lawyer who later took on my father's defense, had come that morning, along with Mr. Esmaili, the director of parks and green spaces, one of Father's colleagues who had taken to visiting regularly. Every day Father spent in jail there was always a

vase of fresh flowers in his room; after his release he discovered that they were sent anonymously by Esmaili. In the months and years ahead I would come to appreciate the loyalty of unlikely people like him and Zia, father's chief of staff, whom I had marked as a mere sycophant.

Father during his incarceration.

Zia was saying that perhaps if Nezhat Khanoom could see the prime minister and convince him of Mr. Mayor's innocence (he never stopped calling my father Mr. Mayor) he might soon be released. "My good man," Mr. Khalighi said with some exasperation, "the prime minister, of all people, knows full well that Ahmad is innocent. You seem to forget that *they* fabricated those charges. What we should do is find out the real reason he is in jail."

Such idle speculation was interrupted by the arrival of Aunt Nafiseh, who made an entrance, evincing no concern that she might be interrupting and accepting the sudden silence as an homage to herself. Aunt Nafiseh had embarked on a campaign in my father's defense. She called on government officials on his behalf and made fireworks of her benevolence, visiting him regularly, sending him his favorite food, even offering to lend him money to see us through the hard times. After acknowledging the company with a general nod and offering me her cheek, she turned toward my mother and Rahman, who followed her out of the room. Her arrival cast a gloomy silence on all assembled.

—

WHILE MOTHER AND AUNT NAFISEH waited at the gate of the Police Detention Center, the temporary abode for ordinary criminals, I stood a little apart, wearing what could have been interpreted by sympathetic observers as a brave little smile. In the car Mother and I had already begun our war—I started mumbling about staying in Tehran and doing my A levels with the help of private tutors and she, for some reason best known to her, wanted me to leave as soon as possible. Only when the car deposited us in front of that huge metal gate, which seemed to stretch beyond the walls into another kingdom, did I suddenly panic.

We did have one privilege: we met Father in the office of the prison director, a long and rather narrow room painted a shiny blue-gray, with a darker blue border. On one side, close to the wall, was the director's desk, and behind the desk a balding man in a blue uniform got up anxiously to greet us. Against this dull background his good-natured round face shone with an expression of frank humility. Opposite his desk, next to the wall, was a row of small chairs and two tables.

My mother and aunt embarked on a polite conversation with Colonel Khorami, the prison director, while I sat in the corner, pressed against the slippery wall, glancing out the window. A pause in the conversation: I turned toward the colonel and, from the corner of my eye, saw my father, looking thinner and younger, standing by the open door with a smile. I lurched forward, stumbling over the narrow metal table. The colonel politely averted his gaze. A small exclamation from my aunt, perhaps a look of disapproval from my mother. I stood there until he walked to me and held me in his arms and as he kissed me he whispered, "It's okay, I'm so happy to see you."

At first they talked grown-up talk while I sat beside him holding his hand, as I had so many times before as a young girl. I am struck in old photographs of my father and me by the way I try to create some form of physical contact between us: I lean toward him, rest my head on his shoulder, or place my hand on his arm.

The first thing he said after he kissed me was, "Never show any sign of weakness, any sign that you are hurt or ashamed. You aren't ashamed, are you? These are just tests of our endurance. This is the time to be proud." *This is the time to be proud.* I would hear this many

My mother, a family friend, Father, and me.

more times from him and my mother over the years. While my father was a promising young mayor who had the ear of the Shah, we were all a little wary of being proud of him. To be proud you had to become a victim of injustice.

"Remember how I used to tell you that you could always rely on me?" Father whispered as my mother and aunt continued to exchange pleasantries with the prison director. "That you could light a feather, like the one Simorgh gave Zal in the *Shahnameh,* and I would come to your rescue? Well, I will still be there for you, no matter where I am. But now, I need your help. You have to take care of your mother. You need to be kind and gentle to her." He said he had asked the same thing of my brother. "You are the man in the family now," he had told him, something my eleven-year-old brother took very seriously. "You know your mother has no one but you and your brother now," he said to me, looking at me intently. "You have to promise me that you will look after her. I have failed her, and I need you to compensate for that. I need you to promise that you will not hurt her or in any way disobey her." I promised I would look after my mother and said I would do my best not to hurt her. It was a promise that I would make and break many times.

Father told me to act as if nothing had happened. We did our best to act normal, so much so that we almost came to believe it ourselves despite the fact that nothing in the world seemed normal. Had we acted with more humility, we would have been lying, because we did not believe in his guilt. We were not at all humbled. And yet acting as if this situation did not affect us was also a lie. Publicly we chose this second lie, but in our private lives we tried both and neither one worked.

I am still grateful to my aunt, who held my hand all through the journey home and pressed it in a friendly manner when the tears started streaming down my face while my mother averted her gaze. Perhaps she felt she could not spare any sympathy for others, even her own daughter, because, after all, was not *she* the real victim? However much she mistreated Father, she never doubted his public honesty. Only later would she repeat the rumors against him which she herself had once vehemently denied while reminding us of Saifi, his honesty, his family's integrity. That she, Saham Soltan's daughter-in-law, had to suffer such public humiliation! How amazing is the capacity of human beings for self-deception: my father's hope for domestic bliss, my mother's illusions about her lost husband, and my brother and I, believing that we could make our parents happy, could protect them from each other.

the prison diaries

THE ADJECTIVES WE ATTRIBUTE to our circumstances—"tragic," "ironic," "humorous"—always come to us with a delay, after we have gained objectivity. When I think of those days now some of these words come to my mind, certainly both "tragic" and "ironic," but mostly I was bewildered, as if walking in a fog. No one had any idea what would become of my father. There were endless rumors that he would be freed the next day, followed by ominous warnings that he would be sentenced to fourteen years (why fourteen, I wonder now—why not thirteen, or fifteen?) or worse, that he would be murdered in jail and his murder would be presented as suicide. This constant vacillation between two extremes was repeated at home, where my mother, brother, friends, relatives, and sympathetic strangers wove stories of hope and despair.

Nine months after his arrest, my father began writing in his diary again: he had stopped writing when he went to jail because every day he hoped that he would be freed. "Today it is exactly nine months since they put me in jail," I read in the first entry. "From the first day they arrested me on trumped-up charges, the worst catastrophe has been that they promised they would set me free. This situation has worsened since the new government took over."

The new government he refers to is that of his old friend Hassan Ali Mansour, who had replaced Alam. Mansour's rise to power had been meteoric: chief of staff to the prime minister at thirty, then chairman of the Economic Council and vice prime minister in 1957, when he was about thirty-four. I remember him as tall and balding, hazel-eyed and tanned. My father spoke with a tinge of envy about Mansour's wife, Farideh Emami, who in my mind's eye appears as a petite woman with long straight brown hair. She seemed to be always hanging from an invisible string connected to her husband. Whenever Mansour's name came up Father managed to mention Mansour's wife's devotion to her husband and his career. Other, less charitable observers saw her as a clinging, ambitious woman who never left her poor husband alone.

I remember a garden party with beautifully dressed men and women, lights around the swimming pool: Mansour strides across the lawn, gracefully pulls my father from the small group he is talking to, and leads him away with one hand encircling his shoulder. I watch them, two young men, confident and sure of where they stand and where they will be going, an intimate pose, almost conspiratorial. A short while later Mrs. Mansour joins them with a serious and busy expression, her gaze hanging adoringly on her husband as she clings to his arm.

Mansour was to become one of my father's obsessions. He writes more about him in his prison diaries than his other "enemies": it was far more difficult to tolerate a stab in the back by a friend. "I have known him for twenty-five years," he writes on page 312. "We had become very close over the past few years. He was a man of taste, talented, polite, humble, but a liar, a flatterer, and extremely ambitious. He would sacrifice everything to advance himself. He constantly dreamed of becoming the prime minister and would do anything to get there. I used to have a great deal of affection for him but soon I discovered his duplicity and dishonesty. In more recent years he considered me his only real rival, despite the fact that I lacked his connections and means."

Later Father reports that an acquaintance who had spies in high places told him that Mansour had seen Father as a rival. By this account Mansour and a contact at the American Embassy, a Mr. Rockwell, cooked up some lies which they fed to the Shah. The Americans would ensure Mansour's success. What were the chances, my father reflects, that a man like him, with no powerful allies and no foreign backing, could survive in such circumstances? This question would come up in numerous conversations my father had with friends and family, as well as in the pages of his diary. Mr. Rockwell resurfaces again some pages later, as Father wonders if the rumors about Mansour's connections to him are true. Could this be why the Iranian government had insisted on Rockwell's transfer before the American ambassador's return from his vacation?

Other friends reported that the Shah had been told that Father had given the list of parliamentary candidates to the Americans (the list was not made public until the Shah approved of it), or else that he had revealed to them the content of a secret conversation with the Shah. "Ahmad Khan, just among friends, tell us the truth," the good-natured Safipur, owner and editor of the popular magazine *Omid Iran*, teased my father. "Are you in jail for supporting the parliamentary candidates that the Americans couldn't stomach or for leaking the list to the Americans? If it is the former we will start contacting our anti-American friends in high places; if the latter, we will lobby the Americans, but if neither is true," he said with a laugh, "then your case is truly hopeless!"

Why was he in jail? Had he offended the Shah? Was it petty rivalry? His own ambition? Few believed the charges against him, not even his enemies. Political dissent in Iran is treated as a form of criminality: most offenders are tried on bogus charges and there is little room for defense. The fact that the charges were not taken seriously made the whole situation unreal, almost a little comic. I was learning my first lesson in Iranian politics and public life: truth mattered very little.

High officials would visit him and wonder aloud as to the "real reason" for his arrest, or send messengers to let him know they believed he was innocent and they didn't know why he was in jail. His prison diaries are filled with reports of these visits. "Around evening, Dr. Jamshid Amuzegar"—a cabinet minister and later prime minister—"came to visit me with Safipur," he writes early on. "We talked about a great many things and he too wanted to know the real reason for my arrest. He said that both in and out of the cabinet, everyone knows for sure that I am not a thief or an embezzler. On the contrary, I've been a great servant to the people. He thinks my problem must be political. Amuzegar and I considered and analyzed whatever came to mind, but God knows we couldn't figure out the nature of my crime!" A few pages later he writes, "At night, when I am alone, I cry a lot. For myself, my children, and this cursed country. Now that we have an opportunity to do something for the poor people, the government has fallen into the hands of prejudiced and feckless youth."

Eager to convince some invisible interlocutor of his innocence, Father details why it would be impossible for "them" to believe that he had stolen from the government coffers. First, they had access to his accounts. They would know about his debts and also that his own personal possessions, after twenty-five years of civil service, setting aside his wife's inheritance, did not amount to much. He gives a meticulous account of his spending and quotes a judge who said that if Nafisi wanted to steal money, he would have done so when he was the vice president in the Planning and Budget Organization, which regulated the country's budget. To the notion that the Shah was displeased with his ambitions, he countered the fact that the Shah knew full well that he had no desire ever to be prime minister. He would have been happy to remain mayor of Tehran, to finish what he had started. He mentions a tape in which his enemies had faked a conversation between him and a woman at a party speaking condescendingly of the Shah.

Where do we go when no amount of careful consideration can provide the answer? The world he lived in was unreal and unreasonable. His highest satisfaction came from responding curtly to his interrogator, not yielding, turning the tables around and pointing out the pitfalls in his arguments. At times the frustrated interrogator seemed to plead with my father to help him find a clue that might justify the charges.

Try as he might, he cannot answer the two most important questions: Why is he in jail and what will happen to him? At some point he takes refuge in the world of dreams. Like a novelist who, having just written a book revealing the most intimate secret of his best friend, states that none of the characters bear any resemblance to real people, Father poignantly writes that he has no belief in superstition, sorcerers, or fortune-tellers, while filling his notebooks with his own and other people's dreams. In these ridiculously symbolic and wish-fulfilling dreams, a world emerges that is far saner and more believable than reality itself. We find a Shah who is forced to see reason, officials who do the decent thing, and my father is able at last to present his case forcefully, logically, and convincingly. Exchanges that have become impossible in reality become the norm in these fantasies. A more equitable world is established in this parallel universe, where all sorts of people are open and independent-minded. They can warn, advise, and even command the Shah to do the right thing. And he does: he listens, he is convinced.

"I AM WRITING THIS first for myself and then for my daughter and son," my father writes some two hundred pages into his prison diaries. "When they have more time than now, and the power to analyze, maybe these writings will be a source of counsel and guidance for them." Five volumes and almost fifteen hundred pages remain of my father's diaries, recording his life in jail until his release and ultimate exoneration four years later. My father used to say half-jokingly that his years in jail were among his most fruitful. Sometimes he said this in reference to the jail he believed my mother had created for him at home. But there was another side to his claim, one that comes out in his diaries, and in his numerous poems and paintings. He had a talent for performing well under difficult circumstances. Something was triggered, something that made him resist whatever was in his way. And so he blossomed in the most unexpected places.

Seeing him on our short weekly visits in a room that was not his own, detached from all objects and places that I associated with him, it was difficult to imagine his actual experiences in the many hours when we were not there. Reading his diaries now, another world leaps off the page, a planet with its own routines and laws and unlikely inhabitants. What seems to have sustained him, other than hope and the love of family and friends, is his enormous zest for life. It is as if jail has squeezed all his love of life into moments of exquisite intensity, so that he learns new languages, writes and reads, ponders history, paints, and sheds over twenty pounds.

In his diary he describes an insane daily routine. "I wake up at 4:30, after washing up I walk around my room until about 7 and while walking I read *Nahj ol Balagheh*"—the writings of Imam Ali— "or books on the interpretation of the Koran or history or religion. At 7 I eat breakfast with the detention center's officers and read until 8. From 8 to 10 I walk around my room, studying German. Between 10 and noon I usually have visitors, or officers and other prisoners visit me. Then until 1 p.m., which is lunchtime, I either

Father in jail, with one of his paintings of a bird.

read or write. After lunch I rest, read, and sometimes take a nap until three. From three to five I take a shower and read in French while walking. From five to six I take a bath, read the papers, have dinner, and engage in conversation with whoever visits me. From then on until I fall asleep around midnight I listen to the radio or read."

He moves seamlessly from his own feelings of frustration, his sense of betrayal and grief, to conversations with the prison staff, other prisoners, visitors, family, and friends, to comments on the country's political situation and events in other parts of the world—Churchill's death in 1965, the war in Vietnam. He celebrates the freedoms of the American people, their amazing capacity to re-create themselves, and at the same time he bemoans American foreign policy. At one point he writes an open letter to President Johnson in which he quotes John Quincy Adams, Franklin Roosevelt, Daniel Webster, and Abraham Lincoln. He explains that he writes as a person who has witnessed "the anxiety and fear in the faces of striking workers in Detroit whom I have seen in the depths of despair lying on the sidewalks with bottles of whisky . . . the ruined and smoky buildings in Harlem and Chicago, the unhappiness and hunger in New Orleans and Baltimore . . . as well as the beautiful new buildings with their automatic doors, the endless blessings of individual freedoms and the beauty, comfort and culture of the country . . ." He talks about the need to acknowledge America's debt to other nations and asks Johnson "not to be deceived by the tyrannical politicians in other countries, not to consider those who think differently from him as his enemies, not to make the mistakes America was making in Vietnam, and not to give condescending charity to other nations—if you are going to help them you should do it based on principle and as equals."

He writes poetry addressed to his children, to his wife, to beloved friends and relatives. He falls in love with Socrates, Voltaire, and the Buddha, and translates Paul Eluard's poem "Liberté," Victor Hugo, and, oddly, a book on the human body, which seems to fascinate him. He creates a collection box to help other prisoners post bail, learns how to paint, polishes his German, and starts to learn two new languages, Russian and Armenian, from another inmate.

In jail he works on the three children's books that he will publish decades later: a translation of La Fontaine's stories, complete with beautiful illustrations copied from the original, a selection of stories by Ferdowsi, and a selection of stories by the great Persian poet Nezami. He describes how he taught me and my brother these stories when we were three or four years old, and how important they are. In most cases his tone is reflective, but in the case of Ferdowsi he becomes at times tongue-tied. "I loved Ferdowsi from the start," he writes at one point. "In my opinion he is the greatest Iranian on earth, and his *Shahnameh* is incomparable. It reflects his love of country, candor, truthfulness. No one teaches humanity, kindness, and goodness better than he does. . . . Every Iranian should honor him. I want my children to learn the love of country, humanity, and to understand the values of the ancient Iranians. Ferdowsi's heroes were all God-fearing and humane. He never praised a tyrant, and did not bestow any evil traits on his heroes."

For a while he gets to discuss Ferdowsi for long hours with another prison mate, a General Baharmast, who was known as General Ferdowsi. The general was arrested on charges of molestation, but, according to my father, his real crime was that he was legal counsel for Haji Tayeb, the boss of Tehran's vegetable market, who was executed for supporting Ayatollah Khomeini during the June 5th uprising.

Strange people keep popping in and out of the pages: a gifted painter who becomes Father's teacher, a young man with four hundred girlfriends who is accused of killing one of them, the frustrated prisoner who hangs himself, the American arrested for killing his wife. He mentions a man who suddenly came to life in the morgue; instead of tending to him the prison officials gloated over the "miracle" until the poor man died of the cold. He remembers how, in the very room where he was confined, next door to the morgue, he had, years before, visited another prominent prisoner. He often complains of how people keep telling him—sometimes by way of consolation—that he is lucky to be in jail. ("Nezhat tells me I am lucky I am in here and that I don't have to work with the new government!" "Rahman tells me I'm lucky to be in prison, otherwise I would have been killed!") He himself used to tell us how lucky he was not to be a member of the radical opposition or like some of the other inmates, without a prominent name and money, whose hope rested on God and God alone. Reading his prison diaries I cannot help but think—with the same feeling of irony and desperation—how jail for him might indeed have been a blessing in disguise.

a career woman

HOWEVER MUCH FATHER WAS ON OUR MINDS—and he was almost always on our minds—we had to live our own lives, and soon the new reality became part of our routine. We would visit him and then leave him behind, like a terminal patient. A great deal of our activity was centered around him, but we each in our own way went about our lives. *Life Without Father* would be a poignant title for this part of my story. In one sense I felt orphaned, or practically orphaned, because his fate, like ours, dangled on a thread. "I feel sorry for Azar," he writes early in his diary. "At this age when she is in need of a sympathetic soul and a guide, she has been left alone. She does not get along with her mother. From the time she was six or seven I tried very hard to make peace between them, but it didn't work. The truth is that I have imposed a lot on Azar and pressured her a great deal. Nezhat unfortunately does not know that a child needs to act childishly and a youth needs to act young. She treats her daughter the same way her stepmother treated her. If you didn't know better you would think she wasn't her mother."

That winter I was forced to leave Tehran again. Mother sent me back to school despite my pleading, Father's objections, and the fact that I could have studied for my A levels with the help of private tutors in Tehran. The only satisfaction I got was that instead of the snobbish Swiss school with its high-class clientele, I was shipped back to shabby, gray Lancaster. Two or three months after my return I fractured my spine trying to climb down from the second-story bedroom—my room was directly above Skipper's living area and I loved to see my guardian's surprised expression as he saw me climbing down in front of his window. I had to lie in bed at first in the hospital, and then at home, for about three months. When I returned home that summer, it was to stay.

I had persuaded Skipper not to alarm Mother by giving her news of the accident directly. Instead, he contacted Aunt Nafiseh or Aunt Mina—I don't remember which. Rahman claimed that before the news reached him he already knew about the accident. "I will tell you something about Azi," he apparently told my mother, appropriating my nickname. "Something has happened to her, but I don't want you to be alarmed." Which naturally made her very alarmed indeed. He picked up her handbag and let it fall to the floor, saying, "What happened to her is like this bag falling. She'll be okay, but you must bring the child back home. She needs her mother," he added, quite cunningly—he did not say her parents, but her mother. "She needs her mother's wise supervision."

And so I returned, but that hardly meant everything would go according to my plans. Without my father as intermediary, Mother and I would be living together in undiluted proximity. If I wanted to go out, I had to plead and beg. It helped if I became hysterical, or even fainted—something to prove the depth of my misery. Then she would let me go. Once, when she had refused to let me go to a party, I told her that the host was an orphan who would feel slighted if I missed his good-bye party. It was true that he was an orphan but he never harbored such petty jealousies and in fact enjoyed the story of how my mother softened and let me go not to have fun but to appease the sensitive feelings of an orphaned child. Sickness and misery always gained me extra points.

By this time my brother and I had grown accustomed to Mother's proclivities: like drug users, we needed a shot of drama to get by. When she shouted and accused us of our various crimes we became hysterical, cried, tore up our clothes, and in some cases even tried to hurt ourselves physically. While we were genuinely worried about my father, she seemed to thrive on his incarceration. She had the satisfaction, so beloved of dictators, of a permanent state of emergency. Later, after the Islamic Revolution, I used to joke that we had prepared ourselves for a time like this by living with Mother. The problem with such a state of affairs was not that you did not get to do what you wanted—sometimes you did—but the effort to appease or resist the reigning deities left you so exhausted that it prevented you from ever really having fun. To this day having fun, just plain enjoying myself, comes at the cost of a conviction that I have committed an undetected crime.

But, as in most cases, there was another side to the story. My

mother must have been riddled with anxiety about my father's fate. For all her stubborn refusal to worry about Father, she was constantly distressed by imagined disasters that could befall me and my brother. I

Mother, during her time as a member of Parliament.

couldn't go mountain climbing because I might break my neck, Mohammad could no longer ride buses or go to the football games he adored because he might be kidnapped by Father's enemies. Then there was the matter of her job. She was now in Parliament, and for the first time in her life she had a job (except for the short period when she had worked in the bank), something to prove that her life's ambitions had not altogether gone to waste. But her moment of triumph was eclipsed by my father's situation. All her activities in Parliament were restricted by the knowledge—on her part and everyone else's— that my father was a hostage in jail. Everyone, including my former school principal Dr. Parsay, now herself a senator, advised my mother to be careful, to keep out of the limelight. She complained about such recommendations, and hardly listened to them. In fact, whenever she found the opportunity she was the most outspoken member of the opposition. Was this another sign of her selfish disregard for my father's situation, as so many friends and relatives claimed? Or was it a reflection of her sense of integrity, her insistence in doing the right thing, no matter what the cost? I think perhaps it was both.

In my father's absence, my mother redesigned her coffee sessions. There was a gradual shift from whispering women to men in ties and suits. Every once in a while she would preside over special gatherings with prominent journalists and officials, whom she proudly called "my men friends." ("I get along far better with my men friends," she would boast, "than with women.") Most of the men came to our house because they were interested in my father's fate, though some did come because they were impressed by her. Since she joined Parliament in the fall of 1963, a few months before Father's arrest, she could claim that her political connections were due at least in part to her own public role. She counted General Pakravan, the former head of the Ministry of Information, as one of her friends. She would talk about what the Shah had told her, how she had argued with the Shah, how such and such was between the two of them.

These coffee sessions were different from the more spontaneous and noisy Friday morning coffee hours, when Mr. Khalighi would jump from politics to poetry. For one thing, they were more self-conscious. There were journalists like Safipur, or the serious-minded Mr. Meshgin. Prominent lawyers came, like Mr. Behdad, Mr. Oveisi, and Mr. Sadegh Vaziri, who later became my father's lawyers; government officials; and members of Parliament. In these sessions the men sat a little too straight, like schoolboys expecting to be called upon at any moment. Mother talked with great passion, blasting the government from the prime minister, who she was sure was backed by both the British and the Americans ("Of course, we know *who* is behind this gentleman"), to the judiciary (the real thieves, from the minister on down). She reserved her most scathing comments for General Nassiri, the former head of police, who was now in charge of Iran's feared intelligence organization, SAVAK, and Pirasteh, the minister of the interior, who was my father's number one foe. She was sure that these two were most responsible for concocting the case against my father. "I am not afraid of these cowards," she would say, "these weak-minded criminals."

Mr. Amirani came only once, or perhaps twice, alone on both occasions. He was the editor of an influential publication called *Khandanyha*. (It is possible I have been left with an impression of the paper's seriousness by my recollection of the man himself.) In his editorials he was bold in chastising the government. It was said that the only person immune from his pen was the Shah himself. Mr. Amirani had decided to take my father's side, at times even published some of his writings. I don't remember seeing him in person while Father was in office, but we heard about him and from him very often once Father had been arrested. "If it is possible to write like Amirani, why don't others do the same?" Father asked in his diary. "And if it is not possible then how can he write this way?" *Khandanyha* published an editorial in his defense that made great waves. Father mentions in his diary that Pirasteh offered Amirani ten thousand *tumans* to publish his own side of the story, but Amirani refused. He continued to publish my father's prison dispatches and to defend him. Father obsessed over Amirani's accounts of haggling with the censors over a line in an article.

For Father what was not written, what was taken out, became more important than what was published.

Mr. Amirani was slim, almost bald, with watchful eyes that peered at you from behind horn-rimmed glasses. His face was thin and sharp, which gave him a scholarly appearance. He reminded me of an emaciated owl. Mother was very proud of her connection to him—she insisted he was *her* friend, and claimed that his support for Father was due to her influence. It was almost poignant, the childish way she competed with my father over these influential men. Years later I saw Amirani's thin, sharp face alongside that of the gentle former head of security, General Pakravan, who had helped save Ayatollah Khomeini after the June 5, 1963, uprising. They were both executed by Khomeini's Islamic regime.

These meetings always left my mother energized, sometimes dangerously so. Usually it was after them that she would pick up the phone and give whoever would listen a piece of her mind. "He might not be a perfect husband," she'd say, "but he has always been a good father, an indulgent father, and a principled man." She would dial a number and say provocatively, "I know Mr. Nassiri's henchmen are listening in, so let me tell you criminals, butchers, defilers of women . . ." Whomever she had called would try to appease her, but she would go on with her barrage of epithets. Later, people would visit Father in jail and ask him to contain his wife, saying that she was the reason his sentence was being prolonged. But Mother would not be contained. Each person would pass her on to the next, like a dangerous explosive, hoping she would blow up somewhere else.

Pᴇᴏᴘʟᴇ ᴅᴏ ᴘᴀʏ ᴀ ᴘʀɪᴄᴇ for their actions, she says cryptically to me one morning. Apparently Pirasteh had been addressing Congress, and a few members, including Mother, kept asking him to speak louder, to raise his voice. He turned to Mother with a smirk and said, "If you are patient enough 'It' will rise in time," making a pun in Persian on the word "rise" and his sexual organ. This caused an uproar on the floor. The session was disrupted, and everyone turned to apologize to her. Soon Mr. Amirani had written a scathing article about the incident, and for a few days we were all basking in the glory of this blunder.

Sometimes I think the years my father was in jail—during most of which my mother was in Parliament—were among the best years of her life. Mother took her job very seriously: she brought to it the same ferocity and determination that she brought to everything she did. She was very proud of the fact that she had been elected secretary to Parliament. Father claims his former colleagues were surprised that Nezhat took her job so seriously, going to her constituency in the small city of Baft in Kerman province and stirring them up with her criticism of the government's neglect and with promises of radical changes aimed at bettering their lives. She used to say that while fate had prevented her from becoming a doctor, now at least she had a chance to show her true mettle. Among the first to experience this mettle was the new prime minister, Hassan Ali Mansour.

Father suspected that his rivals, especially Mansour, had imagined that Mother would be grateful for the job in Parliament and that she would become a willing tool in their hands. How wrong they were! She was fond of telling people about the time when she had been invited with other colleagues to have lunch with Princess Ashraf, the Shah's powerful twin sister, who was said to be close to some of the people (including Pirasteh and Baheri, the minister of justice) who put Father in jail. Mother would relate with pride how, when she was asked to sit at the Princess's table, she refused loudly. Why would eating with *her* be an honor? she asked her colleagues, who I imagine must have done their best to dissociate themselves from her as quickly as possible.

In 1962, before he became the prime minister, Mansour ran for Parliament and was elected as the second representative from Tehran, after Abdollah Riazi, the speaker of the House. He was voted in on the ticket of the Progressive Alliance. Mother's first act of defiance came when Mansour formed a new party, Iran Novin. He expected members of Parliament to join his party, which most did, making him the majority leader. Mother not only refused to join Iran Novin, she made sure that her refusal was well advertised. She would boast that when Mansour suggested that the Shah himself was interested in her active support of Iran Novin, she had responded that, should His Majesty wish to convey a message to her, he could do so directly.

Mansour was not the majority leader for long. He succeeded Alam as prime minister when Alam resigned in 1963. From the start, Mansour's government was controversial. Not long after he took office, he raised the price of gasoline to meet budget deficits, creating a taxi strike that caused so much popular discontent that he had to overturn the decision. In the fall of 1964, the Mansour government brought a controversial bill to Parliament known as the capitulation law, which gave diplomatic immunity to American military personnel, placing them beyond the jurisdiction of the Iranian court for civil or criminal acts. My mother and a few others (only one other person, she insisted) refused to support the law. Those who voted for the act, she claimed with indignation, had no pride in their own country. First the British, and now the Americans. No wonder honest men who have no ties to foreign powers are in jail.

Many admired her courage in voting against the capitulation law, but she puzzled most people with her decision to oppose the family protection law of 1967. This law abolished extrajudicial divorce, permitted polygamy only under limited circumstances, and established special family courts. Her negative vote scandalized those who were pushing for women's rights. She argued that it was hypocritical to pass a law claiming to protect women that stipulated that they would still require the notarized permission of their husband to leave the country. She was too radical, or too inflexible, to accept the compromise that had been proposed, and she preferred to vote against the law than to take what she considered to be half measures. I disagreed vehemently with her about the protection law, and still do, yet I cannot help but admire her hardheaded independence.

LATER MOTHER WOULD SAY you could see it coming. "I was no fan of Mansour," she offered, drawing a deep breath. "I rejected every single bill he brought to the House. Once he tried to reach out to me—of course he was always very polite, not like that goon Pirasteh, who had no manners—where was he educated? I told you what he did in Parliament, didn't I? When he insulted me? People saw Pirasteh for what he was. But Mansour was different. He was a gentleman, always charming. You never knew where you stood with him.

"I had left Parliament," she went on, "and was at the pastry shop. You remember how much you loved those cream puffs? He was very fond of you, the owner. Remember him?" "Yes, Mom, Mr. Tajbakhsh." "He always had a free cream puff for you. I was standing there at the counter, talking to Tajbakhsh, when I heard someone saying, 'May I butt in?' I saw Mr. Tajbakhsh suddenly freeze, so I turn around and there's Mansour, he is smiling at me with this charming smile. It never fooled me. 'Could I divert you for a moment from this very important activity?' he says. 'It certainly *is* important,' I tell him. He leads me toward the door, and asks, 'May I have the pleasure of your company for lunch?' 'No, you may not,' I tell him. He may have been the majority leader, but I wasn't exactly honored because he wanted to have lunch with me. I say, 'If there is anything you want to tell me, please do so right here.' So we stand there, right outside the door. 'I always thought of you as a friend,' he says. 'Well, you have a strange way of showing it,' I tell him. 'Ahmad doesn't help his own case,' he says, 'he likes making enemies.' I say nothing and stand there looking at him. You know, the kind of look I give people when I know what they're up to?" "Yes, Mom, I know." "Of course, I was brought up around politicians—my own father, when he was running for Kerman, and Saham Soltan. . . .

"Then I say, 'So, are you here to insult my family? You want to tell me my husband is responsible for the biggest hoax in the history of this country'—for it was a hoax, accusing Ahmad of embezzling money from that bankrupt institution, or claiming that he conspired against the Shah. Whatever your father may have done to me," she said, addressing me, "I have always been fair to him."

" 'Nezhat jan,' he says softly, 'I am talking to you not as his wife, but as a colleague, an esteemed colleague. Let's put Ahmad aside for a moment. Why can't we work together?' And in truth I could have worked with him. If I had wanted to I could have had a second term. The Shah himself was very much on my side. I gave all that up. I gave it up because my pride did not allow me not to stand up for my husband! I would not have minded the sacrifice, had it been appreciated, or at least acknowledged. . . . The point is, I just refused to comply with him and he was offended, although he tried to cover it, and from that day on he seldom talked to me, he never approached me again. And now this!"

My mother's "now this" referred to Mansour's assassination by a man named Mohammad Bokharaii, said to be affiliated with the Coalition of Islamic Societies, a group created at the behest of Ayatollah Khomeini in 1963. They were supported by clerics nominated by Khomeini, among them his trusted student and follower Motahari, and some of the future leaders of the Islamic Republic such as Rafsanjani and Beheshti. The group had drawn up a list of people to assassinate, among them the Shah; thirteen leading figures in his government; his personal physician, General Ayadi, who was said to have been targeted because he was a Baha'i; General Nassiri, the new head of intelligence; eleven civil servants; and newspaper editors who had attacked clerics and Khomeini. The June 5th uprising had been quashed, but not the religious opposition that had led it.

FROM MY FATHER'S DIARIES: "Friday, Bahman 1, 1343 [January 22, 1965]. Today around noon I heard that Mansour has been shot. At first I didn't believe it. These days, unfortunately, gossip surrounding the government abounds. But soon the news was confirmed. Around 10 a.m., they say, a young man shot him four times. It appears that the bullets were not fatal. Today they announced on the radio that his physicians say his blood pressure is up and he will recover within a month. I feel so sorry for him . . . he was not by nature a bad person, he didn't want to betray his country and he had good reason to serve it, but he had little experience and was ambitious and hasty . . ."

A few days later Father writes, "Hassan Ali Mansour, the young prime minister of Iran, after a week in a coma, full of pain and anguish, left this world on Wednesday, Bahman 7, 1343 [January 27, 1965]. Two days earlier, rumors were circulating around town that he had already died. In a country where the government has never been honest and open with its people, and the real news is kept secret, rumors replace facts. From the start it was obvious that the bullets were fatal, but until a day before his death the new bulletins claimed that he was improving. On Monday they even claimed the danger was gone."

In his diary Father describes how he stood by the window of his room, opened onto the hall leading to the morgue, waiting for Mansour's body to arrive. "His death made me sorry, it brought tears to my eyes. I did not sleep all night. . . . A year and a half ago we were among the most prominent young men in this country; many envious and some hopeful eyes were fixed on us. Tonight one of us is in jail thanks to shameless rivals and their malicious cohorts and three meters away the other rolls in his own blood, his cold body is stuffed into the coroner's fridge. Here is a lesson for us. Both of us might have been useful to our country."

Mansour haunts my father after that. It was incredible that Mansour was assassinated, the one who had been considered so lucky, who had promised hope and created so much controversy during his short term as prime minister, the one who had time and again been compared to the young and handsome John F. Kennedy. His gravesite was made into a shrine, but after the revolution his grave, like that of many others, including Reza Shah's, was razed to the ground by the Islamic regime.

a suitable match

"**N**EZHAT CAME TO VISIT," MY FATHER writes in his diary in the fall of 1964. "Again she was irritated and anxious. Why doesn't Azar leave for England? Why am I in jail? Why doesn't the world turn in our favor? She is one of those who think they are God's chosen people and believes she never makes mistakes. Whatever bad things happen she thinks it is someone else's fault. In this case she considers me the guilty party." His tone, when he writes about the Shah and other government officials, is full of defiance tinged with exasperation, but almost without fail when he writes about my mother a sense of despair creeps into his voice.

"From the day of my arrest I was happy with the thought that Nezhat would be chastised and that she would finally dispense with the illusion that the world should be at her service. I believed that when she saw me in jail, she would understand what I could not make her understand when I was free. But today I realized that she is after my life, my entire existence—not only has she not learned a thing but she thinks I am in the best of places and owe her a great deal."

Many men use their wives and family for political purposes but my parents were so subsumed by their differences that they hoped their political lives would solve their problems at home. I once heard my father tell a friend that his relationship with my mother reminded him of a story by Attar, the twelfth-century Persian mystic poet, about a man who fearlessly rode a ferocious lion. When the narrator followed this brave man to his home, he was shocked to see how easily he was cowed by his wife. How could a man who was not afraid of a fierce beast be so intimidated by his own wife? His host shot back: If it weren't for what happens at home I could never ride a lion.

"You are here, away from all the trouble, doing what you want while all the burden is on me," Mother would say without irony. All this made my brother and me more protective of our father. I bought him what he liked, praised the gifts he bought for my mother, and commiserated with him. I baked him cakes and wrote him little sentimental notes about how proud I was of him. I also lied to him about how good things were at home—statements that would almost immediately be contradicted by my own mournful countenance and half-articulated complaints.

"Nezhat asked me today to tell Azar not to visit me so often," he writes at one point. "Has anyone heard of anything so ridiculous?" He wondered how he had become "not just her husband, but her friend, consultant, accountant, in fact her servant." He would write her poems, which she ignored. I read them avidly and collected them.

I WAS FIFTEEN when Behzad Sari's mother asked for my hand in marriage. Her husband, who had recently died, had been a respected judge, and she, unlike us, had a very orderly family. She was a true matriarch, ruling over her family with an iron fist. My mother had her men friends, and father had his women friends, whom he admired for their character and strength. Parvin Dowlatabadi, a well-known poet, was one of these; Mrs. Sari, Behzad's mother, was another. She was very ladylike and something of a character, too pushy for my taste, perhaps because I detected in her what I saw in my own mother: a will to control—only she was far more successful than Mother. She was the kind of person who was difficult to oppose or resist. The Saris were devoted to their social position, perhaps too much so, but were basically good people.

When she proposed on her son's behalf my father was still mayor of Tehran. Our families had recently grown closer and we saw them regularly, once or twice a week. Behzad was twenty-seven, neither good-looking nor ugly, sober, a hard worker. My parents thought that he would treat me with what was called respect. I had no tangible complaint, except that I thought he was dull and I did not love him. Yet my parents did not discourage the match, perhaps because of our close relations with his family. They left it up in the air, which meant that they politely told Mrs. Sari it was up to me and I was as yet too young to decide, but they encouraged her to think that my will could be changed with time.

When my father went to jail it was a point in Behzad's favor that his family still wanted me to marry their son. Behzad's steadfastness had become a recommendation now that my father was out of favor. I was invited to their house, where small gifts were exchanged and I was subjected to extreme flattery. "I used to think it was her lips, but look at that nose," Mrs. Sari would tell her daughter, scrutinizing me. I felt like a cadaver in anatomy class. Whenever Behzad approached I busied myself with his one-year-old nephew. Everything about them bored me, except for that nephew and the juicy stories about Behzad's sister, who could have easily played the role of a naughty nun. She had an innocent air about her, with her round face, enormous pale blue downcast eyes, and porcelain skin, offset by a generous display of cleavage. Rumors circulated that she had eloped with a Don Juan type, but that her mother had brought her back to the fold through a hasty, well-connected marriage.

Her brother had none of these exciting qualities. He was a successful engineer, stable and straightforward. That is why my parents liked him. When he came to our house one day with a bunch of roses to ask me for my final answer, I panicked and said, "I don't want to marry yet. It's not you, I'm just not ready for it." He stopped me as if he had not heard me and said, "I am getting old. I can't wait any longer, I need to know *now. Soon.*" The longing in his eyes alarmed me.

Before my father's arrest, my parents were content to say that I was too young to marry. They both told Behzad and his family that were I to marry, the one condition was that I should be allowed to continue my education. But suddenly the shock of my father's continued imprisonment made everything plausible. If we lived in a world where fortunes could be made and unmade so arbitrarily, then girls who were supposed to continue their education could also marry at sixteen or seventeen or eighteen, not because they were in love but because there was a decent guy from a good family offering the promise of security. No one would force me, but no one would allow me to go out with boys my own age, either. It was not long before I announced my refusal, which both he and his family reacted to with some disappointment but also with good grace. And the truth was that I was attracted to another man, completely the opposite of Behzad. He was tall, handsome, romantic, and confident. He spoke with a mellow voice about poetry and philosophy. More important, this man was also in love with someone else, which made him more intriguing and desirable.

MOST WOMEN ARE TURNED ON by looks or chemistry, but you can be seduced by conversation. When a friend told me this a long time ago—we were sitting on bar stools at a café in Tehran after the revolution eating ham sandwiches, which were now forbidden and secretly sold to trusted clients, and discussing *A Night at the Opera* and *Johnny Guitar*—the conversation was so intriguing that at that moment I was prepared to vote him, who was normal-looking in the extreme, the most seductive man in the world. "I've never met a woman who could be so turned on by a conversation about Woody Allen," he said.

He had a point. I had a strong attraction to men who stirred my intellect. In one sense I could say I had inherited this trait from my parents. There was Father's love of philosophy and literature and Mother's appetite for stimulating political conversations with her "men friends." Reading my letters from England, written when I was in my early teens, I am amazed at how much I try to impress my father by pontificating and talking about books.

My conversion to Woody Allen had taken some time. Between ten and thirteen my favorite movie star was Yul Brynner, whom I yearned for in part because of his unrequited love for Deborah Kerr—apparently both on- and offscreen. I used to collect his pictures. My father hated this and one afternoon, as one fell from a book I was reading, he made me bring him all my pictures of Yul—as I affectionately called him—and he tore them up. For a while I was (sometimes I think I still am) infatuated with Dirk Bogarde, with that cryptic smile of his and eyes that looked beyond you even as they fixed you. The heartbreaking discovery that he was not interested in women did not deter me from my affection. And then, sometime in my early twenties, I fell in love with Woody Allen. My classmates would look at me with shock and a bit of pity, but I felt superior; at any rate I couldn't help it, the heart does what the heart feels, as the master himself stated decades later.

When I fell for Mehran Osuli, I was in transition between Yul Brynner and Dirk Bogarde. I think that Mehran may have hastened my move toward Woody Allen, though they looked nothing alike. He was good-looking and tall, with light-brown hair and eyes, and a beautiful soothing voice. He looked a little like an American football player, the kind with a secret urge to become a great writer or philosopher. My infatuation began when I was fifteen and he was twenty-one, a second-year law student at the University of Tehran. The wife of one of my younger uncles, Hussein, had four handsome brothers, all very popular with the girls. Mehran was the most serious. He showed little interest in the games played by love-struck girls. I can pinpoint the night I fell for him. We were at his house with Uncle Hussein and his young wife, engaging over dinner in a heated discussion about The Nature of Love. At first Mehran seemed detached. While the rest of us interrupted one another constantly, he sat back and dropped a few choice comments. His beautiful voice took my breath away. As the night progressed, it suddenly seemed as if he and I were the only ones talking. I brought up Rudabeh and Zal from the *Shahnameh*, Mathilde and Julien Sorel from *The Red and the Black,* and suddenly he quoted a well-known Persian proverb. "You have not suffered hunger to forget love," he said, meaning love is for the satiated idle.

Then he turned to leave. To me this most mundane utterance was full of hidden meaning. I was convinced that he addressed it to me and that what he meant was the reverse of what the proverb implied.

Mehran did relish his role as a romantic hero. He led me to believe that he was hopelessly in love with his best friend's older sister. That is how our relation began: with his telling me in detail about her. He loved the idea of unrequited love. I was so docile and easily impressed by his wise remarks. In time he would tell me about the first time he told her that he loved her. What I remember is not so much his recounting of the story as the incident itself, as if I had been there, observing their every move from behind the dining-room curtain. After lunch, everyone leaves except for the two of them. A popular love song is playing—one that I remember to this day. They are standing by the dining-room table and she is about to leave when he says, "Wait, I have something to tell you." In my imagination she turns her head, perhaps surprised, perhaps not, with a silent smile. In these accounts his fickle beloved is always silent, always the recipient of his passionate courtship.

It seems to me now that his stories did more to attract me to him than his handsome features did. For a while I saw him regularly; we met on weekly mountain-climbing expeditions organized by my uncle Hussein. During these few hours every Friday we would walk and talk a little apart from the others. As I scrambled up a difficult rock he would hold his hand out to help me up. At first I refused, feeling brave and independent, but after a while I accepted and he held my hand longer than necessary. Sometimes he would gaze into my eyes as he let go of my hand with an expression of infinite tenderness and concern, as if I were a stray creature from some impossible fairy tale. Pausing at a high point to gaze at a magnificent view of Tehran, he would write her name in the dirt with a stick and then wipe it out with his boots. I stood beside him, distracted, feeling for him and pretending a lack of concern. I never quite knew why he loved this woman. He never described her as beautiful, or intelligent, or possessing any special qualities. She was just the older sister of his best friend.

Gradually the hand-holding became more frequent and we talked less and less about her. Instead we spent hours talking about my "situation." For I did have a situation with my mother. I acted like his little sister and he would give me advice and write me cute little notes. Then at some point I replaced the older sister in his affections, a shift which he demonstrated by becoming highly jealous and possessive and by giving me the Persian translation of Hemingway's worst and most sentimental book, *Across the River and into the Trees*. He addressed me as *Aye Hija Mia* (O my girl). But that came much later.

S OME FAMILIES TRY to cover up their tensions in front of strangers, but for Mother, a woman otherwise so insistent on social etiquette, no such niceties existed. She gave in to her emotions regardless of where she was. I tried not to let her know about my interest in Mehran but she had a hunter's instinct, alert and sensitized to my secret hideaways. Her instinct was helped, in this instance, by daily intrusions into the most private corners of her children's lives. She listened in on my phone conversations, read my letters and diaries, and walked in and out of my room whenever she felt like it. I could never be certain which I resented more, the fact that she read my diary and letters or that she never allowed me to feel indignant about her actions: she would use her new evidence as proof of my betrayals.

Let us pause on one particular day. It is late fall, when the dry cold of Tehran settles on the still-tender leaves. My feelings and emotions are in harmony with the change of season. Fall in Tehran is beautiful, but I loved the winters with their mixture of sun and snow, when one can almost smell the crisp air. I am being driven from Father's jail to another location, to Shahpour Avenue. Parliament is in session, but Mother has sent the car to pick me up. Against my better judgment I tell the driver to take me to Mehran's house. I say, casually, "You need not wait for me, I'm picking up some stuff here and will go straight on to my class afterward." Mother is very much against my visiting Mehran or any of my uncles, but it is something I do regularly. Once, when she discovered I had gone to Mehran's family's house without telling her, she came to their door and demanded that I follow her home. That first time was embarrassing, but afterward, having witnessed my predicament, everyone became actively sympathetic. How to solve Azar's problems with her mother became a topic of endless discussion. They were now not just friends but also coconspirators.

My heart pounds in the late autumn chill. I am wearing my light red coat and pull the collar up, so that it rubs against my skin. The whole situation is exciting and romantic. I tell the driver to drop me off in front of a narrow alley. This is the old part of Tehran, with small spice shops, dusty narrow alleys with dry streams winding into houses with tall protective walls. As I near their house I take out my small bottle of perfume and pat Nina Ricci's L'Air du Temps on my wrists, behind my ears. I ring the bell. The door opens and I walk a few steps down to the cobbled yard with its ancient tree and small round pool and cool ground-floor rooms.

About an hour later the bell rings and there is a pounding on the door. My heart stops. I know it must be my mother; she would have interrogated the driver as to my whereabouts. "Where is she? I know she's here," she shouts. "She's not here," says Morad, Mehran's youngest brother, "you can come in and look for yourself." We have become more savvy and this time she cannot find me. After she leaves I wait for about ten minutes before heading out. I walk a maze of winding alleys into the main street—where I am confronted by my mother.

I lie (I am now good at lying). I tell her I went to the house to borrow some books—I show her the books and say that as soon as I pressed the bell they told me she had been there, looking for me, so I hurried back. "I must have just missed you," I say innocently. "And what were you doing before that," she says, acting unconcerned. "I . . . I went for a long walk!" That did not help me, but the trick was to persevere. Even if she knew I was lying, and she did, I had to stick to my story. After a while the most absurd lie would take on the color of truth. Such encounters were not about facts, anyway: they had their own logic and at some point, when our emotions had run their course, the original reason for the flare-up would be forgotten. Years later, after the Islamic Revolution, I would experience a similar dynamic on a far larger scale. We would play their game. We invented the most preposterous stories to account for why our breath smelled of alcohol, why our lips were stained with makeup, what that tape by a banned popular foreign singer was doing on the dashboard of our car, and, with the offer of a smaller or larger bribe depending on the circumstances, we would be let off. For weeks after that, at different parties, our pathetic victory would become a topic of jokes.

The first thing she does before letting me off at the British Council for my English class is to inform me that I cannot go mountain climbing that Friday. I can't complain to Father, whom I try to shield from our confrontations, though I know she will make a point of bringing up my transgression when she next visits him. ("Why does Nezhat think that I've had this daughter by another wife?" he asks several times in his diary.) But even in jail, despite the private complaints and public fights, my father never forgets to remind me of Mother's hardships, her need for love, and of my duty to understand and support her.

When I get up the next morning I find her busy arranging her coffee session. I follow her from the dining room to the kitchen to her bedroom, begging her to let me go mountain climbing, but she won't budge. Then she turns around and says, "In fact, never again will you go on this ridiculous expedition." I tell her I will go with or without her consent. "What do you want from me?" she starts to shout, "Will you not rest until I die?" I look at her blankly and say nothing. But my mind is not blank. I feel I want to do something terrible—throw a glass at a wall, cry hysterically until my whimpers give way to helpless mumblings and she melts and comes toward me. "There, there," she will say, "stop crying."

"You're not my daughter," she says angrily. Already in my mind a faded image takes hold, of Mathilde in Stendhal's *The Red and the Black* holding Julien Sorel's severed head on her lap. "You and your father . . ." she screams as the image in my mind gains color and detail. Mathilde is in the carriage and the sound of horses' hooves grows louder and louder—I hear my mother's voice, the horses' hooves, and

Mathilde's silence. Gradually I control my urge to shout and cry. But since she has not achieved her purpose, which is to reduce me to hysterical tears, she will not speak to me for the next two days.

I say, "I am going, you can't stop me." Now both of us are shouting. The doorbell rings, but we don't pay attention. She says she has not brought me up to be a tramp. "Is this," she says with fury, "why you wanted to stay in Tehran? Not because of your father, not because you feel anything for him, but to go prancing around the city with God knows who?" At this I finally burst into tears. "I can't live in this house anymore," I say. "I can't stand it." We don't notice my brother emerging from his room, standing in the middle of the hall, nor do we hear the sound of the front door opening.

A few minutes later Aunt Mina comes in. I am still crying. Mother kisses Aunt Mina, who takes hold of my hand. "I can't stand it," I say, "I don't want to stay here anymore." Aunt Mina says, "It's okay, don't worry," and softly moves me toward my room and sends my brother for a glass of water. I can hear my mother's angry voice fading as she walks down the stairs toward the kitchen. Aunt Mina sits down and talks to me like a grown-up, as if she is sharing a confidence. "I don't know," she says, "how Nezhat can be so cruel to herself and to those she loves." "She calls me names," I stammer. "She says I'm waiting for her to die." "She doesn't mean it," Aunt Mina says gently, handing me the glass of water and sending my brother away. "Yes, she does. She says I'm like the rest, after her money." "She says that," Aunt Mina tells me, "because she can't say it to those who actually hurt her."

Mother brought out the best and worst in us. By taking away our private spaces, we were forced to create other secret realms of our own, often by engaging our imagination. My father escaped into his garden, his poetry, and his work. I can still picture his expression in the mornings, when he would bring a plateful of aromatic jasmine petals to the table, or when, on trips to our villa by the Caspian, he would suddenly stop the car and plunge into the woods in search of wildflowers to plant in the garden. From time to time he would call me—deep into some novel I was reading, lying lazily on the couch—

and summon me outside to see some amazing flower in bloom. I escaped into stories: Rudabeh was my role model, Julien Sorel my lover, Natasha Rostova, Elizabeth Bennet, Catherine Earnshaw, and numerous other heroines of literature my ladies-in-waiting, who would help me find that elusive self I hoped to become. How various and wonderful that imaginary world was compared to the one in which I lived!

women like that!

AROUND THIS TIME I STARTED spending hours lying in bed, reading. I underlined passages, rewrote them in my diary, and took to repeating lines from my favorite female poet, Forough Farrokhzad: "All my being is a dark chant that will carry you to the dawn of eternal growths." On Friday mornings I would enter the living room during Mother's coffee sessions with a book that often elicited a comment or an inquiry. This Mother perceived as an intangible affront. She could not put her finger on what was wrong with my love of books. Her excuse was that I was too obsessive, but she never could articulate why my particular brand of bookishness seemed to her to imply mutiny, to be a declaration of some dubious form of independence. When I announced that I would not marry Behzad Sari because I did not love him, she blamed it on reading too much poetry and consorting with Father's family, who conspired to prevent me from marrying him. In one sense she was right. Forough Farrokhzad's poems were embodiments of the potential I had detected in the fictional heroines I loved. She lived what she wrote and paid a high price for it. An invisible thread linked Rudabeh to Forough Farrokhzad. A certain boldness and openness in a culture that denied both.

Farrokhzad was born in 1935 and married in her teens. It was not a forced marriage—she fell in love with Parviz Shahpur, a man well known within the intellectual community and about sixteen years her senior. Soon after her son Kami was born she left her family, some claim because of a love affair. She devoted what was left of her life to poetry and later to filmmaking. She died in a car crash in 1967 at the age of thirty-two. Her most shocking poems—those for which she was notorious—were celebrations of her love affairs, but she also wrote passionately about politics and society, especially near the end of her life. She had the audacity to acknowledge her love affairs without shame in her poetry, to which she owed her status as a much admired and hated icon. She turned the idea of personal "sin" ("I sinned a sin full of pleasure, / In an embrace which was warm and fiery") into a defiance against authority, especially that of God.

Weary of divine asceticism,
At midnight in Satan's bed
I would seek refuge in the downward
    slopes
Of a fresh sin.

Forough Farrokhzad.

"Only the Voice Endures." This was the title of a poem by Forough Farrokhzad that I jotted down on the top of a page in my diary and underlined twice. Underneath it I wrote that I had a huge fight with my mother about Forough (she was always referred to by her first name, a liberty seldom if ever taken with the male poets). Mother kept saying she did not educate me to follow in the footsteps of a "woman like that." I wrote in my diary that I suspected if my mother were more like "women like that" we would all be having much better times.

A few days later, on return from my afternoon class at the British Council, I was summoned to the library. Mother was sitting upright on a soft leather chair. Rahman was slumped on a seat nearby and Aunt Mina, clearly uncomfortable, sat opposite him. The culprit, my diary, with its dull black plastic cover, was on the side table for all to see. Mr. Rahman leered at me with a benevolent and knowing smile. Usually he would rise to my defense, but this time he remained silent, at times clicking reproachfully, his bulging eyes merry with mischief.

Mother wanted to know how I could say that I preferred that woman to my own mother, as I had, in fact, in my diary. Aunt Mina was trying to be conciliatory. I wanted to know why my mother had read my private diary; what gave her that right? Rahman offered piously that a mother had the right to prevent a sin from happening. In Islam even strangers had that right. The more helpless I felt, the more insolent I became. In defense, I offered up a brief consideration of Forough's importance as a poet.

At this point Mother took on that terrible, impersonal, mocking tone of hers. "*You* are of course right," she said sarcastically. "You are a treasure trove of knowledge. How could an ignorant woman such as myself ever hope to reach such heights!" When she was cross with us, her expression was glacial and she deliberately chose formal words. She would call me Madam, as she did when she wrote me admonishing notes. She would write letters which she would leave about the house. Other families talked, we wrote: what we felt or hoped for, our complaints—we wrote all this, as if we could not bear to look into one another's eyes and just talk.

Sometimes Mother's notes would be short and straightforward, congratulating us on our birthdays, on the New Year, or some accomplishment. But mainly she wrote when she was angry. Then she would address us in generic terms: My Model Husband, My Grateful Children, My Dutiful Daughter. It was not uncommon for her to enumerate all the different sacrifices she had made for us. "A mother's task in life is to nurture upright children . . ." she wrote in one. "I am happy that I have raised two individuals," she began, before turning to our misdeeds. She never denied our "accomplishments," as she called them, which she implicitly took credit for. Often she would end with: "I am sorry I was not a worthy mother. I am not wanted in this family, I am an outsider. I wish the best for the three of you." Later she would add the names of her grandchildren to her list of culprits.

I should have seen that there was something essential missing. "It is doubtless that Azar is a brilliant student," she would write, deliberately depleting her writing of any feeling or emotion. Or, "A mother's main task in life is devotion to her children." Now I am saddened by this painfully distant love. At the time, we were too accustomed to these notes to recognize the luminous pain that caused them.

That day I was reprimanded and, after a reluctant and teary apology, exiled to my room. A vivid day in my memory: I spent the whole day in my room, refusing to eat or answer the telephone. She sent the servants, my brother, and my uncle at different times to summon me to dinner but I did not go. I reviewed everything through tearstained eyes, and soon drifted into a narcotic state of self-pity. Not even Mehran could keep my interest. Nor did I waste time thinking about Behzad Sari, whom I had refused to marry anyway. What if I could inhabit a world that was completely different from the one in which I lived? What if I could live a more normal life? I have no idea how I reached the conclusion that I did, but by the end of the evening I had said to myself, Okay then, I'll marry him!

"YESTERDAY NEZHAT AND AZAR came to visit," my father wrote in his diary. "There is a new suitor. Azar has rejected a few suitors. This one is Mehdi Mazhari, Colonel Mazhari's son. I know General Mazhari, his uncle, who is a good man. Their family is prominent in Azerbaijan. But what worries me is her mother's manner and my own predicament and Azar's naïveté and lack of experience on the one hand, and her hurt and anguish because of conditions at home. She may be forced into accepting because of this situation. . . . Her mother is in a hurry to get this done as soon as possible. Perhaps she wants to have the wedding while she is still in Parliament. Azar is constantly tearful and unhappy. She doesn't want to get married until I get out but I don't know when I will be released and cannot keep her dangling."

Mehdi Mazhari came from a military family that was in many respects the exact opposite of ours. He was many years younger than his youngest sister and the only boy in the family, the apple of his mother's eye. When I met him he was a senior in electrical engineering at the University of Oklahoma. His favorite star was Frank Sinatra, whom he appreciated mainly because of what he thought Sinatra represented: opulence, charm, worldly success, gloved servants at the dining table. His family was unabashedly materialistic, while mine was careless about such matters.

At first I did not take his offer at all seriously. I did not love him. I was not even physically attracted to him. My only persistent suitor had been Behzad, whom I had never seriously considered marrying. I hadn't paid much attention to Mehdi until at some point he started paying attention to me. The only boy close to my own age that Mother allowed me to hang around with was her friend Alangoo's son, Bahman. She considered him trustworthy, while she felt that Uncle Hussein's brother-in-law or anyone from my father's side of the family was not good for me. Bahman and his friends were thought to be a much "safer" course. Mehdi was one of Bahman's friends.

IT WAS AFTER DINNER and Mehdi called me into the dining room. I was standing and he was sitting on a chair. He held my hands and said, "I want to marry you."

I said nothing. He said, "Hadn't you guessed?" I said, "Well, I haven't really thought about it." He told me he had always wanted to marry young; he wanted to have fun with his wife—a legitimate enough point—but then he went on to say that his parents were old and he was their youngest child and only son—they wanted to see him married with children before they died. He thought I came from a good family, with excellent connections, although he did not approve of my parents' relationship. (Only one person, he said, should wear the pants in a family and in your house that person is certainly not your father.) He said he liked the look of me the first time he saw me. "But," I said, "there must be many girls whose looks you like." "Yes," he said, "but you are so innocent." "Innocent?" "You've been to England but you still don't know what a French kiss is." He informed me that he was a very jealous person. "I will sleep with a pistol under my pillow," he said. Then he returned to the question of my family. "Despite what has happened to your father, it is a good family," he said, "a prominent family with a good name." I let him kiss me, mainly to be spared from having to give him an answer then. Later, it occurred to me that his proposal should have been a warning of things to come. It vaguely reminded me of Mr. Collins's proposal to Elizabeth Bennet in *Pride and Prejudice*. Unfortunately, I cannot claim that my own behavior resembled that of Elizabeth Bennet's.

That night I came home late, but Mother was still awake. As I tiptoed toward my room, she called me from her bedroom. The room was dark and she was in bed. "So," she said, "what happened?" "He asked me," I said. "He asked you what?" "To marry him." "What did you say?" "Nothing." "What?" "Well," I said curtly, "I need to think."

Later I would blame my mother for my decision to marry Mehdi Mazhari. I would remind anyone who would listen of how she would send me to their house and stay up at night to hear how it went; how without my consent she visited my father and nagged him to give permission for a hasty marriage; how she slyly evaded Father's request that she seek guidance from his elder brother in Esfahan.

I would also privately blame Mehran. His evasiveness, at first so attractive, was becoming tedious. He had broken with the girlfriend he had talked to me about, but was coy, constantly testing me, casually telling me about this or that girl he had met at a party—none of whom, he would say, meant anything to him. Later it occurred to me that my silence, in fact, my whole lopsided attitude, must have been a factor in making him act that way. As soon as I informed Mehran, casually, of my new suitor he became—too late, as it turned out— adamant that I should not marry this man, that he was and always had been "there for me," absolutely and unquestionably.

It can be something of a relief to give yourself over to someone more decisive than yourself. Mehdi knew what he wanted and I felt a foolish pleasure in yielding to the new life he might offer me in marriage. I had always been attracted to men like my father, intellectuals with a vision and a mission, gentlemen who (in theory if not always in deed) were flexible and tender. Mehdi was the opposite. I chose to marry Mehdi not because I expected anything from him but because I wanted to fit into the role he had assigned me. I had graduated from high school and applied to the University of California at Santa Barbara to study literature. He was studying electrical engineering in Oklahoma, and felt, like my mother, that I spent too much time buried in my books. I was filled with doubts about marriage. He had very fixed ideas about it, and had his own strict rules about the different roles a husband and wife should play. I convinced myself that for these very reasons he was good for me, although at times I felt that I was on my way to becoming "another woman gone to waste."

The irony was that both my mother and I chose him for the same reasons: he knew what he wanted and he passed my mother's litmus test regarding suitable suitors. "My daughter is not made to be a housewife, she has to finish her education," she told him when they first met. An educated wife, he assured her, would be a feather in his cap, so long as her parents were prepared to pay for her education. I have now become something of an expert in the ways of "decisive" men. They are not firm, they just seem to be. Because they have a formula for everything, which they forcibly impose, they seem confident. But they cannot face the unexpected. They can be far less capable in a crisis than the seemingly fragile women they bully and are secretly afraid of.

And yet, Mehdi had something that I did not: a stable, happy family. It was so different from mine—there seemed to be no angst, no self-consciousness. They could all gather at home around a big table and laugh or get angry. They spent their holidays together, traveling in huge numbers. Next to them our family seemed so forlorn. In our own way we cared about one another—sometimes we cared too much—but always this caring was anxious and fraught.

I did exactly what my mother wanted me to do. Later she denied it and claimed that from the very start she had been against the marriage, but in my father's diary there are several references to her insistence and her desire for haste. Father tried to delay the wedding, he asked her to wait for my uncle to consult with the Koran, but she would not be deterred. I went around in a haze as she made the arrangements with dizzying speed. Less than two months after I had decided to marry Mehdi, I was in a short white wedding dress, teary-eyed, carrying a small cake, en route to my father's jail. I had decided to go see him a few hours before the real wedding ceremony, which was held at our house. I cried the night before the wedding, on the way to see Father, and up until the last hour before the ceremony.

On the wedding day my mother kept saying how similar our fates were: her father had been absent at her wedding as well. Father wrote in his diary that our fates seemed to be "intertwined," because I had made the same mistake he had. In a strange passage in which he writes in the third person he says, "Finally Azar's fate has become identical to her father's. She has forced herself into marriage. Because of her unhappiness at home and her father's absence she preferred to escape her own home. The one person who constantly thought of me has now transferred her affections to another." My brother spent part of his summer vacation in Esfahan. He was now summoned to Tehran and spent the last few days before the wedding walking around the yard, trying to dissuade me from going through with it. I let Mehran's calls go unanswered. He, like the rest of my father's family, felt that Mehdi and I had very little in common and was bewildered by my choice.

Over a decade earlier Father told me you cannot just be stubborn against something, you need to be stubborn for something as well. Rudabeh did not insist on marrying Zal to resist her parents' wish, or because she was desperate, or to spite anyone, but because she loved Zal. That, my father had said, is what makes her hardheadedness okay, something to be admired. The relevance of what he said came to me too late.

EVERYTHING ABOUT THE WEDDING was melodramatic. Mehran called me up to the end imploring me to change my mind; my brother pleaded with me to call it off. A few days before the event, Uncle Abu Torab called my mother from Esfahan to say that he had consulted the Koran and the result was negative. Layla, Aunt Mina's younger daughter, a stern mentor, sat me down and tried to make me understand that I was now what my mother kept wanting me to be: a lady. I had responsibilities and would have to act accordingly. I nodded in agreement just as I had when she lectured me about my duties as a woman. Perhaps I should have asked Layla what she would recommend for a rather frightened and bewildered teenager masquerading as a confident and decisive adult?

We went for our honeymoon to our family villa on the Caspian Sea with my husband's family. His three sisters, their husbands and children stayed at a popular resort close by. Father had bought the place years earlier, when the whole stretch of land was undeveloped. He loved it and had retreated there whenever he could. If a place can encompass a person's soul, I would say that he put his soul into it.

The beaches on the Caspian Sea are unique in all the world, though to be honest I am merely repeating what my father used to tell me. He explained that few places were blessed with the sea on one side, mountains and forest on the other. He would spend hours deep in the forest, foraging for exotic plants and flowers for his garden. That garden occupied him more than any lover ever would. During my youth, on harsh winter days and in the heat of the summer, even if he had only two days he would travel four and a half hours from Tehran to work in his garden. Gradually the land nearby had been bought by prominent families and our simple house came to be surrounded by sumptuous gardens and villas. My mother always objected to being there. She was a city person, and carried with her its restlessness. Flowers for her were decorative advertisements. From the moment we arrived, she would galvanize the poor gardener and his whole family into scrubbing the place. My father was a social person; he wanted to invite our neighbors and friends over, but Mother would make socializing almost impossible. She worried about what food to serve, whom to invite. She didn't like to swim. She didn't know how to relax.

If I could close my eyes and imagine myself in a place where I can relax and feel truly at home, I would choose that house, that garden. I would resurrect the smell of the sea and the sand, the different shades of green, the moisture in the air, my father's triumphant smile as he showed off his latest discoveries, a flame-colored flower called Ferdowsi, another, with small, fragile blossoms hanging like grapes, named the bride's braids. And that is where we went, my husband and I, for our honeymoon. It was the worst place we could have possibly chosen.

Since then I have erased most memories of our first two nights together. I remember that I could not make love with him. I was scared and I was lonely and suddenly I felt as young as I was and not at all worldly. I wanted to go home. I thought of my parents and my brother and I could not do anything. He was not tender, nor was he rough. I don't remember exactly what he was. He just wanted what he felt, with some justification, was his to claim.

I was afraid and genuinely sad, but he did not understand this. He took my reluctance to have sex with him as a sign that I might not be a virgin. Had he been misled? I see in my imagina-

Mohammad and me, holding a picture of my father, who could not attend my wedding.

tion one clear scene in black and white: the air is moist, his figure distinct, in a white terry-cloth robe, standing pensively by the door, smoking a cigarette. Where was I? I must have been standing next to him, explaining something, reassuring him that I really was a virgin. The next night at dinner, over the sound of laughter and festivity, he said to his youngest sister, "Tell her what to do." She turned to me sweetly—and she was ever so sweet—and said, "Just close your eyes and let yourself go. Imagine you are somewhere else. Imagine anything, imagine you are eating an omelet."

I did as she said. I pretended I was somewhere else, although I could not bring myself to think of omelets. I don't think I quite succeeded in being somewhere else in the way I could when my mother said or did things that hurt me. But I did absent myself from my body. From then on, for decades, sex was something you did because it was expected of you, because you could not say no, because you did not care, could not care, and so you would be coy about it to undermine the seriousness of comments you made, such as Please don't hurt me. None of the experiences of abuse I had suffered as a child made me feel as dirty and guilty as this experience of sleeping with my husband. In choosing to marry Mehdi, I had lied to myself, and in a sense betrayed my own ideals of the kind of woman I aspired to be—my passion for Rudabeh and Farrokhzad now seemed a little hollow.

The first time I visited my father after the honeymoon I wore dark sunglasses and refused to take them off, and for a long time I took to wearing them inside. I was deeply ashamed. It was a shame that would not wear off for a very long time.

married life

IN SEPTEMBER, when we arrived in Norman, where I enrolled as a freshman at the University of Oklahoma so that Mehdi
could finish his engineering degree, quite a few surprises awaited me.
Certain things he had not explained—for instance, that he had lived
for four years with an American woman who people thought was his
wife. I'd always had contempt for men who studied abroad, lived with
American women, and enjoyed not just sex but a kind of intimacy
they never would know with the wide-eyed virgins they married, but
who wouldn't think of marrying these foreign concubines because
they were, as my mother would say, "a girlfriend and not a wife." I
had never thought of myself as that kind of wide-eyed Persian girl,
and the fact that I did not only made things worse.

Our first obvious disagreement was over money. Mehdi was obsessively preoccupied with the things money could buy, and he doubted
my assertions that Father had not stashed away a great fortune, stolen
from the public coffers. Finally Father had to disclose to Mehdi's father and uncle the state of his financial affairs and let them know that
far from having stolen vast sums, he had been living partly off loans
from his brothers ever since he'd been in jail. "General Mazhari apol-
ogized, he had tears in his eyes after we finished talking," Father
wrote in his diary after their conversation. In part their complaint was
legitimate. My mother had agreed to pay for my share of living expenses, but she resented the arrangement and made things hard for me
by never sending the money on time.

Mehdi played poker at least twice a week, sometimes until dawn. He had me dye my hair black, made me go to hairdressers every week (a woman, he said, should always look her best), and banned me from smoking or drinking (women should not smell of cigarettes or alcohol). He himself, of course, both smoked and drank. One night, I accepted a glass of wine as I was talking to a friend: he walked toward us, took the glass from my hand, and poured the wine into the sink. I discovered he had been telling the truth when he said that he was jealous. Of course he did not, as he had suggested, hide a gun under his pillow, but he did make a scene when I showed up at the library with a male classmate.

Photos of that period show me dancing merrily with my husband, my jet-black hair perfectly coiffed. Who was that woman? It was as if I had created a parallel personality whom I watched from a distance with curiosity and dismay. The melodramatic gesture I had adopted soon after the honeymoon, wearing dark sunglasses indoors, like a spy hiding my true identity, or perhaps my sense of guilt, would soon be internalized. I wrote notes to myself that I still have with me: "Do not hurt his pride by constantly disagreeing with him," I wrote. "When you disagree, begin by saying something complimentary and then suggest your own ideas." Or, "Don't make fun of his ideas or fight with him every time he plays poker." Perfect advice, worthy of the *Ladies' Home Journal*. But I never did listen to my own advice.

I hated being cooped up in a corner of someone's living room with the other women, gossiping, while the men played poker until six a.m. I was bored with his ideas and distrusted his taste for black-gloved chauffeurs, and probably I wasn't as compliant as he might have hoped when it came to wearing the pants in the family.

DESPITE MY PIOUS NOTES to myself, I did not become the kind of wife Mehdi wanted me to be. Not really. Farrokhzad's book of poetry, *Another Birth*, was constantly by my bedside. She had come to replace Rudabeh in my affections. I had marked several passages from

"The Green Illusion," about a woman who sat by the window watching the world go by. The first line I had underlined several times.

All day I cried in the mirror.
All day I fixed
My life's eyes
On those two anxious fearful eyes
Which avoided my stare
And sought refuge in their lids' safe seclusion
Like liars.

I had become obsessed with Forough's portrayal of herself as an intimate but frightening stranger, a pair of reproachful eyes judging and condemning her. Rejecting domestic life, abandoning her husband and child, leaving the security of marriage, was not an easy choice, but an inevitable one. Her attitude was not self-congratulatory but one of tortured guilt. She realized that her triumph as a liberated woman could also be perceived as "this fraud, this paper crown."

She believed that staying in a loveless marriage was a sin, but leaving her home and her responsibilities filled her with guilt and made her feel alone. In this and in another poem, "The Awful Visage," she talks of her other self, the self reflected in the mirror that stares back at her, accusingly and without compassion. Later, I discovered the literary progenitor of this reflected image in the poems of Alam Taj, a housewife almost two generations older than Farrokhzad who had been forced to marry a man twice her age whom she found physically repulsive. She hid the poetry she wrote—denouncing the hypocrisy of religion, loveless marriages, wasted lives—among the pages of books by her favorite classical poets: Hafez, Saadi, Nezami. After her death these poems were discovered by her son. In poem after poem she rails against the condition of women like herself, married without their consent, never allowed to experience love, against the religious hypocrisy that denies women the freedoms it so liberally bestows on men. In a poem called "Predicting Women's Freedom," she dreams of a time after her death when women in her country will be free. She says that "tomorrow's freedom" is like a newborn child, resting on her lap. She calls religiously sanctioned marriage a form of adultery; she hates herself because she sleeps with a man she does not love, because she raises a child from a loveless marriage "not with love but with instinct," like an animal. And she too wrote a poem about the experience of staring at a stranger, at her other, damaged self, in the mirror. Hating the conditions imposed on her, conditions beyond her control, she hates herself. This image of an accusing face, reflected in the mirror, stayed with me after my marriage.

B Y THE TIME WE returned to Tehran the next summer, I was ready to ask for a divorce, but I felt I could not complicate my parents' life and add to their worries. Father's case had not progressed much. Every once in a while he was interrogated, sometimes promises were made, hopes raised only to be deflated, and I was not about to trouble him with my personal problems. From championing Mehdi, Mother became his worst nightmare. His pressure for money was reason enough for her displeasure. Now, she said, she realized his family's "greed" and accused him of "lack of respect." How could she expect Mehdi to respect her when her own daughter never defended her? "You went and married against my will, but now I am the one who has to pay the price," she said. The suggestion was so preposterous that I could not think of anything to say. She treated Mehdi coldly and with condescension, quarreled with him ferociously, and then gave me an ultimatum: choose between me or your husband. It was silly—in essence it would have meant divorcing him right there and then. She told me that if I chose him I should pack up and leave the house.

If I could relate the emotion I felt that day to something tangible—the color of the dress I wore; how, when she told me to leave, I was in the drawing room with my back to the window; or how, going up the stairs to my room, her voice gradually diminishing in volume, I felt a sudden pain in my legs—if I could remember this and attach my emotional memory to more concrete circumstances, if I could thus give my feelings some sort of flesh and blood, then perhaps they would not be, even now, quite so raw. But all I can really say is that I went upstairs to my room, packed my bag, and meekly followed my husband out of my mother's house and went to stay with his parents. I don't remember what Mehdi and I said after that. He came from such a different world, and we never learned to speak one another's language. He asked questions for which I had no answer (Why was my mother allowed such liberties? Why was my father so weak?) and others that made me resent him (Why did I need to visit my father every day in prison? Why did I take books so seriously?). But it was not easy to move in with his parents. Although they would not say anything directly about my expulsion from my own home, I felt humiliated and rather forlorn.

"Monday, June 6, 1966. Today near noon Azar and her husband came to visit," Father wrote in his diary the week of our return. "That happy and hopeful girl has been transformed into a bewildered, anxiety-ridden young woman." A few days later I had gone to visit him on my own and the first thing he asked was: "Are you unhappy with Mr. Mazhari? I don't want you to be trapped in an unhappy marriage. It's better to get out of it now." He leaned toward me in that earnest way he had when he wanted to drive a point home. He held his two hands close, the fingers tapping against one another. "You should get out," he said again, "before you have children." My mother, in her usual arbitrary manner, had already visited him and expressed how worried she was about me and that at night she cried for me. Father writes, "I said that it is not enough that parents should cry for their children and in the meantime make their children cry!"

I told him that I'd married Mehdi to escape home, but that I had hopes, I wanted to try to make it work. "I will turn him around," I said. "I'll make him understand." This is how he reports our conversation in his diaries. He adds that despite my reassurances, he is concerned about me. He wrote: "I am afraid there is no happy ending to this story."

———

AROUND THIS TIME, my brother took to questioning my father about the existence of God. (He had been reading Bertrand Rus-
sell and talking to my cousin Majid, who had been immersed in
Jean-Paul Sartre.) Father asked himself why his son should believe
anything he said. His whole career had been devoted to bettering the
country he loved. He had always told us that however vexing the set-
backs, in the end justice would prevail, but now we could see perfectly
clearly that justice did not in fact prevail. In his diaries for that year,
scattered between thoughts about America's blunders in Vietnam, the
constant bickering between Iran and Iraq, the merits of poetry, and
the stupidity of his interrogator, a line would sometimes surface: "I
hate myself and do not wish to remain alive." He was increasingly
haunted by feelings of despair. "My wife treats me in such a way that
I am scared of her," he writes another time. "I am scared of asking her
a favor and she performs it with such delay and so much condescension that one loses the joy. I told Nafiseh today that maybe God had
decided to use my wife in order to test me." After a meeting with one
of the municipal contractors, who offered to lend him money, he
writes, "I have reached the point where the contractor whose offer of
millions in bribes I refused now offers to loan me five thousand *tumans*"—about seven hundred dollars—"because he knows I have no
money. Damn this life! Why should I have to put with up with such
dishonor? I can't take it anymore. God spare me such scenes and just
kill me."

Suddenly, in July of 1966, the tone of his diaries changes. There is
talk that he might be freed on bail. Before that, a number of people
had tried to persuade him to write a letter asking for forgiveness.
They felt that this way the government could save face and speed up
his release. He of course refused. He suspected that the government
wanted to find a way out, and he was not about to provide them with
an easy escape—and then there was the matter of his pride.

It started when a prominent reporter for *The Washington Post*, Alfred Friendly, published a long piece on Iran in which he mentioned my

father's case. "Yesterday the translated version of Alfred Friendly's article in *The Washington Post* was published," Father wrote in his diary in the summer of 1966. "It is an interesting article. While it praises the Shah and considers his projects to be the cause of progress, he is not very optimistic about Iran. He is even terrified of its future. . . . His worries are confined to two areas: the economic situation and likelihood of a crisis and the problems with the implementation of justice, and he mentions my name in this regard. Although what he says is brief within the context of this long article, it is still central." Friendly wrote a series of articles on Iran. In the one published on July 6, 1966, he wrote:

SMELL OF A FRAME-UP

The most notorious case at the moment is the 32 month's imprisonment without trial of the former Lord Mayor of Tehran, Ahmed [*sic*] Nafisi. Once highly regarded and favored by the Shah, Nafisi was accused (justly or otherwise, depending on whom one listens to) of corruption in connection with certain municipal contracts. The case smells of a frame-up by his personal and political enemies. A few weeks ago, after 2000 pages of interrogation were taken down, the prosecuting attorney found no case against him. But instead of his release, the consequence was the initiation of a new interrogation. Nafisi may remain in jail for years without trial.

Mr. Amirani published a translation of Friendly's article in *Khandanyha*. It was said that the secret police had banned its publication but Amirani complained to the Shah, who, pleased by the compliments to his reform agenda, ordered its release. The article created a great buzz in political circles. In a culture dependent on gossip and innuendos, the fact that permission had been given to reprint the article was taken as a sign that my father's case would soon be reactivated. He was visited by excited friends and well-wishers, all of whom speculated that he would soon be free. Despite his own pessimism, these confident predictions had an effect. Sometimes they threw him into panic. What would he do? Where would he go from here? All his life he had worked in the government, climbing one ladder and then another. What now? Would he be forever in debt to my mother now that he had lost his job?

Mr. Jahanbani, a friend of Father's and a close associate of Prime Minister Amir Abbas Hoveyda, visited my father to say that "Amir Abbas" sent his regards and suggested that since the "misunderstanding" had now been resolved, the government would like to close his file and invite him to return to his job. "If they had kept me for only ten days or a month," Father writes in his diary, "if they had produced only some twenty or thirty files against me, if over 300 municipal workers and staff had not been persecuted, threatened, and forcibly interrogated by the justice department, some arrested and their names dragged through the mud, if the amount of money the government claims to have been involved was not six hundred million *tumans,* perhaps the prime minister's proposal would have had some meaning." A month later Jahanbani visited Father again to say that the Shah had ordered the justice department at long last to follow the letter of the law: he would be freed on bail and would be granted a trial where he could defend himself. My mother told him excitedly that she heard from the Shah's mother-in-law that the Shah had ordered the prime minister to wrap up the investigation. Rahman returned from a visit to Esfahan around this time and claimed that he had communed with my grandfather's spirit, who said that this jail term would be beneficial to my father. According to Rahman, Grandfather's spirit recommended that he pay more attention to his mother.

At this point, General Nassiri, the head of the hated secret police, who had played an active role in framing Father, came to visit him in jail. He said that Father was in jail because of his own stubborn inflexibility. He then told Father to write a letter of contrition addressed to the Shah, implying that such a letter alone could bring about his freedom. In his book, my father published the letter he ultimately wrote to the Shah. In it he reviews every charge brought against him and refutes them. Then he writes: "I would like to apologize for whatever crimes I have not committed, or whose nature I am not aware of, because I have perturbed His Majesty's peace of mind. I leave the true criminals to the wrath of God, for as the Koran says, 'Those who deceive should know that there is no authority higher than God, who will return to them the fruits of their own deceit.' "

General Nassiri told my father that this letter was obviously no apology and would not solve the problem. Rather than apologizing, he had accused the government, and by implication the Shah himself. When Father was finally released on bail, the general sent him a message saying Father's letter was responsible for the extra time he had spent in jail.

General Nassiri was one of the people most hated by our family, right there next to Pirasteh, the minister of the interior. When Nassiri became the head of the SAVAK, our hatred went beyond personal reasons. I never thought of him as a man with a heart. Yet in my father's diary he appears as a naïve and simple man who sheds tears to see my father in jail. I was learning how things were more complicated than I thought, that men who shed tears can also be cruel and unjust. After the revolution, when I saw his battered face on the television screen and later came across photos of his cadaver, alongside those of other executed officials, I felt, to my surprise, an immense sorrow. For years I had dreamed of revenge, not just for my father, but for those dissidents who had been arrested and tortured, for the fear that SAVAK had incited in the hearts of the people. For years I had thought of this man as a vile oppressor and I had waited for some sort of retribution. And when I saw him on television, I began to realize how easy it was for us to be as vengeful and brutal as those we had denounced.

FATHER WAS SET FREE on bail in late August of 1966. The court, to make things as difficult for him as possible, set the bail at 55.5 million *tumans* (roughly 6.5 million dollars). Father writes with excitement and evident pride that he was shocked to see how many people flooded the justice department to put up his bail. "I feel like crying," he writes. "I did not know the Tehranis to be so kindhearted.

داستان تلخ !

۳۳ ماه زندانی شهردار تهران و ۳۴ مهندس وشخصیت تشکیل صدها جلسه محاکمه
و بازپرسی ـ ترتیب ۳۷ هزار برگ پرونده ـ نوشتن وقرائت ۲۵ صفحه رای دادگاه ـ
تحمل میلیونها ریال خرج برای نگهداری این زندانیان همه وهمه بر اساس :

یک اعلام جرم پوچ وواهی !؟

با اعلام رای در مورد برو ندهٔ نفیسی وهمکار انش دادگستری باز هم ثابت کرد که دادگستری واقعی میکند

تمدنامه و نیمخواص بدائم اعلام جرم کننده یا اعلام جرم کنندگان چه کسانی بودم اند ولی آنها بهتر است امروز بنشینند و قضاوت کنند که واقعا چه کرده اند. خوشی نیست. بهمال همه جماعهٔ فعال وشاهدوست وهمین پرست باورند است.

سالها وبتهای او فعالیترین خنگمکاران اندیشگاه قضائی برای روشن شدن حقیقت تلاش کرده اند. پرونده ها تا بیست و هفت هزار صفحه تشکیل خدمات ک قطور تن پرونده های قضائی است . لاقل رهزحه چندین جلسه بازپرسی و محاکمه تشکیل شده است ودود نماینده این ماجرا کمیسلم قید ببال برای دولت خرج برداشته به فراوان کودکانی که همان بی اسفاق بباطر نبودن پدر و خرخلکاه بباطر در آغوش نکشیدن ادود کنارق آرمنهند کریسهاند. چه زنانی که دور از خودر انتشان تیرمردران نادرا واماجراک به میزلترین کنانشان خورده بوده است تحل نبودن وبرانوبوداه چهامیهها وآرنروها که بباد نرفته است ... چرا و کس یا کسانی خواستهاند حسابشان با کسانی آلومسازند وزندگی شریفترین کنانی با خدمتگذاری به درمهمر خدمهانداشتهباشنده باور بنده.

بازم میگویم از مهمین پرونده هر در بار دادرس قطبه احمد نفیسی ویشان و آقمی بماطر علاقه است که بکار وجوانمردش بمضق خلل ناپذیری بهمین و شاعدامیهر و ولی حیفوکنستکه در فراق پدر فرزته احمد نفیسی میگرسته و فرزندان کارهنشمهرواردش او نبی اید گریه میکنرد نیزا پدری بماطر گیی این حفیقتدر رای دادگاه روشن وملاد نا ضرف دادگاهری تفاذنان رمه ماله آمست دانیل ...

نا بهام چه بوده است . آخر با چمامیهدی میوان اسارق به کوربخخت بست ولاری کرد که از مونز عرایلیای وهل برخت یاد داده و آن ترنب برشکوهروزی کنگره تاریخ ایران . کنگره آزاد زنان وآزاد مردان است بعد از این خدمتگذاری به سال دگرهده زمان دادگستری نشست . تا ثابت شوه که بیگانه است .

روزنامه این که تمام شد و روزشیه خبرسمیح منتشرگفت احمد نفیس شهردار اسبق تهران وهمکارانش که بیش از پنجاه نفر بنوجب اعلام جرمی درتبهاجی بودند از اتهامات منتسبه تبرئه شدند و آزاد گردیدند. این افشاء دربرخی موارد پیش میآید که برخی دادگستری را درماجرای این پرونده نفس میداشته ولی ایا . حرفور سالنمی میخواشته بوت فرغریطق بعد بعداو دادگستری نآچار بود در نهایت وقت با این اعلام جرم رسیده ای که و حتی اگرخهاللول میکند، نظرتیا اعلام نمایند با بن منبها ی عدالت بود مقافا اینکه دادگستری بن آناملا رای در موند وبرونده مهمین شهردرتان دادکه است ویس اما دران میان زندها تیمنده انزوی بجاری میکرد که تا بساین نتیجه رسیداماآند که همان کی خلکانا و با در رفته تا بیاین نتیجه رسید هماانند که احمد نفیسی و حنگایانش بیگنه بودهاند . آخر چرا ۱؟

چرا با بر بابه یک اتهام وامی جمی از برجسته ترین شخصیتهای شهررا رأکه از نفیس گلفته که خوش مطبوعات عیدقبی است که هنوز خبرکی بود «ایرانآباد اورا داده با خوشروی خلط میکند. بیش از بست نفرهمین تحسیل کرده دا بند بکنند وبی ازنه سال، بابی بیگوند شما که اسی نداشتهاید . بن چه کمی کاماظلم بوده است ؟

اعلام چه کنندها !

پایه اتهام چه بوده است . آخر با چمامیهدی میوان اسارق به کوربخخت بست ولاری کرد که از مونز عرایلیای وهل برخت یاد داده و آن ترنب برشکوهروزی کنگره تاریخ ایران . کنگره آزاد زنان وآزاد مردان است بعد از این خدمتگذاری به سال دگرهده زمان دادگستری نشست . تا ثابت شوه که بیگانه است .

دراهده جای دنیا اصل بین ترله وبگانی است مگر آنکه نابگان با یک کبرومرده تبسط آشاکت وحمی کبی .

ناگهان شب متر تیرآهن ماشین ناله باورد آهن روی خانه چند بارکر جلوی شماسبز میشود و ایستلسد ن ماشینجلوی خیابان یماسر مساوست با د روبیخت شدن وروبست باخان در باکلکر ازمیدان بی بایخانها سعدی...

ولی باز می پاید بنگویم که این دویستصفحهمقاله است که دربارهباره کارلامای مسافری دریا باری و کأخلشهردان دکهای آهن ... فروشی میننوبسد زیرا کبه خود بعد از این خدمتگذاری خودمان نیست ذیرا آله وآن رحب خان خبردارند کهبیعا لهنستانبجای تااحت که کهپموزنهادستجهانی

رشادنآنهاکه ازوجود این بیماری سود میبرند نگذارند شما هم در درمان آن توفق یابید . اینده وجود دهها کارآزاد باریکهوساظر بركهخط اولخباجهای عازکری شهربون ناصرخسرو . وبزرخمیر سیه . چهرابرتری وفردر سی آست . از جلوی مسجد شاه تامماهاهمرروه فقط سیزده گارداهشت نم کدام بابه تا بست اتوبوخودددردز در ترآفک علوفنرین نقطه شهر را بهم میبریزد و بدون هلا اتعال این کارآزاد بخارج شهر که تنها اعضای یکریان تنواهدد بلکه باعث خواهد شدکه یکبار قلب پایتخت خلوت شود .

آقای رئیس ترآیکتهران شمابایمال بهمین خیابانزودرجمهور

This nation is very strange. It watches tyranny in silence and in time it proves its own will—the fact of its existence—through passive resistance. Among those here today to bail me out there were people from different walks of life and different religions: the grocer up the street as well as the owner of the Iran Super Market, a Jewish man with hundreds of millions in capital. Friends, colleagues, relatives close and distant were here. By noon they had offered nearly one hundred and twenty million *tumans*." In his diary, he lists the names of the people who helped him so that we children would later show them our gratitude.

He was finally released on bail, pending trial. No trial date was set. My husband and I were due to return to Oklahoma any day and I could neither sleep nor eat out of the fear that I might have to leave before seeing my father's release. I had made up with Mother and returned home. Our telephone rang day and night and people came in at all hours. Aunt Nafiseh spent most of the daytime hours at our house and Rahman kept trying to get hold of my hand, which he would pat and say, "Mark my word, you'll see your dad before you go. And what will you give me if that happens?"

A rumor circulated that the new head of the fruit and vegetable market had organized all the vendors and shopkeepers to greet my father on his release. The justice department was overrun with supporters. We had waited so long for this moment that when it happened it seemed like a figment of my imagination. I was filled with nervous energy and could not stay in one place. But I also felt curiously numb and drained, the result of three years of anxious waiting. Phone calls, flowers, running to the door. When will he be here? We were all bumping into one another, like spectators at an overcrowded show. It was not until eleven at night that he was finally released from jail. Despite the fact that it was late and people had been discouraged from waiting for him, Father writes that he saw the shadowy faces of expectant supporters lining the street outside the jail. He had been told by government sources that he should not go straight to our house because it might attract crowds. So his first stop was Aunt Nafiseh's house. This must have cost my mother some pain. She resented her half sister and at the same time craved her favor like a younger, blundering sibling. They would quarrel and not talk for months, but when they made up, my mother would assume an almost sycophantic attitude toward my aunt that made my brother and me feel angry and almost ashamed.

Three days after my father's release I left Tehran. The first night he spent at Aunt Nafiseh's and the next day was spent with crowds of visitors and flowers, but he went home that night. I spent my last night at home to be close to my father. "Thursday morning Azar left for the U.S.," Father wrote in his diary. "In the airport Nezhat and her son-in-law had some confrontation. Unfortunately this young man is in love with money and anxious to get his hands on it, exactly the opposite of Azar. I am afraid these two will separate in the end."

MOST SERIOUS CONFRONTATIONS in life are not political, they are existential. One can agree with someone's political stance but disagree in a fundamental way with how they came to that position. It is a question of attitude, of moral configuration. My husband and I had plenty of grievances, but it all boiled down to a fundamental difference in the way we perceived life, the context within which we defined ourselves and our world. For that, there was no reconciliation or resolution, there was only separation or surrender.

At some point I could not take it anymore. It was not that I could not take him, but I could not take myself. If I did not leave immediately it was partly out of guilt, because I felt I was the one who had been untrue. When we married I knew a lot about the kind of person he was. He had not hidden his ambitions from me. It is true that he had never told me about the woman he had lived with and so easily discarded, but otherwise, I had made my choice with open eyes, although they were the eyes of a girl still in her teens, and under great pressure.

He told me he wanted to return to Tehran after graduating, because his parents were old and he wanted to be close to them. He didn't want me to stay and finish my degree on my own, nor would he wait until I graduated. The truth was that whether we stayed in Norman so that I could finish my studies, or went someplace else, I was tired of the role I had been playing. I had started to cultivate friends of my own who did not go to hairdressers—mostly classmates studying philosophy and English literature. These friends were hip, they read poets like Ferlinghetti and Ginsberg. I, like most of the girls in the group, was infatuated with a classmate named Charley, who had fashioned himself after the hero in Robert Heinlein's *Stranger in a Strange Land*. My husband disliked my friends and did not want me to visit them. So I did what I had learned to do with Mother: when he came for me, they would tell him I was not there.

And then we fought. I wanted to have the freedom to wear jeans and long dresses. My private notes had gone from *Ladies' Home Journal* to Betty Friedan, in part under the influence of a professor who had become a friend and mentor. I will always remember her litmus test for love. You know you love him if you love even his dirty socks, she said with a smile that was genuinely sweet. If you can't tolerate the dirty socks then you should get out.

Mehdi refused to consider divorce. At first he would say, You came into my house in a white gown and you will leave it in a white shroud (in fact it was not his house, but a rented apartment, for which I paid half the rent). And so I took revenge. I did what I wanted. I wore moccasins and jeans instead of the prim and proper little dresses he liked. I did not go to the hairdresser, and I had a glass of wine whenever I felt like it.

One evening, in the midst of a fight, he slapped me. After that I left the house. I had said that we could never live together if we raised our voices against each other and now our relationship had deteriorated far beyond that. So without telling my parents the real reason for leaving Norman, I packed my bags and followed my professor friend to a ranch in New Mexico, where she had moved to start a new career as head of the philosophy department at a small college.

In some ways I felt sorry for Mehdi. He did not get what he had bargained for, while I had the advantage of not having expected anything. "You were never going to be a good housewife," he said, "so it was not for those qualities that I loved you, but for yourself." And the terrible thing is that I believed him.

I WAS IN NEW MEXICO when my father's trial started in earnest, in September of 1967, one year after his release on bail. It was a closed session, although the government had announced that it would be open; not even my father's brother was allowed to attend. The evidence presented in court was mostly laughable. The prosecutor offered up a fabricated tape of my father with his greatest detractor, Seyyed Mehdi Pirasteh, the minister of the interior, having a conversation in which Father insulted the Shah. The purpose of this recording was to prove one of the allegations against him: that of insubordination. Pirasteh's voice was his own but Father's was clearly fake; the tone and his manner were all phony. The tape was representative of the case against him.

Father composed and delivered his own defense. It is one hundred and twenty-eight pages long. It starts with a quotation from Ferdowsi and is interspersed with anecdotes from Rumi, Saadi, and other classical Persian poets as well as from Imam Ali, the Koran, Voltaire, and Dante. Later my father told me his decision to draw from the classics was deliberate: he chose the best of Iran's heritage, in order to show his enemies that they were not the true sons of this country, that Iran did have other traditions, other values, and that he, my father, represented them.

Early on in his defense he cited an anecdote from Mullah Nasreddin, the popular fictional satiric figure. One day the Mullah was invited to give a sermon. When he got to the pulpit, he asked his audience if they knew what he was going to say. They said no. He was offended—what good would it do to speak to such ignorant people? The next day he repeated his question. Some in the audience said yes and others no. This time the Mullah said, "Those of you who know what I am going to say can tell those who don't." The third day he repeated his question again, and all said that they knew what he would say. "Why am I wasting my time telling you what you all already know?" he asked as he stepped down from the pulpit. My father told the court that this was his story: "I don't know why I was arrested. If no one else knows either, then we are all in the same boat. If, however, there are some who know they should inform the rest of us who don't." Father denounced the court and accused certain officials by name, including Pirasteh, of malicious conspiracy. He went over every single charge and refuted them one by one and closed with a poem he had written for the occasion.

The trial ended on November 27, 1967. Father was exonerated of all but one charge, insubordination, as a result of which he was banned from government service. That decision would eventually be reexamined and overturned by the High Court, which exonerated him of all charges. The press was overwhelmingly on his side; three major publications, *Sepid Seyah*, *Khandanyha*, and *Omid Iran*, published the introduction to his defense. After his exoneration the prime minister offered him a job, which he refused. He had decided never to enter government service again.

I was in New Mexico when Father called to tell me the news. I congratulated him and after we had talked for a while, I suddenly said, "I want to divorce Mehdi." My tone was neutral and formal. I was afraid of becoming too emotional. I think Father realized this. He paused. "Are you sure?" "I am," I said. "I am sorry, I didn't want to bring this up now." He said, "I would have asked you what you were doing in New Mexico anyway. Don't worry, we'll talk about everything later. Don't worry," he repeated.

I was surprised that neither my father nor my mother asked me to reconsider. The next summer, when Mehdi and I returned to Tehran, my parents did everything in their power to make the process easy for me. At first Mehdi would not grant me a divorce. My father reminded my husband of my power to ask him for alimony at any time, even if we were not divorced. Alimony in Iran was the money both sides agreed on at the time of marriage to be paid to the wife in case of divorce, but that she could claim at any point during the marriage. Many women used this to get out of terrible marriages. In the end, an agreement was reached that if he would grant me a divorce I would waive all requests for alimony. It worked. My parents were so supportive that I could almost forget I had been married and divorced. "My poor Azi, you never enjoyed your life," Mother said, looking at me, her eyes filled with pity. "I could tell from the start this match wouldn't work," she said. "He was not our type. No one would listen to me."

THOSE FOUR YEARS my father spent in jail changed our lives forever. For the first time we realized the fragility of life, how easy it is to lose everything, and that changed the way we looked at all that we had taken for granted. My mother was a changed person. Over the following months, as life settled down to our new routine, she would read, with tears in her eyes, my father's poems to her. She even tried to watch his favorite television shows with him, although more often than not she would fall asleep in the middle of a program. Her fears and anxieties remained: she worried if he came home a little late, if the phone rang late at night or the doorbell early in the morning. It took the machinations of several of the most powerful men in our country to make my father's dream of a happy marriage come true. He could now look back with some satisfaction on that day when, at eighteen, he fled his parents' home with its traditions and their demand that he marry a girl of their choice in order to start a brand-new life for himself.

Let me start again:

I can say in all honesty that my father's imprisonment brought on a new era in our lives. I married and divorced, losing my faith in marriage and marital fidelity. I believe that was when my father decided to be seriously unfaithful to my mother. He had lost all hope of a desirable public life. He was still young—not yet fifty. Mohammad and I had grown up. When he was released he must have decided that since politics were out of the question, he would try to fulfill his dream of a happy domestic life. But my mother did not change at all. And as it turned out, there would be certain personal as well as political consequences to my father's imprisonment, but it took us eleven more years to find that out.

PART FOUR | REVOLTS AND REVOLUTION

*What gets left of a man amounts
to a part. To his spoken part. To a part of speech.*

—JOSEPH BRODSKY

a happy family

AFTER MY DIVORCE I APPLIED to and was accepted at the University of California at Santa Barbara. I thought it had a great English department and for some reason had set my heart on going there before I married Mehdi. I was lying on my bed reading the letter of acceptance when my father came in. He sat by the bed and told me that if I went to a new college in the middle of my studies I would lose too many credits and it would delay my graduation. He wanted me to finish up at the University of Oklahoma. I protested that I had always wanted to go to Santa Barbara, but he went on to say that he had been hoping he'd have a chance to spend time with me before he got too old, that he wanted me to graduate early and come home as soon as possible. Remember, he said, you didn't want to leave us in the first place. I had drawn the curtains and there was no light except the bedside lamp. He had positioned himself at the foot of the bed and I half sat, resting on one elbow. An intimate portrait, father and daughter, illuminated by the artificial light from the lamp.

So I stayed at the University of Oklahoma. I do not regret it. But I probably would have returned home sooner had I gone to U.C. Santa Barbara, where there was no nascent Iranian students' movement to get involved in, and where I would have focused more on my studies than on organizing demonstrations.

I started life over in Oklahoma, as if I had never married—that at least was my perception, though it wasn't what others felt. Not some of our old friends and acquaintances, who either tried to pick me up or

kept their wives away from my bad influence. Not the young American men who equated a young divorcée with an easy lay. Not even my
former husband, who would write me loving letters from Iran, advising me how to behave, where to go, what to do, how to preserve my
integrity.

When I returned home the following summer, my father introduced me to the woman he had fallen in love with. "Nezhat is looking
for her own unknown and invisible self," he wrote in his diary just before his release from jail. "Something she lost from day one and
doesn't know how to find. I might have been that thing, but I am not.
It might have been the children, but they're not. It could have been
position, wealth, or fame. I don't know what it is. She is always anxious, tense, and restless. She thinks of herself as the center of the
world! What should I do?" Of all his siblings, he had taken the greatest risk by rejecting his father's worldview. It was essential to him, to
that dream of success that had propelled him to leave Esfahan at eighteen, that he find a woman to love. "I wish I had a beloved," he wrote
that fall, "a space to be alone with her, loyal to one another and joyous
together, but regrettably I am getting old and am afraid that these few
remaining days will also pass and the imaginary happiness I dreamed
of will always be inaccessible."

Not long after he left jail, he accepted the executive directorship of
a private textile factory that had been owned by a dear friend who had
recently died. At the textile factory he met Shahin, who was his secretary, and later, when he left to become vice president of the Iranian
Bank, she left with him.

I had been in Tehran for a few days when he took me to meet her.
We had tea and discussed the virtues of modern poetry, especially
Ahmad Shamlou—perhaps the most influential living poet in Iran—
and the twin vices of hypocrisy and materialism. It was a common-
place conversation full of platitudes and big words, a way of affirming
the other person as your kind of person. Whether consciously or not,
we both wanted to like one another and to please my father. And
pleased he was, basking in this mutual bonding.

She was not as beautiful as my mother, only younger and more confident. Perhaps poised is the right word. What attracted my father to her, I believe, was the fact that she appeared to share his interests: she gathered his poems, empathized with his plight, offered seemingly wise remarks gleamed from books of psychology. "I talked about this to my beloved friend who is both beautiful and wise," my father wrote. "She said, from a psychological point of view, women who reach an age when they are no longer attractive, will do anything to draw attention, even if it means wishing their husband's death."

It is too obvious an irony that my father's women were at first welcomed by my mother. She adopted them. They tolerated her extreme attentions because of their interest in him. None of my father's women had much in common with my mother and yet she tried to form personal bonds with them. The fact that by constantly bringing up Saifi she had openly demonstrated her own emotional infidelity never occurred to her. So it was with Shahin. Mother, who could not keep away from Father's office, had taken a liking to Shahin during her regular visits. She found her charming, a serious and well-mannered girl, and often invited her to lunch or coffee. In my mind's eye I see it all again, sitting in our bright, spacious living room, my father, Mother, Shahin, and me. Shahin sets her porcelain coffee cup on the table, politely listens to my mother, murmurs something appropriate in response. She is wearing a simple brown suit, her hair pulled back severely in a tidy chignon. Large round gold earrings gleam against her black hair: ladylike, attractive, attentive. My mother has on the friendly smile she reserves for her protégés. Instead of empathizing with my mother, I am embarrassed for Shahin for having to tolerate this. Every once in a while she averts her eyes and looks sideways, not toward my father, but to a point away from him. I catch their glances, as he looks toward the same point and smiles awkwardly—happily.

I WENT BACK TO OKLAHOMA in mid-August, after yet another big and bloody fight with my mother. I vowed never to return to Tehran, and wrote my father a loving letter in which I called Mother a lunatic and said that she should be committed. Mother discovered the letter, opened it without his knowledge or permission, and all hell broke loose. What was extraordinary about these incidents was not so much the extent of the emotions on display as the fact that we went on without breaking contact for good, without ever really taking permanent offense. Mother seemed to find these discoveries uplifting, providing proof, as they did, that she had been right all along. Years later she still had a copy of that letter, which every once in a while she would wave in front of my eyes with an expression of bitter satisfaction, or refer to with acid neutrality.

Not long after that, she discovered the truth about Shahin. Father constantly vacillated between his urge to start a new life and his fear of it. He kept threatening to leave and never followed through. At different points he left the house for a while and made my mother consent to a divorce, but at the last minute she reneged or he was persuaded to return. "My wife says she would never consent to a permanent separation," he writes in his diary, "because that would bring me happiness and she does not want me to be happy!" Later Father told me over lunch at a restaurant that Rahman had informed my mother of the liaison after Shahin had refused Rahman's sexual advances. He told me this after Rahman's sudden death in the summer of 1973. Father grieved for his death and felt that had he not abused his extraordinary powers Rahman would perhaps have been useful for himself and those close to him.

Aji maji, latrajii: I hear Rahman utter these nonsensical words, supposedly magical invocations, as he laughingly tries to grab hold of my hand. He was such a physical presence, when he entered the room one could almost feel his bulky body fill the space around him, so that even I in some strange way missed him—or felt his absence, the emptiness, as if space itself had bulk, and a piece of it, in the shape of Mr. Rahman, had been scissored out.

My parents stayed together for another decade. Shahin married a wealthy suitor who she later claimed was a gambler who refused to give her access to money because he feared that once she had it she would leave him. Father told me they spent most of their time abroad.

CHAPTER 21

Demonstrations

ACK IN THE UNITED STATES I FELL IN LOVE with Ted, who read Beckett and played the classical guitar. He gave me my first book by Nabokov, *Ada*. In the mornings we marched against the Vietnam war and ROTC, Ted carrying his camera to document the proceedings. I can still picture those young men our own age who looked so vulnerable as they tried to ignore our jeering. In the evenings we drank wine and went to Ingmar Bergman and Fellini movies. Ted helped me make a film for a class based on my unhappy marriage—my teacher said it was truly Bergmanesque and gave me an A. Such were the times. When Ted and I broke up I had fully matured into believing that relationships do not, perhaps should not, last.

In 1971 I watched on American television the lavish twenty-five-hundredth-anniversary celebrations of the Persian Empire near the ruins of Persepolis, to which Alexander had set fire after his conquest of Persia in 330 B.C. Celebrities and royalty, including Prince Philip and Prince Charles of Britain, Prince Rainier and Princess Grace of Monaco, and King Haile Selassie of Ethiopia, participated in the sumptuous extravaganza in a tented city near the ruins designed for the occasion by a group of French architects. Food and wine were imported from France, and the city was walled off from ordinary Iranians. A procession of men dressed as ancient Achaemenid soldiers paraded by the assembled grandees. The Shah, in an address to Cyrus, the great Achaemenid king, that became a joke among Iranians, declaimed, "Cyrus, sleep well, for we are awake!"

Earlier that year opposition to the Shah had taken on a new urgency as it shifted from the mainly peaceful methods of the old groups to the more militant means of the two new armed revolutionary groups, one

The tents for the 2,500th-anniversary celebrations at Persepolis.

Marxist and another Muslim. In an armed uprising in the village of Siahkal, a group of Marxist guerrillas, called the Organization of Fedaian-e Khalgh—all young, educated, middle-class men and women—were either killed in a clash with the police or apprehended and later executed. Meanwhile a militant Muslim organization named Mojahedeen-e Khalgh called for an armed struggle against the regime.

All through the early seventies the country was living a paradox: it enjoyed an economic boom thanks to the skyrocketing cost of oil (which soon would lead to numerous economic problems) but was

deeply divided by the socially liberalizing measures initiated by the Shah. At the same time it became more polarized and closed politically. The middle class, which had benefited most from the political and social transformations, was alienated by this increased repression. In March of 1975 the Shah eliminated the nominal two-party system and asked the whole nation to merge into one party, called Rastakhiz (meaning resurgence, or resurrection). Those who advised him to do this hoped that the different forces and factions would come together. The Shah's new party was unpopular from the start, as was his terse statement that whoever opposed it was free to leave the country. The following year he quixotically decided to shift from the Islamic calendar, which starts with the prophet's flight from Mecca to Medina, to a new one based on the establishment of the Persian Empire by Cyrus the Great, bringing the year from 1355 to 2535. Iran's history was being divided by two polarized political powers: the Shah, who more and more identified his rule with ancient pre-Islamic Iran, and the religious establishment, who defined Iranian history as beginning only after the Arab Conquest.

In this context our campus activities in the U.S. and Europe became more militant and polarized. In the seventies it was easy for a young Iranian abroad to be antigovernment—inside Iran, of course, it was a different story. Gradually I found myself drawn into the Confederation of Iranian Students, one of the most active campus movements in the United States. There I was not treated as a young divorcée, but was invited to participate in reading groups on Engels's *The Origin of the Family, Private Property and the State*, Marx's *Eighteenth Brumair*, and, later, Lenin's *State and Revolution*. Strange bedfellows for *Tom Jones, Tristram Shandy, The Rise of Silas Lapham, Persuasion*, and *Winesburg, Ohio*, books I devoured so quickly that by the time classes started I had finished most of them.

The Confederation was an umbrella organization, composed of groups with different ideological viewpoints, but with time, especially in the U.S., the most militant and radical ideologies became dominant. In our group it seemed as if everything could fall into place, all questions could be answered: the world could be controlled, polished, purged, and purified. There was a clear line between the bad guys—the Shah and his imperialist masters—and the good guys, those like us who were the champions of the oppressed. We were consumed by the inflexible ideological trends of the time, turning the teachings of Che Guevara, Mao, Lenin, and Stalin into romantic dreams of revolution.

The Iranian student movement in the U.S. was on the whole militant and as time went by increasingly puritanical: family ties and sexual intimacy were denigrated, and in some cases driven underground. A far cry from the liberating poetry of Forough Farrokhzad! The feminist movement was called bourgeois by the more militant segments of the Confederation; women were comrades, and the desexed images on posters from China were our ideal. But since man cannot live by ideology alone, I, like others, gave in to relationships, and like them I hid those relationships and told myself that it was all for the good of the movement. And so the problems that had started with childhood and intensified with marriage found a haven to fester without a challenge.

Every once in a while Father would ask me to take Mother off his hands for a few months, so that he could "breathe a little." She would descend on me in Oklahoma with suitcases full of nuts, dried cherries, Turkish coffee, woolen scarves, and sweaters, and would immediately start cleaning my apartment and making me food. She mixed and mingled with my friends, offering them coffee and mocking our activities. I was at this point a teaching assistant in the English department. Mohammad had enrolled at the University of Oklahoma for a year; he then transferred first to Paris and then to the University of Kent, where he got his degree before returning to the U.S. for graduate studies at the New School for Social Research.

Somewhat surprisingly, Mother did not make a scene about my political activities, despite the fact that they had already caused trouble at home. Father had been summoned by the secret police and forced to make promises about my future conduct that were not his to keep. I was active in a group called the Third World Committee, organized by a Chinese student who was at once quiet and persistent. We were all in love with Chairman Mao, or at least with the romance of his legend. When Mao died, in 1976, Mother was in the U.S. on one of her visits. We made quite a to-do about his death, vocally mourning him and staging memorial meetings. I remember the scornful expression on my mother's face when I came home teary-eyed and inconsolable. She said, with incomprehension, "You cry as if one of your parents has died!"

WHEN I MET BIJAN NADERI, he was the leader of a student faction headquartered in California with which we had chosen to associate ourselves. His group was more cerebral and less ferociously self-assured than most of the other factions. It also had few members in the U.S. With other men I was not challenged. I had somehow abdicated responsibility by hiding my relationships. But from the very start there was no evasion and concealment with Bijan. He was not shocked by my fear of monogamy, or my secret affairs. Our relationship was the first I avowed in public since I had broken up with Ted. By then I was convinced that marriages did not last and that those that did were very unhappy. At no point in our courtship did he ever really tell me why he had decided to marry me. "Isn't it obvious?" he would say. He knew very little about my background and circumstances, nor was he particularly interested. To my annoyance, he was not even much interested in my first husband. According to family lore his father, a kind and temperamental man, picked up one day and left home, never to return, leaving behind a short note addressed to Bijan, in which he asked Bijan to take care of his mother and sisters. All he took with him was a small suitcase and the suit he wore. He had waited for his eldest daughter, Mani, to marry and arranged for Bijan, at the

age of seventeen, to join her in America. Bijan's younger sister, Taraneh, was put under the guardianship of her maternal uncle. Bijan's father was never found, and although he was always mentioned with kindness, no one ever discussed his strange vanishing act.

Me with Bijan Naderi,
my second husband.

Mother met Bijan in 1976, on her last trip to Oklahoma. She liked him: she said he seemed responsible and far more "together" than my cousin Mehdi, who was then involved in the same student movement. It helped that her main priority was to protect me from my father's family, and being overly cordial to Bijan meant snubbing Mehdi. "He is just a friend," I said.

She very much wanted him to be more, or at least that is what she implied when we were alone. Over dinner it was more difficult to deflect her. "He has a job," she would drop casually as I focused on my plate, examining each morsel with great interest. "He is not like all those vagrants who are sent here to study and become useful members of society and what do they do? They wear patched-up trousers and act like illiterate hoodlums. He does have a job, doesn't he?" she would continue, following me to the kitchen with the dishes. "No, no," she'd say with a sense of urgency, "first wash the sink." "Mom, why do I need to wash the sink?" "Is it a good job?" she asked.

I had by now a whole new armament to help me shut out her voice—Fielding, Lenin, Wharton. Later, as I sat, book in hand, she asked again, peeling an orange: "He *does* have a job, doesn't he?" "Yes, Mom," I finally said, holding the book closer to me as if for protection. "He is a civil engineer and I don't like engineers." "What *do* you like?" she asked in exasperation. "Are you waiting for another Chairman Mao?"

AFTER A SHORT ENGAGEMENT, we announced our wedding date—September 9, 1979. My parents flew to Washington, D.C., and Mohammad and his girlfriend, Janet, came from New York. Mother arrived full of plans and energy, pushing me aside to such an extent that one might have been forgiven for imagining that it was her wedding. She wanted everything I didn't: the customary alimony, a proper wedding dress and ceremony, a proper diamond ring. She brought with her all the material for a traditional Persian wedding—rosewater; huge sugar cubes, a staple of traditional wedding ceremonies; jewelry—and fell into arranging everything with a vengeance. It did not take me long to understand that wedding ceremonies are the exact opposite of what they are made out to be: joyous and harmonious celebrations of love and family.

Almost from the start I had developed a loving and flirtatious relationship with Bijan's family, especially his two sisters. I was almost dazzled by their unpretentious generosity and sense of moral integrity.

During these warlike preparations, Bijan's mother and sisters treated me as a beloved eccentric. They begged me to comply with my mother's demands. My mother-in-law, justifiably distressed by the ultimatums my mother and I exchanged, designated Mani and Taraneh to act as emissaries of peace. I hear Mani's footsteps coming down the stairs, I sit up straight and prepare to confront her requests with strong counterarguments. Her voice is gentle and cautious. "Azi jan?" Behind her I see Taraneh, smiling and saying nothing. "All mothers are like this, look at Afahg joon," says Mani, who is known to throw herself and those closest to her to the wolves in order make peace. Her husband, Kioumars (whom we call Q), is the best husband in the world, but if a friend complains about the indifference or cruelty of her spouse, Mani will say, with all the sympathy in the world, "I know exactly what you mean," provoking Q to good-humored exasperation. Taraneh interrupts: "Let's go shopping for a dress and we'll get away from of all this." "We can get a coffee at White Flint Mall," Mani adds, perhaps trying to bribe me into joining them. Half an hour later, like the defeated generals of a losing army, they head back upstairs.

Bijan begged me to let Mother have her way—he pointed out that my obstinacy only resulted in making a bigger deal out of not wanting to turn the event into a big deal. "What," Mother would ask him sarcastically, "do you have to say to all of this? You and I need to have a serious talk." He would nod his head, concede with a smile that she was right, yes, they should have a serious talk, and then he would disappear. Finally I gave up, more out of exhaustion than anything else, and she won on all counts. "We will anoint you a saint," Bijan said with a smile, "for all your sufferings, but now please be a good girl and let us get on with our lives."

For three days, Bijan's patient sisters dragged me from Montgomery Mall to White Flint and all around D.C. in search of shoes and an appropriate wedding dress. What we found was not ideal, too cute for my taste, but that was not the point. The wedding went on as planned. Despite the bloody battles preceding it, the ceremony itself was warm and intimate.

The morning before the wedding we went to the State House for a civil ceremony and, in the middle of it all, I suddenly plunged into irrepressible laughter. To this day I still don't know why, but at least it was better than the tears at my previous wedding. Mani was embarrassed on my behalf. Bijan gave me a dirty look, and Mohammad's girlfriend, Janet, who was one of the witnesses, started laughing with me.

My second wedding day,
September 9, 1979.
From left: Bijan's mother,
me, Father, Mother.

The morning after the civil service we held two more ceremonies, first a Baha'i ceremony presided over by an Indian woman, then the Muslim marriage. Bijan's family was Baha'i, a fact that my parents accepted with surprisingly little reluctance. That night some twenty friends and family gathered at Mani's house. While my sisters-in-law danced, our family stood on the sidelines with silly smiles, looking on with admiration and perhaps even some envy at their ability.

revolution

BIJAN LEFT FOR PARIS RIGHT AFTER our wedding to talk with the leaders of our group there. Armed militant organizations and increasing repression polarized the opposition's political discourse, radicalizing the student movement abroad. Mother stayed on for two months. She rented an apartment in New York, where my brother was studying, and since Bijan and I had not had time to find a place of our own it was agreed that I would move in with her to work on my dissertation until his return. New York, the locus of most radical activities in the 1930s, was a good place for me to get back to writing my dissertation on Mike Gold and the Proletarian writers of the 1930s.

Mother never failed to guilt-trip Bijan's family about his leaving. "Married two weeks and he leaves my daughter for no good reason," she'd lament, muttering under her breath that he was following in his father's footsteps—like father, like son. She called his mother to tell her that I was in poor health and overworked and who would have taken care of me had she not decided to stay on? "Is this what is in store for my poor daughter?" Bijan's mother was in a terrible state for her own reasons. She genuinely believed that government agents might kill Bijan, especially when he traveled in Europe.

That year, President Jimmy Carter established an office of human rights in the State Department, signaling a change in U.S. foreign policy. At a Hungarian pastry shop on Amsterdam Avenue, not far from Columbia University, my comrades and I discussed the effects of what some called "Jimocracy" on the dissident movement in Iran. A group of nationalists wrote a letter to the Shah asking him to implement the constitution and to limit the role of the monarchy. A human-rights committee formed in Tehran demanded that the rights outlined by Carter should be respected in Iran. Some political prisoners were released and the treatment of those in jails improved. The Writers' Association held a series of poetry nights at the Goethe Institute in Tehran to overflow audiences, where the lack of freedom of expression was loudly denounced. On the last night, soldiers stood outside in the rain while poets and writers spoke of suppression. The soldiers had been instructed not to use force unless violence broke out and the evening ended without any problems. But a second series of readings at Arya Mehr University was derailed by SAVAK.

Although secular forces had initiated the protests, Ayatollah Khomeini and his followers were by now gaining prominence in Iran. Too arrogant to think of him as a threat and deliberately ignorant of his designs, we supported him. And yet everything was there for us to see: Khomeini's book *The Rule of Jurisprudence* called for the creation of a theocratic state ruled by a representative of God; he had denounced women's suffrage as a form of prostitution; he had made countless pronouncements against minorities, especially Baha'is and Jews. We welcomed the vehemence of Khomeini's rants against imperialists and the Shah and were willing to overlook the fact that they were not delivered by a champion of freedom. Khomeini himself very shrewdly refrained from making his plans widely known. He had implied in his public statements that once he returned to Iran he would retire to the holy city of Qom and leave the affairs of the state to politicians.

For the first decades of the twentieth century, Amoo Said and his generation—men like Dehkhoda, Hedayat, Nima, Dowlatabadi, Rafaat, Iraj Mirza, Eshghi—had all been only too aware of the reactionary role of some clerics. Many wrote scathing satires, criticizing their religious hypocrisy and backwardness. We young revolutionaries had their writings to refer to, but we were inebriated by the moment and blinded by our own passions. Thus, as uprisings spread to key cities like Tabriz and Qom in 1978, we in New York, Washington,

Demonstrators protest against the Shah, near the White House.

and Berkeley attributed them to "our" forces. At a party given by my brother and his roommates in New York, attended by Paul Sweezy and Harry Magdoff, the editors of the *Monthly Review,* Sweezy offered to drink to the health of "the first real workers' revolution." It took a few months before disillusionment set in. Two years later I published my first essay in English, in the *New Left Review,* about the dire condition of women after the revolution and signed it AZ.

The Confederation of Iranian Students planned huge demonstrations in Washington, D.C., on November 15, 1977, during the Shah's state visit to the United States Bijan, who had just returned from France, went directly to Washington and I joined him there. Nearly two thousand students gathered around the White House, escorted by mounted police. I along with two other women from different factions gave speeches and shouted out slogans. A few of the Shah's defenders had gathered close to the White House lawn, their voices drowned out by our slogans: Death to the Shah; CIA agents, U.S. advisors out of Iran; Iran the next Vietnam; U.S. get out of Iran.

The next day *The Washington Post* published the famous picture of the Shah and Carter on the White House lawn. The tear gas used

The Shah and President Carter at the White House.

against the demonstrators had spread to the lawn and the Shah, bending his head with a handkerchief to his eyes, looked as if he were crying. We did not know then that he had cancer, nor could we imagine how confused he had become as he watched (back in Iran) hundreds of thousands of what he thought had been his loyal subjects protesting his rule. When I returned to New York the next day, I had almost lost my voice. I concealed my participation in the demonstrations from my mother, who would have strongly disapproved. She made another phone call to Bijan's family to complain about her daughter's frail state and her son-in-law's utter disregard for her well-being.

A few days later she returned to Iran and I went to D.C. again to join Bijan. We finally settled in D.C., where he went to work for a construction company and I started, at last, to focus on my dissertation. I turned the living room of our rented apartment into my office, and as soon as I woke up and showered I would take my coffee back to bed and read the news about Iran. One corner of our bedroom was soon filled with old coffee-stained copies of *The Washington Post* and *The New York Times*. Some mornings I would go to the Library of Congress, where I spent delicious hours looking through old microfilms of *The Masses, The New Masses,* and other publications from the thirties for my dissertation. Usually Bijan picked me up after work and we would walk around Dupont Circle, eat something, and go home.

IN AUGUST 1978, Cinema Rex in Abadan, a port city on the edge of the oil fields, was set on fire by arsonists and over four hundred people were scorched to death. The Shah's government denied any involvement in the incident and claimed it was the work of the religious opposition. Both the secular and religious opposition fired back, accusing the regime of committing the crime with the express purpose of blaming them to undermine popular sympathy. It was significant that the fire had taken place during the holy month of Ramadan. Few people believed what the government said, and the atrocity became a symbol of the lengths to which the Shah's regime would go to preserve power. For weeks Cinema Rex was evoked to remind us of the fact that there could be no dialogue, no compromise, with a regime as brutal as this. Photographs of innocent victims who had gone to the movies that afternoon stared at us from the pages of newspapers and the pamphlets that appeared denouncing the perpetrators of this most heinous crime. The callous brutality of the act was another argument for the overthrow of the Shah's regime.

After the revolution, the families of the victims demanded justice. To their dismay and surprise the new Islamic government ignored them: their protests and sit-ins were attacked, and several prosecutors resigned in the middle of the investigations. Because of public pressures, many people, guilty and innocent alike, were arrested and executed. In some cases it was blatantly obvious that the charges were trumped up—one officer who was found guilty and executed had not even been present in the city at the time. A young man who had been directly involved claimed he had confessed to the authorities but no one would take him seriously. Hysteria and outrage eclipsed all facts. People believed what they wanted to believe.

Later it emerged that the fire had been planned not by the Shah's government but by sympathizers of the religious opposition, who felt that with this act they could accelerate the revolutionary process. Because the investigation had been muddled from the start, the truth came out piecemeal. The Islamic government and the official news organs hid the evidence and tried to blame the Shah. The greatest crime the Shah's police had been guilty of, in this case, was bad judgment. Panicked and overwhelmed, they had acted foolishly: seeing a group trying to light a small fire in a corner and hoping to catch the culprits before they could escape, they ordered that the doors be shut until the firefighters arrived. By then, the fire had spread to the whole building and burned almost everyone.

Where was I when we discovered the truth? What did I do? Did I read the papers, discuss the news with friends, express outrage, and go on eating my ice cream? Was that the day I returned home pleased with myself because a class on *Tom Jones* had gone particularly well? The worst thing about such acts is that they leave no innocents: everyone is implicated, even the victims, or bystanders such as myself.

Not long after the Cinema Rex tragedy, Bijan made another trip to Paris, to discuss the future of our group. He returned disenchanted with the leaders, who immediately started a Stalinist-style campaign against him. While he was in Paris his mother was diagnosed with uterine cancer that had metastasized to her brain. Some in the leadership used Bijan's mother's illness against him, accusing him of reneging on his political commitments in order to tend to his mother. Tending to one's mother was seen as a bourgeois affliction.

For someone as committed and loyal to his political beliefs and to his family as Bijan, this was exceptionally difficult. Although he seldom spoke about it, he did not sleep much at night. His mother died within a few months. I too was pressured to make a choice between my political commitments and personal loyalty to Bijan. In the end we were both isolated and disenchanted. Perhaps I owe my dissertation to that disenchantment, as I was finally forced to focus on my writing.

The more I delved into my dissertation the more disillusioned I became with its subject, a proletarian writer of the thirties, and his ideological stance. I started to read Richard Wright, Arthur Koestler, and Ignazio Silone, whose experiences of communism resonated with my own activities in the student movement, and I began to wonder, how can one remain loyal to one's progressive ideals without clinging to a destructive ideology?

IN THE FALL OF 1978, Iraq expelled Khomeini in a bid to improve its relations with Iran. From his obscurity in Karbala, where he had cultivated a network of clerics and allies, suddenly he was thrown onto the world stage. His projected image as a man of God, at once imposing and otherworldly, was perfectly encapsulated by a photograph of him sitting under an apple tree in the small French village of Neauphle-le-Château. Soon international media and all manner of Iranians—seculars, nationalists, even radicals—would make the pilgrimage to Neauphle-le-Château to pay their respects, to appease their curiosity, and, for some, to size up a potential future leader of Iran. The paradox of the man of God turning his back on the world while at the same time conspiring and planning to take it over would fascinate his millions of admirers.

In January the Ministry of Court in Tehran had published an article in the official newspaper, *Etelaat*, under the title "Black and Red Imperialism." The two enemies of democracy and freedom were identified as communists (red imperialism) and the radical clerics led by Khomeini

Ayatollah Khomeini, in exile in Paris.

(black imperialism). The article had triggered demonstrations in the holy city of Qom that left six dead. Forty days later, in keeping with the Muslim cycle of mourning, there were demonstrations in Tabriz and three more deaths. In demonstrations in the city of Yazd on the fortieth day commemorating the deaths in Tabriz, the Shah was compared to Yazid, the murderer of the martyred Imam Hussein. Throughout the early part of 1978 the Shah vacillated between crackdowns and reconciliation. On September 6th, several thousand participated in demonstrations on the festival of the Eid al Fetr, ending the month of Ramadan. The Coalition of Islamic Societies added to the slogan "Liberty and Independence" the words "Islamic Rule."

When I spoke on the phone with my father, who was in Paris on business, he sounded excited by the changes in Iran. He kept repeating that for centuries Iran had suffered at the hands of absolutist monarchs and reactionary clerics, and this was a chance to get rid of both. "I almost feel sorry for the Shah," he said, "with all the sycophants surrounding him, telling him he is the shadow of God on earth." Ill with cancer, confused and hurt by the people's reaction, insecure about international support, especially that of the Americans, the Shah seemed to have lost his will. He did not want more violence, and he refused to act upon the advice of those who suggested he crack down on the demonstrations and let the army loose on the people. It was, as so many suggested at the time, a little too late for this gesture of goodwill.

On January 16, 1979, the Shah left Iran. Before leaving, to appease the opposition, he appointed a liberal nationalist ally of Mossadegh, Shahpoor Bakhtiar, as his prime minister. That was when I had my first serious fight with Bijan—if one can call it a fight. About a month before we'd had a falling-out, one whose cause I cannot even remember. Since then Bijan had given me the silent treatment. He did not argue or shout, he simply withdrew. When I say he withdrew I mean not just from the fight but from everything. While he was growing ever more reserved, reducing our communications to the few necessary words, I had been brooding. I would wake up in the morning exhausted, having carried on into the night the fight we had avoided during the daytime. This desperate situation was further proof to me that marriages did not work. At least they did not work for me. Better cut your losses, I thought, while you still can.

That night we drove to a friend's house in silence. During dinner there were the usual arguments about the Shah and Khomeini. We all gathered by the television to hear about Bakhtiar's appointment—the fifth and final prime minister in less than two years. "I think if the left and the secular forces in Iran are wise," Bijan said mildly but firmly, "they will gather behind Bakhtiar. He is a genuine democrat and a seasoned politician. We all must rally behind him."

"That is bunk," I said. "Bakhtiar is a compromiser." "And what has he compromised?" Bijan asked. "He is disbanding SAVAK, he will bring forward a liberal government, and he will prevent Khomeini from gaining more power." But I, like so many others, was for a complete break with the Shah. Nothing less than the overthrow of the regime would do. I started to recount, with the righteousness attendant on such extreme positions, all of the crimes committed by the Shah. Bijan looked at me and said with disdain that I need not trouble myself telling him about the Shah's crimes. He did not pursue the argument, which of course fired me up even more.

On our way home, after driving in silence, I blurted out, "I want a divorce." There was a pause: Bijan was genuinely shocked. Whatever he had expected, it was not this. "Why?" he said, "why on earth would you think that way? We have such a good relationship." "We have hardly been speaking," I said, "for the past month." He tried to convince me that he loved me and that no matter how angry he might have been—and when he was angry he could not speak about it— nothing had happened to make him think for a moment that we should divorce. He said, with some desperation, "There are other ways of expressing yourself, you know, than with words."

On FEBRUARY 1, 1979, Khomeini made a triumphant return to Tehran, where millions flooded the streets to welcome him. When asked by a journalist how he felt about being back home after almost eighteen years, he said, "Nothing." Ayatollah Khomeini had been elevated to Imam, a title given in Shia Islam to the successors of the prophet Mohammad. To use his name in vain or insult him would now entail serious consequences. Thousands of Iranians, some of whom I knew to be perfectly sane, including my secular and reasonably educated aunt Nafiseh, had spotted his image in the moon. Later, when I

An Iranian woman with a propaganda poster of Khomeini.

made a derogatory comment about him, she said, "Darling, please don't say such things. My mother told me about a woman who slandered him and a cat jumped out of the garbage can and bit her arm so severely that she died."

If my aunt saw Khomeini in the moon, there were others in my family who saw possibilities that only a year before might have seemed equally illusory. My cousin Hamid, the least political of Uncle Abu Torab's children, who, after getting his master's degree in media and film from UCLA, had returned home to help build the film and media department at the Open University,

now found little room for himself and his American wife, Kelly, in Iran. They picked up and left for America, while his younger brothers Majid and Mehdi, who had been associated with a radical Marxist group, returned home from the U.S. For the young generation, my generation, we who had such romantic longings for revolutions and upheavals, the image we saw in the moon was that of a future where, in unison with the proletariat, we would liberate the country and live happily ever after. Except that there seemed to be something terribly wrong in the way the dream was shaping up.

Majid, who had surprised everyone with his precocious poetry, had become the young hope of a group of influential intellectuals in Esfahan. He was a perpetual rebel, repudiating his parents' faith and way of life. Majid never did anything halfway. In his twenties he dropped poetry and picked up politics, choosing to follow the most militant form of Marxism. He vowed that he would not write another poem until after the workers' revolution. "What have you done for the revolution?" he would ask me seriously, even before we had any hint that there might actually be one. Studying, reading literature, all this was bourgeois and antirevolutionary. Once we had a fierce argument over his claim that ironing was a bourgeois activity. He drove me crazy, but I admired his tenacity and single-mindedness, both of which I felt I personally could do with more of. He pursued poetry, and later politics, with all his heart and soul. I wish now that I had asked him then, "Why did you abandon poetry? How could you forget that the greatest changes in this country were brought about as much by its poets as by its politicians?"

Back in Tehran, Majid fell in love with a young woman by the name of Ezatt whom he met through his revolutionary activities. His youngest sister, Noushin, also met her husband, Hussein, in this way. The four of them participated in the shantytown uprisings on the outskirts of Tehran in 1977.

In a manuscript addressed to his wife, Majid describes how their romance flourished during those unreal days between February 1, 1979, when Ayatollah Khomeini returned to Iran, and February 11th, when he asserted his power over the country. I never met Ezatt. In photographs she looks slim and boyish. He describes her as a tomboy, with a slender neck, slim, but not short like his sister Nafiseh. In a poem he has her in a khaki coat, "Small, slender, with bony cheeks."

On February 8th, Majid and a dozen university students went to a factory on the outskirts of Tehran. Because of the unrest, the plant had had no sales for the past eight months and the owner had not paid his workers their wages. Two workers brought the owner to the front yard. "He was chubby and tall, with big red cheeks." Majid writes. "He was scared and could hardly talk. We didn't know what to do. Some of the workers talked boldly and the owner listened politely. The government was dying and could no longer back him. But the workers had our support. Finally it was decided that the workers would elect a council to manage the production and sales." As Majid went home, a group of soldiers shot into the air and cyclists with covered faces belonging to the Marxist Fedaiyan Khalgh Organization asked people to go to the Farahabad Garrison to support the rebel airmen's uprising. Majid passed a young man teaching his eager pupils how to make Molotov cocktails. The next morning he opened the door to his wife, Ezatt, who had just returned from Esfahan, and he clasped her, shivering from the cold, in his arms. "The moment of uprising had come," he writes. Love and revolution, what could be more romantic?

That day Majid, Ezatt, Hussein, and Noushin rode their motorcycles to the Farahabad Garrison to support the insurgent soldiers. They climbed inside a tank and drove to the dreaded Evin Prison, which had been overtaken by protestors. The jailers had left in great haste and in the kitchen they found huge colanders, half-filled with rinsed rice. "A group of armed civilians tried to push the people out and control the prison," he writes. "They were trying to organize the first prison unit of the new regime." Next they went toward another prison, Qasr. "I saw that power is not a divine gift. The magic was gone. Prisons, garrisons, and royal palaces had all become naked buildings with no extraordinary protection. The Shah, ministers, SAVAK agents, and military generals were of the human race with no noble blood in their veins. Now the new power has sprayed a new magic potion in the air. It put on a clerical turban and garb and grew a beard to hide its human origin."

WHILE WE INDULGED in the euphoria of playing around with tanks and Molotov cocktails, increasingly the slogans focused on Ayatollah Khomeini and his emerging role as the sole leader of the revolution. Leaders of the Nationalist group, whose mentor, Mossadegh, was betrayed by Khomeini's mentor, Ayatollah Kashani, now deserted their old ally, Bakhtiar, and rallied around Khomeini. There was an air of smug certainty to all of this: so many believed that once Khomeini was on Iranian soil, he would retreat to the holy city of

Qom. He did return to Qom for a while, but not to retreat, and soon the violence that he had first advocated against the Great Satan and its domestic lackeys would be turned against his own supporters, both secular and Muslim.

Bakhtiar went into hiding and finally left Iran secretly in April of that year. (He was murdered by the agents of the Islamic Republic in his apartment in Paris on August 7, 1991.) There was chaos in the streets and the only force that could sustain order was the now divided army, whose barracks were stormed by the members of militant armed organizations and thousands of ordinary people overtaken by revolutionary zeal. On February 8th Khomeini announced a provisional government headed by a moderate Muslim dissident, Mehdi Bazargan. In his speech introducing Bazargan, he referred to himself as a person who had authority "through the guardianship [*velayat*] that I have from the holy lawgiver [the Prophet]." He said that the provisional government must be obeyed because it was not ordinary government and that "Revolt against God's government is a revolt against God. Revolt against God is blasphemy." To consolidate his power, Khomeini began to form parallel organizations to the army and police forces: revolutionary committees and revolutionary militia, armed organizations whose power was unspecified and unlimited. At first the revolutionary committees were unarmed groups whose role was to help suppress the chaos and protect communities, while at the same time arresting counterrevolutionaries, which at first meant supporters of the old regime but soon extended to liberal and radical forces. It wasn't long before the committees became the guardians of our morality and began arresting citizens for a whole range of crimes, from blasphemy to possession of alcoholic beverages and Western music. On February 11th, the Supreme Military Council unanimously decided to declare itself neutral and ordered all military personnel to return to base. That day Ayatollah Khomeini and his provisional government declared victory. For several weeks, despite the protests from human-rights organizations and from the moderate elements within the new revolutionary regime, hundreds of officials of the old regime were summarily executed.

The Islamic vigilantes roaming the streets were declared by the new leaders to be voices of the people. Khomeini issued an edict making the veil mandatory, which he was forced to retract after women organized huge demonstrations and sit-ins, shouting, "Freedom is neither Eastern nor Western. Freedom is global." But the vigilantes attacked unveiled women, sometimes with acid, scissors, and knives. The family protection law was soon abrogated, and religious laws became the law of the land, lowering the legal age of marriage (for women) from eighteen to nine, legalizing polygamy and "temporary marriages," defrocking female judges, and introducing stoning to death as punishment for adultery and prostitution.

Women protest against the Islamic dress code, 1980.

the other other woman

By THE TIME I FINISHED DEFENDING my dissertation, in the summer of 1979, and left with Bijan for Tehran, I had few illusions about the new government in Iran. My parents had been summoned to the revolutionary tribunals. Mother was ordered to repay the wages she had received as a member of Parliament and most of the property in their name was confiscated, but they were not jailed or executed like so many other government officials of their rank. My mother's votes against the capitulation law and family protection law were counted as points in her favor. Father's life was saved because of his jail time and his secret service records, which revealed his alleged sympathy for the protestors during the June uprising of 1963. Sometimes he would remind us with wonder that Mr. Rahman had told him that his time in prison would save him from a bigger disaster down the road. Mother would shake her head knowingly. "Who believed in him?" she would say, as much to herself as to any of us. "Who kept him around, despite all your efforts to throw him out of the house?"

While I was in America, my parents moved to a new house in the northern part of Tehran, opposite what was once called the American Hospital, which would soon be turned into a hospital for the veterans of the Iran-Iraq war. When we moved back Bijan and I decided to stay with them. The arrangement was intended to be temporary, until we both found jobs and a place of our own, but like so many temporary arrangements it soon devolved into the norm. Mohammad had his own place but he visited often, especially on Fridays for my parents' coffee sessions, which were in full force.

The large room on the ground floor of the new house saw many charged and heated debates: the fate of the country was at stake and everyone, except our charming and lethargic colonel, had something to say. Father still had high hopes for the revolution: he kept repeating his thesis that if we could get rid of the two oppressive forces of absolute monarchy and orthodox religion by strengthening the moderate secular and religious forces, we would be on the right course. He felt that Prime Minister Bazargan had the power and the will to unite the democratic-minded groups and individuals into one front—an illusion that was soon put to rest.

At this point both Shirin Khanoom and my mother were admirers of Khomeini. Mother furiously defended him against a growing contingent of young skeptics composed of my brother and me and our friends. She could find nothing wrong with a leader who practiced her religion, as she put it. "Your religion!" someone shot back. "Nezhat Khanoom, if he could he would have you and your daughter and every single woman in this room wrapped in black from head to toe."

My mother rejected such conjectures, passing around bowls of fruit and handing out the coffee and small pastries. "It isn't right to peddle in rumors," she said. "He is firm, he knows how to rule." Impatient recitations about the latest outrages committed by the revolutionary guards did not move her. She insisted the violence was not Khomeini's will but the work of a few extremists who would soon be punished.

It was not long before she could not remember a time when she had defended Khomeini. News of the atrocities committed by the new regime ate away at our festive mood, and dashed our hopes for change. A number of colleagues and friends were killed by the regime— Mr. Amirani, the editor in chief of *Khandanyha*, who had supported my father so bravely during his years in jail, and the soft-spoken and good-natured Mr. Khoshkish, my mother's bashful suitor, who had been the head of the central bank, were both murdered without trial or formal charges. There were others: my former school principal Dr.

Parsay; General Pakravan, who had been instrumental, incidentally, in saving Ayatollah Khomeini's life in 1963; our old foe General Nassiri; and many others who had in fact been against the Shah's system, including some, like my cousin Said, who had spent time in the Shah's jails. Later the killings would extend to ordinary people whose sin was simply slandering Khomeini or Islam. The regime rounded up gays, adulterers, those it deemed to be prostitutes, as well as some minorities, especially the Baha'is. By the time the American Embassy was seized, on November 4, 1979, and the moderate prime minister, Bazargan, fell, my parents' honeymoon with the revolution was over.

O N THE FIRST FRIDAY after our return to Tehran, Mother was eager to introduce me to a new guest. She explained that the woman in question was an associate of Uncle Ali, who headed a well-known hospital in Tehran. "I have heard so much about you," Ziba Khanoom said with a meaningful smile, her tone too intimate for someone I had just met. She stayed for lunch after the other guests had left, and was joined by her husband and her ten-year-old daughter, a pretty, shy girl who despite her shyness seemed to be quite at home and whom my mother pressed with chocolates. After lunch Father took us out to the garden. "Your father has spent so much time on this garden," Ziba Khanoom said with admiration. "Every single flower he has planted with his own hands."

Mother had been the first to discover her. She met her on a visit to Uncle Ali's hospital, where Ziba Khanoom was on the administrative staff. Mother had taken an instant liking to her and invited her, and later her family, to our house. By the time I returned with Bijan to Iran, Ziba Khanoom and her husband were among my parents' closest friends. Apparently the affair had started when my father and Ziba Khanoom took to complaining about their respective spouses. "He is cold," my father told me in confidence, "and surprisingly indifferent to the charms of a passionate and loving woman." Nothing like two disgruntled spouses to bring about a conspiracy of affection.

Ziba Khanoom was prettier than Shahin, and more conventional.

A little plump, overdressed, a great cook, and an efficient housewife who worked hard and well, without any of Shahin's pretensions. At the start of the revolution, when the new government was arresting functionaries of the old regime and my parents worried that Father would be called in, Ziba and her husband had given him shelter for a few days.

Shahran (my good friend and Mohammad's first wife), me, Bijan, and Mohammad, 1983.

We saw much more of her than we ever had of Shahin, because she was a family friend (and a close one at that) and because she was my mother's "find." While I was away, Mother and Aunt Mina had had a falling-out for reasons that were never quite clear. In response to my inquiries, my mother would make vague references to lies and being made a fool of, and how she could not take it anymore. Mother had been impressed with Ziba's "ladylike demeanor," her proper sense of respect and deference, and she began to take Aunt Mina's place. It irritated me, the innocent and persistent way my mother had of being attentive toward this woman and her family. It made us all uncomfortable, since we all knew what was going on—Bijan, Mohammad, and later Mohammad's new wife, Shahran, who quickly became a good friend.

when home is not home anymore

I CAN CITE THE DATES WHEN the war with Iraq started (September 22, 1980) and ended (August 20, 1988), and I can tell you the casualties were high, but I feel helpless when it comes to describing the subtle changes that transformed the fabric of our lives, so that I could walk down the familiar streets of my childhood and feel like an utter stranger. In a diary I started in the fall of 1980, somewhere in between my teaching notes for classes on *Huckleberry Finn*, *The Great Gatsby*, and Gorky's *Mother*, I wrote, "Home is not Home anymore." Our lives altered, not just by catastrophe and carnage, but also by a different kind of violence, almost imperceptible, that wormed its way into our normal everyday lives.

Like my cousin Majid, who roamed the streets of Tehran in the hope of bringing about a revolution, I had dreamed of change in the political system, but at the core of everything I did was the idea of returning home, to those mountains, to the night sky under which I had slept throughout my childhood, to Naderi Street and the scents of fish, leather, coffee, and chocolate, to the movie houses and restaurants and cafés with their lively music, to my father who, holding onto my hand as we walked along the wide, tree-lined avenue toward the mountains, would say, "One reason we should believe in God is that poetry like Rumi's or Ferdowsi's exists." Nothing is more deadly than crushed expectations: the revolution was supposed to change the political system, to bring more freedom, to make us more at home in our own home. Now I had returned and nothing was the same. Or, more disturbing yet, everything seemed the same but was in fact different: the streets had new names, Iran had become the Islamic Republic of Iran. Even the language sounded oddly unfamiliar, a language in which citizens were either emissaries of God or Satan, and women like myself were "prostitutes" and "Western agents." The face of religion was changing from the gentle teachings of my father to the ideological rants of a group of people, staunch followers of Ayatollah Khomeini, who called themselves Hezbollah—the Party of God. Their slogan was "Only one party: Hezbollah."

Religion was no longer just a part of Iranian culture, shaping it and being shaped by it; time and again Ayatollah Khomeini reminded us that not Iran but Islam was our real home and that Islam's borders stretched from Iran out into the wide world.

I CANNOT THINK OF the Iran-Iraq war without remembering that this was a war between two governments who were simultaneously carrying out a brutal campaign against their own people. Ayatollah Khomeini had called the war a blessing; for him it was a great diversion from the mounting domestic problems and opposition. In his mind, now the whole nation would gather against the foreign invader while at the same time the state could suppress any voice of dissent in the name of national security. During the eight years that the war lasted, Tehran was bombed several times, never as heavily as some of the border cities in the province of Khuzistan, but in the intervals between the bombings the fear remained. Every time there was a victory march on the radio announcing the bombing of another Iraqi "nest of spies" in Baghdad, we knew all too well that those spies were ordinary people like ourselves, as we knew that soon Tehran would be targeted and Saddam would announce the destruction of "nests of spies" in Tehran. I felt a great deal of empathy for those ordinary Iraqis, forced to be our foes, but in reality our kin in distress.

About a month after my return to Iran, I started teaching at the

University of Tehran and a girl's college whose changing name was symbolic of the constantly changing times: during the Shah's time it was known as Farah Pahlavi, after the Shah's wife; then it became Mottahedin, after a female member of the militant Islamic Mojahedeen Organization who had been killed during the Shah's time. When the divisions between the Mojahedeen and the new regime deepened, the college's name was changed again to Al Zahra, to commemorate the prophet Mohammad's daughter. The first day I entered the cavernous hall of the faculty of Persian and Foreign Languages and Literature at the University of Tehran, I was struck by the buzz of different voices rising and falling. Several tables were laid out with pamphlets, books, and leaflets, each table representing a different political grouping. I soon got used to the noise, the crowds that swelled and receded at the tables, the constant motion.

After a while I myself would become part of that motion: I would rush from meeting to meeting, protesting the expulsion of a professor, attending demonstrations and sit-ins. But my point of focus was always my classes. From the moment I stepped, with fear and anxiety, into the immense room to teach a class irrelevantly called "Research," and wrote on the blackboard the required reading: *Adventures of Huckleberry Finn*, I felt at home. No matter how contentious the atmosphere that reigned over the university, it was somehow calming to know that these books had survived wars, revolutions, famines. They had been there long before we were born and would be there long after we were gone. (What was it that Ferdowsi had said? "I shall not die, these seeds I have sown will save / My name and reputation from the grave.") The novels of George Eliot, Jane Austen, Flaubert, and Tolstoy became a vehicle to express the need to foster a democracy of voices. *Tom Jones* taught us the value of humor, *Tristram Shandy* of irony, and each novel we read seemed to offer a lesson in the complexity of moral choices and individual responsibility. All became somehow deeply and urgently relevant to the reality we lived in. Sometimes I mixed in examples from Persian literature, drawing mainly from banned books such as Sadegh Hedayat's *Buf-e Kur*, Forough Farrokhzad's *Another Birth*, or from our classical past, discussing Rumi's exuberant playfulness, or Hafez's mischievous delight in undermining orthodoxy. We discussed the tyranny of bad writers who impose their own voices on their characters, taking away their right to exist. Why is it that in novels with a message, the villains are so reduced that it is as if they come to us with a sign on their forehead saying: Beware, I am a monster? Doesn't the Koran state that Satan is a seducer, a tempter with an insidious smile?

On March 21, 1980, on the occasion of the Iranian New Year, Ayatollah Khomeini issued a harsh statement, accusing the universities of being agents of Western imperialism. At Friday Prayer on April 18th, Ali Khamenei (who was to replace Khomeini as the Supreme Leader in 1989) attacked the universities, saying, "We are not afraid of economic sanctions or military intervention. What we are afraid of is Western universities and the training of our youth in the interests of West or East." This was a signal for what came to be known as the Cultural Revolution: the plan to close down the universities in order to Islamize them, create a new curriculum, and purge them of undesirable faculty, students, and staff.

The students and faculty did not give up without a fight. I remember the fiery speeches, the demonstrations and sit-ins, the vigilantes who would suddenly appear with knives and stones to attack the demonstrators. I remember running for cover in dusty alleys. I remember finding a refuge in a nearby bookstore seconds before the owner locked the doors and we all scrambled away from the window to avoid the bullets. Every day we heard news of murdered students, their bodies snatched away by agents of the regime. These scenes appear out of nowhere, still disturbing my sleep.

Soon the tables of pamphlets in the hall would be removed. Many of those who stood behind them, representing different student groups and tendencies, would be expelled, arrested, and in some cases executed. All organizations except the Islamic ones would be closed—though not without bloody protests, sit-ins, more arrests, jailings, and executions. In our faculty, me and two other colleagues would refuse to wear the mandatory veil and soon I would be expelled from teaching along with many other colleagues.

In time, many of the students who pressed for the Islamization of the universities would become disillusioned and start criticizing the regime, staging protests and demonstrations. Could any of us have foreseen how some would become enamored of Jane Austen and F. Scott Fitzgerald, Spinoza and Hannah Arendt, and begin to question the tenets of the regime they had so ardently supported? Soon they would be asking for secularism and democracy, the ones arrested, jailed, and executed.

I WAS LEAVING AL ZAHRA, the girls' college, for home, admiring as I often did the way the garden with its mown lawn and flower beds, carefully arranged to appear haphazardly strewn together, made one feel secure and serene amid all

Teaching in Tehran; the veil was mandatory at the university.

the turmoil just outside the gate, when I heard a loud whisper behind me: "Professor!"

I had not noticed anyone following me and was startled when I turned around to see her standing so very close to me. "May I speak to you?" she asked. "Of course," I said. "That day when you were talking to Miss Bagheri about *Wuthering Heights,*" she said, "I was there." Miss Bagheri, whose sensibilities had been offended by the novel, was an aggressive defendant of morality on campus. She had waylaid me one day after class to protest the book's immorality: she said it set a bad example by condoning adultery. "Novels are about life, they embrace all aspects of existence," I said. I asked her, "When you read Ferdowsi, do you start believing in demons and people living for four hundred years? Do you decide to go whaling when you read *Moby-Dick*?" "This is different," Miss Bagheri said. "Adultery is a sin." "That is the point of novels," I told her. "The only thing sacred about them is that they are by nature profane. It is a great love story. Can you tell me of one good love story that sticks to the rules?" By the end of the term this same Miss Bagheri had told me enthusiastically that she was now so in love with Catherine and Heathcliff that the girls in her dorm made fun of her.

"And so," my stealthy stalker said, "I want to know what you meant when you said that the only thing sacred about a novel is that it is profane." She was dressed in a black chador, revealing only the "oval of the face," as the edicts on proper dressing indicated. Her face evaded description. It was rather long, rather pale, almost bloodless, and bony. Serious eyes that, unlike those of so many other students, looked at you directly. I don't remember her name. She was different from Miss Bagheri. There was a tenaciousness, a certain stubbornness in her that I liked—she would not change her mind about *Wuthering Heights* in a matter of months. Her tenacity did not come only from prejudice or her religious beliefs; it seemed to me as if she was trying to solve something as she talked to me. Despite her faith, she appeared to be driven by an inner puzzle, so wrapped did she seem to be in some interior world. The pause between my last sentence and her response was at times so long that I thought she had forgotten we were conversing. Her serious demeanor made me feel frivolous. I wanted to joke and lighten her burden. This was not the kind of discussion I was used to having with my religious students about the morality of a work of literature—I had discovered how boringly similar their arguments were to my own and my comrades' reasoning when I was a radical activist, in the way they reduced all literature into an ideological message.

I said to her, "Perhaps if you and I discussed some of these so-called immoral novels my meaning would become clearer." She asked for a list of books. She said she had read Forough Farrokhzad, and I reminded her that her works were banned. She said, "Everything is permissible, I think, if it is in pursuit of knowledge." Pursuit of knowledge! That was one way of putting it. "Anyway, Forough Farrokhzad was more Western," she said. "She did not follow our traditions." I suggested that she should perhaps take another look at the women in the *Shahnameh* and other classical tales. After all, adultery is not a Western construct, nor is love. In *Vis and Ramin*, the lovers openly commit adultery, because their main moral commitment is to love. But while we are on the topic of adultery and the novel, how about starting with *Madame Bovary* and *Anna Karenina*?

Over the next two months this student and I met at least once a week. We sat on the lawn or walked up and down the leafy street on which the campus was located. Once or twice I brought a cream puff or two and she made sure the next time to bring a big box of pastries. She read *Madame Bovary* and some of *Anna Karenina*. She said these women were repentant in the end. "Not repentant," I said, "desperate. Anna's heart was broken, Emma had reached the end of her rope." "You said it's about love," she said. "That too, but with Emma it's more about illusions, the dreams we impose on a drab and harsh reality. She married because of that dream and she cheated on her husband for the same reason. She had read too many romantic novels and wanted to be a romantic heroine."

"She broke her contract," she said; "she had a contract to honor." "She did," I said slowly, "but Charles Bovary was also partly a victim of his own romantic illusions. He loved the idea of Emma as much as, if not more than, he loved Emma herself. He was blind to who she was and what she wanted from him."

I asked, "Why don't you think women who marry without love are adulterers? It seems to me they are worse." "They are bound by their duty," she said, "they don't lie." "There are so many different kinds of lying," I said. "I know a woman, a very morally correct woman who would never dream of adultery, yet for almost thirty years she has been cheating on her husband, emotionally, with her dead first husband." (Once I asked my mother why she never danced again after that dance with Saifi and she said, "Because there was no one to dance with.") When I told my student about that woman, she said, "I feel sorry for her and for everyone else too. This woman you talk about, she suffered from the absence of love"—my student said this as if the absence of love were a form of malady. I registered that phrase and returned to it every once in a while when I thought of my mother and grandmother, of Aunt Mina, the poet Alam Taj, and so many other women who felt their lives were wasted not just because of their aborted social ambitions but also because they suffered from an absence of love.

We trailed from there to the meaning of loyalty and self-respect, and, inevitably, time and again to women, women in Europe, in America, in Egypt, in Turkey, who had fought the same fights, tolerated the same humiliations. "But why aren't we told about all that?" she asked. "Why is it never mentioned in school?" We ended up talking about women in our country, who could go to school and read *Wuthering Heights*, but were deprived of the right to make the most basic choices about their lives: whom to marry, how to dress, where to work. Her intelligent eyes took on a new light. "It's funny now that I think of it," she said, "before the revolution I most probably would have given in to an arranged marriage, to spite the government, but now I am not sure anymore. I guess this is what the novel is, it makes us think about these things—or something like that."

Suddenly she stopped coming to classes and the term ended. I left Al Zahra and was immersed in the campus battles that flared up at the University of Tehran. I wanted to ask Miss Bagheri about her, but I did not. Only from time to time I returned to her and wondered what became of her. Did she marry a man of her choice? Was she ever tempted by another man, or the idea of another life?

O FTEN IN THE MORNING we would wake up to some new and unexpected event. My mother's sources (she had her "eyes and ears" in every corner of the country, like the emperor Darius) had informed her that soon there would be a reversal of fortunes for the new rulers. She would wink at my husband, who, along with my father, she called Mr. Churchill. For some reason she considered Churchill very sly (which he probably was) and diplomatic (which at times he was not). "He is so diplomatic," she would say of Bijan, "saying nothing, just smiling, but very dangerous all the same. Soon," she confided, "the grand Ayatollahs will rebel against Khomeini."

And they did rebel. Many clerics did not believe that the religious establishment should interfere directly with the affairs of state. For centuries the clerics had exerted power by pressuring the state and posing as supporters of the poor and the needy. Although Khomeini seized power in the name of tradition, his ideological interpretation of religion was modern and, according to some, antitraditonal, influenced by modern totalitarian ideologies. Around the country traditional religious leaders, further up in the hierarchy than Khomeini, were making their unhappiness known. The most prominent of these, Ayatollah Shariatmadari, began to openly criticize the regime. In Tabriz a million people reportedly participated in demonstrations in support of Ayatollah Shariatmadari, who was calling for the separation of religion and state, which he insisted was one of the cornerstones of Shia Islam.

These rebellions were quashed violently. The venerable Ayatollah Shariatmadari was defrocked and jailed. His supporters were arrested and some murdered, and he died while under house arrest. ("Remember that when Khomeini was in trouble with the Shah this same Shariatmadari sat under a tree weeping in protest," Father would remind us with an ironic smile. "Our new Imam knows how to show his gratitude.") A message was sent by the regime to the faithful: to survive they would have to be loyal to only one interpretation of the faith, and to accept the new political role of the clergy.

Father felt that this spelled the end of Islam in our country, and he did have a point. "No foreign power," he said, "could destroy Islam the way these people have." Later a friend would say, "How can you believe in a religion when, from politics to plumbing, it is held responsible for everything?"

Mother was becoming increasingly interested in my activities at the university. Now, when she called me down to join her and her friends for coffee, she would say, "Tell them, tell them what 'they' are doing at the universities to women." She would count all the injustices committed against women: banning them from serving in the judiciary, from participating in sports, abrogating the family protection law (she conveniently forgot that she had herself voted against it), lowering the age of marriage, and on and on she would go. Then she would turn to me and say, "Tell them." She wanted me to describe the demonstrations and sit-ins staged by women, the battles over the veil.

Mother on her pilgrimage to Mecca, in the mid-1970s.

"And then what did your friend Haideh say to the committee on the Cultural Revolution," she would ask, egging me on, and before I could say anything she would turn and say triumphantly, "And this woman, Azar's colleague, gets up and says, 'You have turned the universities, the bastions of knowledge, into torture houses.' Of course, she, Azar, and two of her colleagues went to the meeting without the veil," she would add, with evident pride. "My poor daughter, is this what I gave up my life to educate her for?"

On Friday mornings my mother would brutally attack anyone who objected to my protests about the regime's infringements on women's rights. Many felt that this was not the time to fight for such unimportant matters when the question of independence and the anti-imperialist struggle was at stake. On one particularly memorable morning, Shirin Khanoom raised the question of "authentic Islam." It was said that Ayatollah Khomeini represented the true faith (*Eslam-e rastin*) while the Shah and Khomeini's opponents embraced a false version, "American Islam." This infuriated my mother. "Who are these people to tell us who is a true Muslim, or a true Iranian, for that matter? My family served this country for over six hundred years," she said with mounting indignation. "I went to Mecca because I believed in this religion." Casting what can only be defined as a withering look at poor Shirin Khanoom, she said, "Who made these people the representatives of true Islam?"

Later, as she became ever more indignant, my mother said, "These people are not true Iranians." She would remind us, interrupting anyone who tried to get a word in, that for almost two thousand years we had been Zoroastrians. A few years later, she would often point to Tahmineh Khanoom, my children's nanny, who was Zoroastrian, and say, "Our Tahmineh Khanoom here is more Iranian than any of us. You need to take over the country," she would tell her jokingly. "If I were born into your religion . . ." and she would leave it to our imagination to conceive of what she would then have done.

reading and resistance

▲FTER THE CLOSING DOWN of the universities, in 1981, some of my faculty colleagues and I formed a fortnightly dinner group. We had become close during the confrontations with the university officials and took to meeting in restaurants and coffee shops to strategize and plan our next move. Once the reason for these meetings was gone, once we had either resigned or been expelled, they evolved into social forums and extended to our families. Bijan had his weekly poker nights with his male friends and I had weekly afternoon meetings with the women from our group, a more sophisticated and perhaps less spontaneous version of my mother's coffee sessions. We talked about our past, our mothers, husbands, and lovers, our problems, and sometimes we indulged in just pure gossip. Later, in my last years in Iran, I joined another, similar, woman's group. We were very frank in our willingness to talk about ourselves, moving naturally from the personal to the political or the intellectual. Sometimes it appeared that although we had far more opportunities and freedoms than our mothers had, our problems were basically the same: abusive husbands, aborted love, guilty feelings about the conflict between work and family, unresolved sexual problems and resentments. These different groups became surrogate families, some closer, some more distant, with all the problems and attractions and contradictions that families entail. There were unexpected loyalties and betrayals. We fell in and out of love, traveled together, and our children grew up together.

On a sunny day in the early fall of 1979, my friend and colleague

Haideh and I were leaving the University of Tehran when a slight man with dark features, a shock of tightly curled black hair, and a large mustache followed us and invited Haideh to join his literary group. His eyes, even behind the glasses, were filled with amusement, as if he had been engaged in a secret conversation with a particularly mischievous elf, while the rest of his body carried on in our normal, ordinary world. That is how I first met Houshang Golshiri, one of Iran's most prominent writers. He was born in Esfahan, and had been part of a group of intellectuals and writers who greatly influenced Iranian literature in the sixties and seventies. Golshiri and his group had discovered and encouraged my cousin Majid when he first started writing and publishing poetry.

Haideh never joined Golshiri's group; she was too involved in the political struggle to devote her enormous talent to literature. But I did. I was in desperate need of conversations that did not end in ideological polemics. I had come to be preoccupied with the relationship between democracy and the novel, inspired by the fact that the rise of the novel in Iran was simultaneous with demands for democracy and freedom. I felt there must be a relationship between the celebration of individual voices in the novel and the polyphony of a democratic society. As I prepared for my class, I was also avidly reading and taking notes on modern Persian literature. Sometimes I drove Bijan crazy. I

Bijan with the writer Houshang Golshiri.

would get excited, kiss him affectionately, and then go on maniacally about my latest find ("The Constitutional Revolution wasn't just a political upheaval," I would say breathlessly. "Do you realize what immense quarrels were fought over language, starting with Mohammad Ali Jamalzadeh, who insisted that we had to find a new democratic language—and he wasn't alone. Look at Dehkhoda and Hedayat, they helped create this new democratic language. This was the time novels, plays, and journalism came into being, so the Islamic regime's targeting of culture isn't altogether arbitrary. . . . They're going back to the source, don't you see?") That evening I told him that I had met Houshang Golshiri. Yes, the very Golshiri who had written *Shazdeh Ehtejab (The Prince)*.

WHEN I FIRST MENTIONED *The Prince* to my father, he came close to rolling his eyes. "Oh no," he said, "as if *Buf-e Kur* [*The Blind Owl*] was not enough." He wanted to know why I was making such a fuss over two thin books. "The whole country is going to the dogs and my daughter is excited about these two treasures, these 'novels' as if they were going to solve our problems." "You have only yourself to blame," I said.

He was right: the country did seem to be going to the dogs. There was no end in sight to the war, and to the rampages of the regime. Ever more relatives and friends were in hiding, escaping the country, or in jail. Nor did I have many illusions about my own situation. Not long after that, Haideh and I were expelled, along with other colleagues, squelching my dream of teaching. My passport was confiscated and I could not leave the country. I was having frequent anxiety attacks.

From the moment I could communicate with him as a human being my father had been telling me stories. When he taught me to search for an understanding of my country, its history and culture, in the tales of Ferdowsi, he gave me literature not as a pastime but as a way of perceiving and interpreting the world—in short, as a way of being in the world. And now that the world had become so puzzling, so hostile, where else could I go? For Father, Ferdowsi was the key to the past. The *Shahnameh* was the only evidence of that magnificent Persian Empire that haunted our dreams and nightmares. What was it in Sadegh Hedayat's *The Blind Owl* (written in 1936) and in Golshiri's *The Prince* (written in 1969) that could unravel for us something of the Iran we lived in? These novels were too barren ("Nowadays, barren and modern seem to go hand in hand," he offered), too convoluted for his taste. "If you call *War and Peace* or *A Tale of Two Cities* a novel," he said kindly, "then you cannot call these books novels as well, without a plot, with such vague characters . . ."

Both novels were banned by the Islamic Republic for their sexually explicit scenes and their authors' critical outlook on orthodox religion. At the start of the twentieth century the struggle for modernism in many ways had been accompanied by an aversion to religion and in some cases, as in Hedayat's, by an infatuation with pre-Islamic Iran. Hedayat's anti-Islamic sentiments were at times as extreme and virulent as his views of ancient Iran were romantic and nostalgic.

I had read *The Blind Owl* at an early age, maybe when I was fifteen, around the time I went about quoting Jean-Paul Sartre's *Nausea* or Albert Camus' *The Stranger*. Like other young people of my age in my father's family, I felt an affinity for these angst-ridden, alienated texts. *The Blind Owl* was the kind of book parents forbade their children to read. Hedayat himself had committed suicide in Paris in 1951, and many associated the book with the suicide. It was said that it incited young people to kill themselves, or to smoke opium, and all sorts of terrible things. All this had turned the book, as well as its writer, into a cult object. *The Blind Owl* was well known for its similarities to European Expressionism. Critics had discussed the influence of Novalis, Nerval, and Hedayat's beloved Kafka. But on rereading it I was struck not by its famous pessimism or links to modernist Western thought, but by its affinities to classical texts. I had the same feeling about *The Prince*. A thread linked these two very modern works: they seemed like nightmarish replicas of classical tales of star-crossed lovers, like *Vis and Ramin* or *Layla and Majnun*, nightmarish because they combined and restructured mutilated images of a robust past experience.

While in Gorgani, Ferdowsi, and other classical poets we dealt with an earthly world, openly celebrating the pleasures of life and of flesh, in later mystical poetry this world was replaced by a heavenly one. But in *The Blind Owl* and *The Prince*, both Earth and heaven are in ruins, the spiritual world has crumbled, and reality is bereft of pleasure and full of menace. Hedayat and Golshiri were deeply influenced by both modern Western thought and classical Persian literature, and were unique in their ability to mix and mingle the two.

The plot in both novellas is centered around the relationship or nonrelationship of the male protagonist—a displaced and frustrated weakling—with two women, one representing the ideal inaccessible woman (called "ethereal" in *The Blind Owl*) and the other symbolizing the earthy erotic woman (called "slut"). In both stories this relationship and the protagonist's frustrated desire to possess the women lead to their and his own destruction. There is a sense of hopelessness and desperation in these two books, a sense that they have lost the past while the present is incomprehensible and therefore dangerous and hostile, a far cry from Ferdowsi's poignant homage to the past.

In Golshiri's book, as in *The Blind Owl*, there are no lines of communication between the male narrator and the female protagonists: all dialogue has broken down, turning to fear, resentment, and the kind of cruelty only the very weak are capable of. What has happened to the women of *Shahnameh* or *Vis and Ramin*, with their pomegranate breasts and ruby lips, who confirm their existence by announcing their names and boldly naming the object of their desire? I could not help but detect some similarity between the impotent torturers and the tortured murderers of the two novellas and those vigilantes who flogged teenage girls for showing a bit of hair. Did they not yearn to muffle these strong and unpredictable women in order to mask their own impotence?

It seemed to me, in my more lucid interludes, that the psychology of our particular political moment could be clarified by the mischievous light of these stories. Where would we go from here? Something new needed to be said. And this was an urgent matter, just as it had been urgent a thousand years ago for Ferdowsi to respond to the conquest of Persia, and for Hedayat and a whole host of other writers and poets to respond to the Constitutional Revolution and the radical changes in its wake. We *needed* a cultural revolution—not the fake one imposed on us by the regime, but a real one.

WHEN I WAS EXPELLED from the University of Tehran in the early eighties, Golshiri suggested that I teach a short course on *The Blind Owl* to a small group of interested young people. Not too long ago, out of the blue, a student from that class sent me a copy of his notes, bound in dark blue, thirty-seven handwritten pages. On the cover he had written with a flourish: "About *Buf-e Kur,* A Novel of Consciousness, Dr. Azar Nafisi." Leafing through those pages, I can retrieve the almost naïve excitement we felt jumping from Ferdowsi and Zoroastrianism and the myth of the first man and woman who were bound together as a single plant to the modernism of Hedayat, the influences of Nerval and Novalis.

After that class I wrote several articles on modern Persian fiction and joined Golshiri in his literary group, composed mainly of his disciples. Each week an author was invited whose work would be discussed by the group. Sometimes the writers he invited were insulted by the harsh way he treated them, and there were often verbal sparring matches, mainly between Golshiri and his guest, offering some insights into the rivalries and animosities that were so very strong among us despite the fact that we had all been forced to unite in the face of the regime's constant threats and harassments.

At the same time, I participated in a different reading group made up of friends, most of them from academia, including Mohammad and Shahran and Farzaneh Taheri, Golshiri's wife, a prominent translator who had studied English literature at the University of Tehran. Some left the group to migrate abroad, and new members were admitted, but, amazingly, over those years of perpetual flux, these meetings were one of the constants in our lives. Living in revolutionary times, when everything was so malleable, when facts were immaterial and all old certainties questioned, we drew a certain comfort from the exigencies of fiction.

We read the classics—Hafez, Saadi, Ferdowsi—but invariably other matters intruded and our study group often stretched long into the night. Golshiri insisted that we take turns reading line by line the passages and poems he had assigned. This often bored me: I was the wayward student, the one who did not do her homework properly, who would make jokes when we were supposed to be reading. Later I was grateful for his method: reading the poems aloud brought out their enticing tempo, and I came to appreciate the way words flirted or sparred with one another, transforming their meanings. Now when I read Hafez or Ferdowsi, almost instinctively I read them aloud, to savor the music. It was not just the beauty of the language, or the artfulness of concept and structure, all of which I had noticed before. What I discovered was the playfulness of these canonical texts, their irreverence. The literary critic Terry Eagleton wrote that great fiction always pushes against the boundaries of existing reality. Reading the classics of Persian literature we caught a glimpse, through the cracks they made in the walls of our existing reality, of the brilliant world of our poets' imaginations.

At times i felt as if my whole life had become a series of variations on my parents' coffee sessions. Since almost all aspects of public life had been either restricted or banned, our private domains took on the functions of public forums. Our houses became our restaurants, bars, movie houses and theaters, concert halls, public forums on literature, the arts, and politics. True, these free zones were threatened constantly by a state that could at any time of day or night raid our houses and confiscate the alcohol, gambling cards, makeup, forbidden books, and videos. They could arrest us on charges of immorality. And yet in those days there was a suppressed excitement that belied the anxiety and fear—or, now that I think of it, perhaps the two fed off and strengthened each other. While the country was torn apart by war and besieged by repressive laws, daily arrests, and executions, beneath the surface, just underground, there were mutinous acts and shows of resistance that constantly frustrated and subverted the power of the state. An act as normal and mundane as having a party with men and women where drinks were served, music was played, and perhaps a movie was watched—*A Night at the Opera* or *Fanny and Alexander*—had to be undertaken with caution, curtains drawn, so that it became something very special, like a stolen éclair. We were like exile communities in a country whose language and culture we did not fully grasp, creating our own home away from home with its own lifestyle, norms, and mores—and of course with nostalgia for what, until the revolution, we would have called the bad old days.

In some ways these gatherings were vaguely reminiscent of those meetings in the late eighteen- and early nineteen-hundreds that I had read or heard about, when plays were performed in private houses, and women were banned from public appearances. Like revolutionaries, people thrived through secret gatherings. Amoo Said writes in his memoirs of the excitement and anxiety he felt when he first came across such a group in the house of one of the prominent women's rights' activists, Mastoureh Afshar. He describes how dangerous it was for a man, a young man at that, to join a meeting with women. He mentions that at the time the sidewalks were still segregated and women were forced to cover themselves in public in black robes. "I kept plotting in my mind, how to confront the impeding danger and threat. Was I going to rob anyone? Was I endangering anyone's life and wealth?" he wrote in his memoirs. "I was not doing any of these, but what I was going to do was not less of a crime."

Amoo Said shared in the exhilaration of what had not existed before. In our case we were trying to preserve what had been taken away from us, and there was a sense of jaded desperation to this. Our revolution had closed a door when it attacked the individual rights that had been so desperately fought for. We had reached a stage where we wanted to preserve what we had, not strive for what we might dare to imagine.

broken dreams

For my father's family the revolution should have been the herald of a new era, their era. They had been highly critical of the Shah and were staunchly religious; now the Shah was gone and the government was Islamic. But already on our first visit to Esfahan, I could detect divisions and hostilities among cousins and uncles who had for decades lived in such intimate proximity. Harsh words were passed between my cousin Said, who supported the militant Mojahedeen organization, and my cousin Jaafar and Uncle Hussein, who favored the more extremist elements among the emerging ruling clerics. Amoo Hussein's daughter, whom I had seen in Berkeley, California, a few years earlier in short sleeves and jeans, had donned the chador, changed her name from Shadi to Zahra, after the prophet Mohammad's daughter, and married a member of the revolutionary militia. The rifts that had seemed mendable a few years back had grown insurmountable.

Said had not talked to me for about seven years, since he had followed his brother Majid, Mohammad, and me to a restaurant (he was about thirteen at the time), and had fulminated at us for drinking and singing along with the orchestra. He refused to speak to us after that. Instead, he wrote long pages denouncing the decadent intellectuals, and left them around the house for us to see. In the meantime he had been jailed for two years because of his activities in the Organization of the People's Mojahedeen. When I saw him after the revolution, in the fall of 1979, he was friendlier. He had married a distant relative,

Fariba, whom I remember as a fragile girl, shy and reserved, in long shirts and baggy pants. They lived in a small studio at the end of my uncle's garden and kept mainly to themselves.

It did not take long for many Muslims, including Said, to feel betrayed. This was supposed to be their revolution. We, the decadent seculars, had been defeated, and yet here was Said, as much of an outsider as ever. The revolution hurt many of the believers in a more fundamental way than it did the nonbelievers—not just militants like Said and his organization, but devout Muslims with no political agendas, people like his parents. The Mojahedeen organization had been banned after confrontations with the Islamic regime that culminated in a bloody demonstration during which many of their group's supporters were arrested and summarily executed. The Mojahedeen were armed and they retaliated, in part by bombing the headquarters of the Islamic Republic Party, leading to the deaths of more than eighty people, including some of the high officials and leaders of the regime. Soon after this, the leaders of the Mojahedeen fled the country, as did Iran's first president, Abdolhassan Bani-Sadr.

Just over a year after the revolution, Said and Fariba went underground. They left Esfahan and moved to Tehran. Suddenly they had become fugitives, spending their days and nights at different safe houses. Said held a high position in the organization. He was more flexible, more accepting, but very firm in regard to his group, which soon became as violent as the Islamic regime itself, responsible for many bombings and the assassinations of government officials and their collaborators. What cousinly love had not resolved, the revolution did: we found ourselves if not on the same side, at least against the same enemy. Some of Said's religious relatives, including cousins and uncles he had lived with, now considered him an infidel, worthy of the terrible punishment planned for his ilk. Ironically, it was now their godless, decadent relatives and friends who walked in the same marches as them, feared the same guns, and gave them shelter in their homes.

In Tehran Said and Fariba were taken in for a few months by a couple, who were also our close friends. These friends, like us, were secular, and she opposed the ideology and tactics of the Mojahedeen organization. But such were the times, when everyone's mettle was being put to the test, so that you could find kindness and solidarity in unexpected places, and discover a sudden intimacy with relative strangers and with those who opposed what you stood for but would give you shelter at great risk to their own lives.

They spent two nights at our house. I found Said more tolerant of criticism and also perhaps more melancholy than I remembered. All his life he had avoided what he thought of as upper-class clothing and now, because of the need for disguise, he always appeared in suits, to distinguish himself from the Mojahedeen cadre, who wore long shirts over their trousers. I remember a light-brown suit that brought out the honey color of his eyes, which even his thick glasses could not hide. And next to him sat Fariba, prim and proper like a recent high school graduate, still awkward, not yet having found her style, in her pleated light-green skirt, long-sleeved white shirt, and bright scarf with a bit of hair showing. She wore a light shade of pink lipstick and sometimes bit her lips, as if to wipe the color out without seeming to.

My mother, who seldom warmed up to anyone in my father's family, now suddenly was all commiseration. I remember her bringing her Turkish coffee upstairs on a tray—four cups, for Said, Fariba, Bijan, and me. They humored her, and after drinking their coffee turned their cups over so she could tell their fortunes. "There will be a long travel to a distant land," Mother began. "Look, come closer, come. Don't be afraid, I'm like your mother. You see, at the top of the rim, these lines? You see this figure? A camel. You will be traveling," she said again. "Ah, your future is bright! Look at this side of the cup, it is clear. Only anxiety on this side, but the other side, nothing. Your cup is stuck to the plate," she told Fariba. "This means either wealth or love. I have a feeling, in your case, it is love." They both laughed a little uneasily, and Fariba nervously extended her hand and picked a tiny cookie off the plate.

That was the last night we spent with them. The next morning, at the top of our winding staircase, we all shook hands, despite the ban on touching a person of the opposite sex, even a cousin. We shook hands formally and awkwardly. Then they walked down the steps, and I stood up there watching them appear and disappear at each bend, until I heard the front door slam and they emerged, like two orphaned children in a terrible fairy tale, walking very close to one another, almost touching, he with his ivory shirt, she with her multicolored scarf. We never saw them again.

"Objects have tears in them," Virgil's Aeneas said. I wrote this down, just as I impulsively write down certain words and phrases that won't let go. I have in front of me a birth certificate, a dirty brownish color, with a photograph staring out at me. There, with her dark scarf (no smile) is Fariba. The first name and the last name on the certificate, though, do not belong to her: she was in fact Fariba Morovat, married to Said Nafisi, but here she is called Fereshteh Bagheri, married to Abdolah Saidipur. It is a fake birth certificate. Date of birth: 1956, date of marriage: 1975, date of death: blank. How did I end up

The birth certificate.

with this birth certificate? I can no longer remember. I found it when I was going through piles of diaries and notes I had brought with me from Tehran. What tears are hidden in its pages?

For almost two years their parents would come to Tehran from Esfahan every month and make their way to Evin Prison in order to inquire about Said and Fariba. Had they escaped the country, they would have let their families know, so their parents had no reason to doubt what the officials implied: that they had been arrested. I remember these visits. The parents usually stayed in a small hotel. At the appointed time, they would take a taxi to the dreaded prison. There they waited for long hours to be told that there was no new information about their children. As long as there was no information, there was also hope. But if they were alive, why did they not call home? Those were anxious days. The confrontations had spilled over to the streets. The Mohajedeen had been banned, people were daily arrested and killed. Many, some among my own family and friends, had been killed or had escaped the country.

After eighteen months they were told that their children had been spotted by the revolutionary guards in the early fall of 1982. They were killed in a street confrontation with the Islamic militia. Fariba's mother refused to believe this. They are safe and sound, she kept repeating, but don't want to cause us trouble because the phones are tapped.

Mourning those killed by the regime was officially banned, but the family in Esfahan held a private ceremony for Said and Fariba. Two of my uncles and a cousin refused to offer their condolences—one uncle called to congratulate Said's parents on their son's death. "They deserved to die as infidels, and now that they have been justly punished, maybe they will be forgiven in the afterlife and be saved from hell," he said. Later, when Uncle Abu Torab, famous for his prodigious memory, was diagnosed with Alzheimer's, one of his granddaughters would say that he decided to forget after Said and Fariba's deaths. He kept his faith in God at the cost of relinquishing his memory.

LESS THAN TWO YEARS AFTER storming the prisons, my cousin Majid was also on the run. His sister Noushin and their spouses, Hussein and Ezatt, had been arrested. Hussein was executed. Noushin's execution was delayed because she was pregnant. I remember the day they brought Cheshmeh, Noushin's infant daughter, to my brother's house. My uncle and aunt had come to Tehran to pick her up, a silent one-year-old. Her mother, a painter, had put small painted pebbles in her pockets. Several years later, Noushin was given amnesty and freed. She told us that when she was called in that morning, she didn't know whether she was to be freed or executed.

Ezatt, Majid's wife, was executed. She was only twenty-four. Majid writes of wandering around the city after her arrest, the same city that he and his comrades had felt they had conquered. Now his wife was in the prison Majid and Ezatt had triumphantly occupied back in February 1979. After her execution she was buried in a special cemetery assigned to political prisoners and minorities, called the cemetery of the infidels, where bodies were thrown into unmarked graves. Majid visited the spot with her father, who told him that he had his own way of marking her grave: it is eight paces from the gate and sixteen paces toward the wall. She was executed and buried collectively with two women and fifty men. For a while I kept a copy of her will in the drawer in my desk and from time to time I'd take it out and read it. Then I lost it and found it in Majid's manuscript. She wrote:

NAME: Ezatt Tabiian
FATHER'S NAME: Saied Javad
BIRTH CERTIFICATE NUMBER: 31171

Hi,

Life is beautiful and desirable. Like others, I loved life too. However, there comes a time when one must say good-bye to life. For me that moment has arrived and I welcome it. I have no specific bequest; I want only to say that life's beauties are never forgettable. Those who are alive should try to get the most out of their lives.

My dear father and mother, hi,

During my life you suffered a lot to raise me. Until the last moment I will not forget my father's calloused hands and my mother's work-worn face. I know that you did your best for me. Nevertheless, there comes a time of separation. This is inevitable. I love you with my whole existence, and I kiss you from a place from which I cannot see you. My warm regards to my sisters and brothers. Kiss them for me. I love them. In my absence do not suffer for me and do not be hard on yourselves. Try to carry on your lives with the usual love and tenderness. Give my regards to all who ask for me.

My dear husband, hi,

I had a short life and we had an even shorter life together. I wish I could have lived longer with you. But it is no longer possible. I shake your hand with a salute to all whom I have loved, love, and shall love.

> *Goodbye,*
> *January 7, 1982*
> *Ezatt Tabiian.*

Writing about those years I am reminded of my father, who used to read passages from the *Shahnameh* about the conquest of the Persian Empire by the Arab army in the seventh century. The warrior Rostam, son of Hormozd, gives a poignant speech, predicting the results of that war, known as the battle of Qadesiya. Who says our present is not already written by our past? Father would ask. He had underlined some passages, I don't remember them all. These are the ones I do remember:

But when the pulpit's equal to the throne
And Abu Bakr's and Omar's names are known,
Our long travails will be as naught, and all
The glory we have known will fade and fall. . . .

Men will be mutual thieves and have no shame.
Curses and blessings will be thought the same.

What's hidden will be worse than what is known,
And stony-hearted kings will seize the throne. . . .

No pleasures, no musicians, none of these:
But there'll be lies, and traps, and treacheries.
Sour milk will be our food, coarse cloth our dress,
And greed for money will breed bitterness

Between generations: men will cheat
Each other while they calmly counterfeit
Religious faith. The winter and the spring
Will pass mankind unmarked, no one will bring
The wine to celebrate such moments then;
Instead they'll spill the blood of fellow men . . .

Majid went into hiding and later fled the country. He ended up in L.A., where his older brother Hamid lived. He had not written poetry since the early seventies, when he went into politics, but he started to write again three days after Ezatt's death, when he went with friends to the Alborz Mountains to pay homage to her. In the evening he was sitting by his brother Mehdi, tears streaming down his face, and he started to write nine poems for her. "I wanted to avenge your death," he writes, "I wanted to have you close to me. You spoke to me through the Muses. I turned back and told Mehdi, Now I understand why early men drew those buffalos on the Altamira caves."

father's departure

IN THE SUMMER OF 1982 my father left my mother, this time for good. She had lost Saifi, she had lost her uncle and her mother, but she never thought she would lose my father. I remember the day I walked in on them in the kitchen. She was dressed in an old pink dressing gown and he was holding a knife to his throat, threatening to kill himself. Later she would use this against him, as further evidence of his lunacy, his lack of control. She could not see how she led him, as well as my brother and me—otherwise reasonably sane individuals—toward the edge of desperation. I don't remember what they were arguing about. It really did not matter. They both turned to me as witness to what each was doing to the other. "This," he said, "is the last time I will suffer such indignity." "Indignity!" she shouted. "A man your age, acting like this, threatening me with a knife." "Not you," he said, exasperated, "not you. Myself."

After numerous fights he had managed to set up a separate bedroom for himself (the final humiliation, my mother would claim) because, he reasoned, he could not sleep at night and he ended up disturbing her, as she was a light sleeper. Every night, after Mother went to bed, Father would talk on the phone for long stretches with Ziba Khanoom. Later Mother would criticize his childish behavior. "Acting like a teenager," she would say, "falling in and out of love. He has no shame, at *his* age, a seventy-year-old man." He wasn't seventy, he was sixty-two, but that's how it was with her—facts were malleable inconveniences. And yet she was right, he did act like a teenager, and so did she. Aborted relationships seem to keep us in a state of perpetual immaturity; to grow up we need in one way or another to pass on to the next stage. My mother had remained frozen in time after Saifi's death, and my father never quite let go of the dream of his youth. So he acted like a twenty-something-year-old man, about to marry the girl of his dreams, and she acted like a young jilted bride.

The next day my father left. He had threatened to leave before, and had even gone a few times, but he never stayed away for more than two or three months. Several times they had agreed to a divorce, but she always reneged and he always returned. She had come to count on this, because the truth was that she never intended a permanent separation. Almost a decade and a half had passed since the day he had written in his diary about his fear of going to his grave without experiencing a true and loving relationship. For her these fights seemed like necessary rituals; for him they were fatal. Like so many husbands and wives, she took him too much for granted.

Why did he leave her at that particular moment? Would he have left had there been no revolution? In his diaries he says that every time he wanted to leave, some consideration prevented him: first, the children were too young. Then, when he was a successful public figure on the rise, it didn't seem right to leave the woman who had shared the hard times with him; when he was in jail there was no time to divorce; later it seemed ungrateful to leave someone who had suffered through his jail time with him. Before the revolution, divorcing my mother would have meant alienating the social group they both belonged to. For a different kind of man this would not have mattered, but my father cared. He was trapped by his own image of himself as a good man. And what good man would leave his wife? It took the Islamic Revolution, the crumbling of the old social order, to facilitate a decision that he had been unable to carry out a decade and a half before.

He had been planning for this for a while. Soon after Bijan and I returned from America, Father sold the house and built a three-story building with three separate apartments, one each for my brother, my mother, and me. His attitude was: for years I have taken care of her, now it's your turn. My brother never moved into his apartment. He and Shahran rented an apartment while they lived in Tehran and then they left for England in 1986. I accepted my task without questioning. I didn't have the heart to say no to Father despite the fact that Bijan was opposed to our living in such close proximity to my mother. He felt that more distance would not prevent us from taking care of her. But there we were, and the apartments were built so that each had access to the other. The kitchen and hall opened into an internal staircase. There would be endless quarrels if I locked these doors, which meant that my mother had access to our apartment at all times, even when we were not there.

For three decades I had empathized with my father, hoping that one day he would lead a happy life with someone who appreciated him. I had not thought of my mother, of what would happen to her. And now that he was gone I felt for her in a way I never had before. Always when I was angry at her and derided her for ruining our lives, some fair observer, Bijan or Shahran, would understandably say, "Things are not exactly how you see them." "Your father is charming," Bijan would say, "and fed up, but he also charms his way into justifying his bad behavior."

Shahran, who had become my third eye, saw a side of Mother I had seldom paid attention to. "You don't appreciate your mother's honesty," she would tell me. "She has been either neglected or lied to by everyone close to her. It started in her father's house, but the tragedy is that even Saifi, the faultless first husband, lied to her when he concealed his illness. I love your dad, I'd rather spend time with him than with your mom, but my heart goes out to your mom."

Suddenly Mother seemed genuinely alone. The revolution had taken away her peer support group, her freedoms as a woman, and now, without her husband, who for decades had acted by his account as father, steward, accountant, and friend, she had no one to fend for her. Her husband could leave her to start a new life with a far younger woman, but for her there was no such option. She had no way of fulfilling her longings and dreams. "I should have been a man," she'd said for decades. "I always wanted to continue my education, to go to medical school." My father speculated often that had he encouraged her to find a job, she might have been far happier. Her time as a member of Parliament had been temporary; its end left her more embittered. She had been left alone with her pride and her anger and her sense of solitary injustice. Did we ever defend her? Did we ever empathize with her?

For a while after Father left, Mother, ignorant of the truth, would confide her grievances to Ziba Khanoom. She cursed my father in front of her, telling Ziba Khanoom that she was sure the whore Shahin had returned to his life. But it wasn't long before she discovered the truth. Ziba divorced her husband and stopped visiting Mother. Later, Mother blamed us for hiding the truth from her, and we guiltily denied knowing anything about the affair.

When Father left, a great silence seemed to fall over us, like the silence after a major explosion. All around our apartment house there were new craters of silence that gradually gave way to my own muted questions. I started to ask myself some of my mother's questions. What if she were a man? What if she had continued her education? What if she had never married? What if she had not given up dancing?

In 1982 MOHAMMAD and Shahran's daughter, Sanam, was born, two months early. The doctors were not sure the baby would survive, and when I was first told the news I didn't want to go to the hospital, as if not going there would somehow prevent any harm from coming to her. When I finally arrived the first person I saw was my brother. He escorted me to the room where his daughter was kept under a respirator. He said, "Our brave little baby, she has been hanging on. She seems very determined." That is how she came to the world, determined and with a haste that would stay with her. She was a miniature baby who broke my heart every time I looked at her, I loved her so much. She and I grew very close. When she was barely two, we walked hand in hand up and down the long winding hall, past her parents' bedroom, the library, her grandmother's room, toward her room at the very end of the hall, and I would tell her stories to which she listened attentively, bending her head, eyes focused on the ground, firmly holding onto my hand. When we went into Shahran's room in the hospital my parents were

Father with Sanam and baby Negar.

there along with her mother, who was fussing over her. My parents made us very aware of their feelings toward each other. Every once in a while Mother would throw my father angry glances which he tried to ignore by looking elsewhere. "There we go again," I thought, "their hidden agenda taking over every event."

Two years later, in January 1984, our daughter, Negar, was born. "Her eyes are open!" was the last thing I heard my

doctor say before I passed out. She was held by the scruff of the neck like a kitten, wide-eyed and alert, an image I took with me before losing consciousness. The night before I went to the hospital, my father called. Mother was in our apartment and she picked up the phone. "You bastard . . ." she shouted, and I knew it must be my father. "It's for you, Madam," she said, her tone changing. She held out the receiver at arm's length like a dirty dishrag. "I have no right to call my own daughter," Father said. His tone was bitter, resigned. We didn't speak much. It was impossible to do so with Mother going on about his sins and my ingratitude.

When Negar was exactly three months old, when I had just fed her and was changing her and she was lying on my bed, looking at me with a mixture of mischief and seriousness, it suddenly struck me that she had come to me as a gift. Opening up to her I opened up to myself—I could not be that bad if this miraculous creature depended on me and seemed to love me so. By the time my son, Dara, was born, on September 15, 1985, the bombings of Tehran had resumed. I spent the months before his birth in fear that something would go wrong with the baby. There were rumors of children being born retarded or paralyzed because their mothers had been overanxious. So I became overanxious about my anxiety. I stayed up at night during blackouts and I would read by candlelight, book after book, exchanging Raymond Chandler for Henry James, Sadegh Hedayat for Bahram Sadeghi, with one hand on my stomach as if my hand could prevent the fetus from seeing or hearing what was going on in the world outside. Suddenly an unconquerable fear would overtake me. What if he is stillborn?

Bijan, Negar, and me at the Caspian Sea.

One night, I remember, I suddenly felt that I was having a heart attack. I couldn't breathe and at that moment I did not think of my husband, who was sleeping next to me, but of my mother. I took a candle and walked down the stairs (her door to the internal staircase was always open when she was home). I did not knock, I just went in and woke her up. She did not protest or ask why I had woken her up at three in the morning. She called a heart surgeon who was a distant cousin, woke him up, and explained the symptoms. She came back with a glass of water and a Valium in her hand. "Now, now, you'll be okay," she said. "Just take this, one pill won't hurt your baby, and you'll feel better." She sat by me, massaging my back. I said, "Mom, what if this child is harmed, what if he is already dead?" She laughed lightly. "Nothing will happen to the child unless something happens to his mother. Let's take care of you first." She made me sleep in her bed that night, while she slept on a light mattress at the foot of the bed.

Dara's birth put an end to my fears. The war continued for another three years, and during the last year, when Tehran was the target of incessant bombings and many fled the city, we stayed on. Never again did I feel the same kind of fear or anxiety from the bombs that I had experienced in the years before he was born. Contrary to my morbid prognostications, Dara was not only healthy but exceptionally tender and calm ("Just like Mohammad," my mother said, "such a good-natured baby"). He was so calm that his passionate persistence about certain things always took us by surprise. When he was barely two, almost every time he looked at a picture book he either wanted to enter the book or to catch certain objects in it. He loved the moon. He would not let me turn the page, and kept pointing at the moon, and saying, "Mah, Mah." I think in fact they have not changed much, Negar with her infinite curiosity, and Dara with his quiet desire to catch the moon.

WHEN I THINK OF MY father's dream of a happy marriage, I am often reminded of a recurring theme in fiction: how our dreams become tainted by reality, how we can turn them into desperate obsessions for which we sacrifice that essential sense of dignity and integrity that we yearn for when we indulge in a dream. Had he never left my mother, my father's personal life might have been considered tragic, but now that he had taken this step—too late and not in the right way—he had lost his chance and with it his good name. Both my parents claimed they wanted their problems to remain private, but Mother's outbursts in front of perfect strangers and my father's protests and grievances made their relationship a matter of public gossip and speculation. "So many men leave their wives every day," he would complain. "They remain friends long afterward, but I can never tear myself free of Nezhat; forever I am to be her slave."

I remember the day he told me with excitement that he had a great surprise for me as we drove to the Independence Hotel—the Tehran Hilton before the revolution. When we arrived at the hotel, Shahin was sitting there, chic and upbeat. I was a little bewildered because I knew he had planned to marry Ziba Khanoom. Father explained that

Shahin and her husband had been in London. He went on to say, in a tone filled with sympathy and understanding, that her husband was a horrible man who squandered his wealth on gambling and did not give her enough to live on because he was concerned that if she had enough money she would leave him. She lived in an apartment in Tehran while her husband spent most of his time abroad.

Almost twelve years had passed since I had last seen her; small talk about materialism and spirituality did not excite me anymore. I preferred the simple Ziba Khanoom, who had no such pretenses and whose possessiveness of my father was up-front and genuine. Ziba Khanoom had shown a certain regard for him. She had destroyed her own marriage, and when there was a danger that my father might be arrested by the revolutionary guards, she had given him shelter and driven him to the revolutionary court. I had heard her speak, her voice still filled with emotion, of the hours she had spent in the car with tears welling up in her eyes, waiting to know his fate. With Shahin I had seen no such emotion. "She seems altogether too pleased with herself," Bijan said when he first met her, and he didn't see much reason why she should be. Once, when Father was giving me a lift home, he casually asked me, "Which do you prefer, Shahin or Ziba?" It was a startling question, and I was rather dismayed that he would ask it of me. I said, "I don't know, they are two different people." I wanted to ask him why he asked me such a question, wasn't he going to marry Ziba? But I said nothing and he did not pursue the subject. When a few weeks later he broke off with Ziba, I was amazed. Later I asked him the reason, and he said she was too jealous of his love for his children.

After that, Father would take me and the children to Shahin's house while her husband was away—and he seemed to be away most of the time. We would eat, and inspect the clothes she had designed. Private trunk shows had become fashionable, especially of clothes designed with traditional Persian motifs. I bought some from her and felt slightly guilty. At first he paid for her trunk show, then she and her mother bought a small apartment and he paid for the bedroom furniture as a housewarming gift. He tried to convince me that she was oppressed by her horrid husband, who held her prisoner and did not allow her to use her talents. My father always seemed to need an excuse for his relationships. With my mother it was her dead mother, her terrible stepmother, her dead husband; with Ziba, her husband's indifference; and now, with Shahin, we had the gambler husband, a profligate, uncaring father, a brother who was an addict, and a mother—like your own, he would say with a winning smile, you and Shahin are so alike—who loved her son far more than this dedicated daughter.

Mother drew up a long list of complaints. For starters she claimed that their divorce was not legal: she had never consented to it. "He has friends in high places," she said, "he's in cahoots with the government and he had them forge phony divorce papers." My father insisted that she had been granted a divorce in absentia. The court had served her many notices and she had ignored them all, including the last notice, which informed her that if she did not appear in court the divorce would automatically go through. I can imagine her feeling of humiliation at being summoned to court by her own husband.

One thing my parents had never quarreled about was money. She had accused him of not standing up for her against her stepmother over her father's inheritance and she gave him a hard time about money issues while he was in jail, but she did not question his integrity. She trusted him with her money, and never asked for deeds and documents. My parents' apparent disdain for money had made my brother and me careless too. We vaguely knew that our mother had inherited land and that, as time went by, some of the land she had been left had sold well. We knew that our father had bought our villa near the Caspian Sea out of his own money, and later two islands which he shared with some friends and some acres of land by the Caspian with my uncle, some of which he had been forced to sell to pay his debts when he left jail. He made more money in business than he ever had in government, and my brother and I knew that our parents had transferred most of the land and property they owned to our names, including a large apartment in one of the best locations in Paris. Mother believed that all of this should be in our names because it was all ours anyway. It amazed me that here was a woman who would not give me a favorite vase for fear I might break it, but who trusted us with all her property. After the revolution I think this was done out of prudence as well. My parents were unable to sell anything under their names and some of their property by the Caspian was appropriated by the Islamic regime.

My father had left my mother in an apartment which, she never failed to remind us, was not in her name. He also sent her a small monthly stipend. For her to be on such a stipend, dependent on my father's generosity, was another humiliation. For the first time she demanded the deeds to the property. Father explained that he had been her accountant all his adult life and he had taken his share and given her hers. He sent in letters with detailed accounts of what had been purchased and what had been spent and insisted that he had not taken anything with him. But in the meantime he had us authorize him to sell the apartment in France and he had power of attorney over all the other property. She blamed me and my brother and, after my brother left Iran, me alone for not defending her, for conspiring with Father to take all her money. Despite my sympathy and the fact that for the first time I genuinely felt she was justified in some of her grievances, I could not bring myself to extract the power of attorney from him.

Father was careful to keep in constant contact with us. He called almost every day, usually from his office. Apart from his weekly visits to us, he would sometimes come by in the afternoon or on weekends, when we took the children to the park. He bought Negar a canary when she was three years old. She claimed that every time Babaii (their nickname for my father) visited, he whistled to the canary and the bird would start chirping in response. One morning she found the canary dead in its cage and that whole day and night she cried. It was a day after the Persian New Year and Father took Negar to the garden, where they buried the canary by his favorite rosebush. He promised to buy her a new one but she woke me up that night and said, "I don't want another canary or any other animal, because they die."

I remember one day, at the very start of spring, there is a chill in the air. Our son Dara is crying—very rare for him—and stamping his feet as I try to get him to put on a light jacket. Negar is in her red hand-knit jacket with small yellow flowers (courtesy of Maman Nessi—my children's nickname for Mother) and is standing obedi-

The cousins: Sanam, Dara, and Negar.

ently, ready to go, looking at Dara as if to say, Look at me, here I am, making no fuss, ready to go. "What's wrong with this child?" Father asks, "I've seldom seen him cry." "He wants a Zorro costume," Negar volunteers. Zorro? Apparently one of the kids in his kindergarten class had come to school with one.

Dara is an even-tempered child, he gives up his toys to others with equanimity, but every once in a while he is caught by passion for something—a football, red boots, his dad's pipe, the moon—and then a little devil seems to take over, his soft chubby cheeks puff up with excitement, his eyes glow, and his entire body is focused on the object of his desire.

"He is being a spoiled brat," I say. His nanny, Tahmineh, who cannot tolerate his tears, already has tears in her own eyes. "Here, here," she says, as she gently buttons his jacket (another gift from Maman Nessi, dark blue with a red dog knitted on the right breast and two small pockets that Tahmineh joon has filled with candy). "I will make you a Zorro costume," she says, "and a Superman costume. Just wait a few days, we'll go shopping for the material together."

Soon, Dara has calmed down and is talking to my father about Superman and Zorro. "I want to be like them," he says, "when I grow up." "Why Zorro?" my father says with disbelief. "There are so many great Iranian heroes, why don't you want to be like Rostam, or

Kaveh?" he asks. "You know who Kaveh is? He saved Iran from the terrible rule of Zahak. When you were born, I was hoping you would be named Kaveh."

Dara says, "I don't like Iranian heroes, they hurt my mother. They have guns and they want to kill us." My father is visibly startled. "Things were not always like this," he says quietly. "When she was a child, your mother could go anywhere and do anything." "Then I want it to be then," Dara says, and we leave it at that.

I believe Dara's behavior was triggered by an incident a few weeks earlier. It had been a national holiday, and Bijan and I had decided to take the children to the mountains, near the village of Darakeh on the outskirts of Tehran, about twenty minutes from our house where there was an easy trail. We had a lovely day, the children sang, Bijan joked, we ate kabob, sitting outside despite the slight chill. We were the picture of a happy family.

On our way back down the mountain, Negar and I took the lead. My daughter was telling me a story about the misadventures of a vain-glorious cock when suddenly a voice shouted out, "*Hey, Hejabeto dorost kon*" (Hey, adjust your veil!). I turned around and a young man was walking very close behind us. I ignored him, holding tightly onto Negar's hand and walking faster. "Hey, didn't you hear me? I told you to cover your hair." Negar looked up at me with apprehension. "Don't pay attention," I said, "just walk on." "Hey, hey you! Are you deaf?" he called. I stopped. "I am not deaf," I said slowly. "It's none of your business how I wear my scarf." I don't know what got into me. Sometimes I wondered what was the point of not wearing a scarf properly, and why I did not just shut my mouth and do as they said.

"We don't want sluts in this country," he said. "Haven't you heard, there has been a revolution."

That was when I started shouting. Bijan and Dara had now quick-ened their steps to catch up with us. Bijan is a very calm person, he al-ways keeps his cool and his dignity. Time and again he has told me that I should accept where I live and voice my protests differently. We have had fights when I accused him of being insensitive, of not em-pathizing with my predicament as a woman, and he tells me, with a

calm that makes me want to shout louder, that I am being unreasonable and childish, I never see the good side of things. He hates these
thugs as much as I do, he says, with some desperation in his voice, and
yet, Azi jan, this is our country. I love it, I take both the good and the
bad, and I try to change it. But this time Bijan was not so philosophi-
cal. Turning to the young man, he shouted, "How dare you?"

"Why don't you do something about your wife?" the man said
scornfully. "It's your duty to keep her in control." (Unruly women
were supposed to be kept in check by their men.) From that point on,
Negar, Dara, and I stood to one side, watching my soft-spoken husband lose his cool.

"Let's take this to the committee," the man finally said. The
regime encouraged upright citizens to perform their religious duty by
reporting acts of immorality to the proper authorities. The local revolutionary committee was at the end of the trail, near the parking lot
in the village of Darakeh. As the young man walked ahead with a bel-
ligerent swagger, Bijan and I trailed behind, each holding on to a
child's hand all through that interminable walk. At some point first
Dara and then Negar burst into tears, dragging their feet reluctantly
as we pulled them along. Bijan and I were arguing, while the customers in teahouses and restaurants along the way, who were quite familiar with such sights, came out to cheer us and boo our assailant.

As we walked down through the village, shop owners and passersby
joined the protest: "Let 'em go, let 'em go," they chanted, cheering us
and cursing him. "Look what you've done to Islam. You call yourself a
Muslim, treating God's creatures in this manner!" Three or four young
boys followed our procession, gleefully booing until we reached the
committee door. To our great relief, there was no one inside.

We were lucky: everyone had gone to the city for the big demonstrations. The man said, "You stand here, I'll be back." We stood as
instructed for a few minutes, and then bolted out the door and ran to
our car. All through the drive back home, the children sat tearfully in
the backseat and Bijan and I kept repeating how lucky we were to get
away. Others had spent days in jail or been flogged for lesser offenses.
I turned to the children and asked Negar to sing her song about

Khroos Zari. I said something silly to Dara, but unlike earlier, the children were very quiet.

That day when Dara chose Zorro over Rostam and Kaveh, I believe he must have been thinking of our day in the mountains. My father said, "Your children were born in this land where you were born, and your father and your father's father and those before them. We each have gone through hardships, through bad times and good times, but that has never made us turn our backs on this country. This regime can confiscate our possessions but we cannot let it take away our culture and our faith."

THROUGHOUT THE EIGHT-YEAR WAR, when Tehran had been the target of Iraq's off-and-on bombings and rocket attacks, Bijan went to work as regularly as possible, even after a rocket fell close to his offices, causing the building considerable damage and breaking all the windows. Under the circumstances, hanging on to normalcy seemed the most important imperative. It is easier now to see various events in relation to one another, but at the time everything seemed to happen in fragments, without the continuity implied by a routine.

I started teaching again around 1987. I had not taught since my expulsion from the University of Tehran in 1982, spending the intervening years writing, mainly about fiction and modern Persian literature. I never returned to the Uni-

Negar and Dara at kindergarten.

versity of Tehran (too many bad memories), and chose to teach at Allameh Tabatabai University, an amalgamation of twenty-three colleges and small universities that had been centralized after the revolution. This university was more liberal than others, and the head of the English department was a wonderful linguist, respected in his field and interested in keeping the quality of work high. During the war classes were held irregularly; I taught two days a week anyway and spent most of my time at home either writing or preparing for my classes.

The last two months before the peace treaty, Iraq escalated its bombing of the cities, especially Tehran. Sometimes as many as six rockets would simultaneously fall on Tehran. What did those who had not left the city do? Some tried to create shelters out of their basements, others pretended that nothing extraordinary was happening and everything was normal: the blackouts, the huddled gatherings in one room with friends and family who had come to visit but now had to stay the night, the blankets hung against the windows, taped with surgical tape to prevent a barrage of breaking glass, the sound of warning sirens, which usually came only after the attack had happened.

In a strange way, life took on an almost festive mood. Neighbors and friends all gathered together. In between blackouts we watched movies and drank bootleg vodka and homemade wine, trying to feel secure by the strange sense of intimacy that urgent conditions create. I slept either in the children's room or in the small hall that separated our bedroom from theirs. The hall had no windows and I could read by candlelight during the blackouts. I wanted to be there with them whatever happened—that was my main anxiety, that I might not share their fate. Almost every time after the bombings, no matter what the hour of night or day, my mother would knock on the hall door and come in, saying, "Are you all right? Don't be afraid."

And then one day the bombs stopped. The sleepovers were over and we put the candles back in the drawers. No more blackouts, the sirens were not bomb alerts but simply ambulances—but the fear lingered; there seemed to be something deceptive in our newfound sense of security. The silence that peace brought with it had the same heavy impact as a bomb. Iran had signed a peace treaty out of desperation, knowing it could not win. Ayatollah Khomeini, who had promised his faithful troops that they would soon triumphantly march into Iraq and capture the holy city of Karballa, announced that the signing of the treaty was like drinking a cup of poison. It was a visible blow to his dream of exporting his brand of Islam to the rest of the world. Almost a million casualties, eight years of war. What does it mean to say: The war ended on August 20, 1988, and a year later, on June 3, 1989, Ayatollah Khomeini died, a quarter of a century after the June 5th uprising that propelled him into the center of Iranian politics?

What now? The discussions at our dinner table and the conversations at our coffee sessions were colored by talk of transformations within the regime. This was the time to articulate our disillusionment with a revolution that had not delivered, with corrupt leaders who had failed to bring freedom and prosperity to the country, and with a war that had not been won. The peace treaty with Iraq had dashed the hopes of those who had sincerely believed that this war would end in the victory of the Islamic regime. Those who felt cheated were not the secularists, but the former revolutionaries, the ones who had guarded the streets with guns, tried to purge the universities of undesirable elements, gone to war and returned mutilated and without hope. Who was to blame? No longer the imperialists and their modernizing agents.

It may be ironic but it is also true that disillusionment can breed hope. Some of the former young revolutionaries began to turn to new ideas and espouse heretical views, quoting Karl Popper and Spinoza, criticizing regressive religious ideas and reaching out to secular intellectuals. They were part of the movement that was later called the religious reformist movement. What they had shunned at the start of the revolution—secularism and Western ideas—was now what they increasingly turned to. Once they started to feel like aliens in their formerly secure world, they sought out new kinships. Some among the secular intellectuals also questioned their own ideological inflexibilities and welcomed new dialogue and exchanges. Some among the intellectuals who were disciples of the Islamic thinker Abdol Karim Soroush published articles by secular intellectuals, among them my articles on modernism, formalism, and Vladimir Nabokov. They also published translations of works by Western liberal thinkers.

The truth was that Iranian society was far ahead of its leaders, and those targeted by the regime, especially the women, instead of retreating had become even more prominent on the social and cultural scene. I had started in jest to draw up a list of things we should be thankful to the Islamic Republic for: making us appreciate the feel of the wind and the sun on our hair and skin, the freedom to read Virginia Woolf or Forough Farrokhzad, the joy of walking down the street in a flowery summer dress, listening to music. Never again could we take these for granted. But the list went beyond that. We had to be thankful to the Islamic Republic for making us question our past, and therefore to learn about it. Even those the regime targeted, like women, minorities, intellectuals, and writers, had something to be thankful for: the realization of their own hitherto untapped powers: if a woman's hair, or a film by Fellini or Beyzaii, a book by Farrokhzad, could destabilize the political system to such an extent that they had to be eliminated, then was this not indicative of how strong these targets were and how fragile and insecure their oppressors?

Ironically, we had to thank the system for the disillusionment of the country's youth and former revolutionaries with the system itself. The ideological barriers that divided people into East and West, outsiders and insiders, were falling. My father believed that, as in the case of the Constitutional Revolution, change would come to Iran through an alliance of the progressive religious and secular forces, and that there would be no real political transformation without participation of both these forces now.

I had come to agree with him. In this manner the past intruded and now colluded with the present. Shirin Ebadi, the first woman to be named to the circuit court of Tehran, when defrocked by the new laws that barred women from becoming judges, would become a human-rights lawyer. Another woman, Mehrangiz Kar, who had been a successful journalist and lawyer, would not only fight in courts but collaborate with a young cleric, Mohsen Saeedzadeh, in writing a series of inflammatory articles regarding women's rights which led to endless harassment of Kar and her family and to the defrocking and the jailing of the cleric. A religious intellectual named Akbar Ganji, who in the first years of the revolution fought for the Islamization of universities, the suppression of dissent, and celebrating the implementation of religious law, now, over a decade later, found more affinities with a Jewish woman of German descent named Hannah Arendt, to whose work he would turn to describe the Islamic Republic. Or a filmmaker named Mohsen Makhmalbaf, who at the start of the revolution showed his films to political prisoners, hoping to convert them, and claimed in an interview that the older filmmakers who had been prominent during the Shah's time deserved to be executed, would now tell me of the change in his attitude and say, "Perhaps art can give us the possibility of living several times. Every individual can live only once, and only from one perspective. Art can create other and different perspectives." Every time I think of this statement I thank the Islamic Republic of Iran: by depriving us of the pleasures of imagination, of love, and of culture it had directed us toward them. No power, no amount of force, could make this genie go back into the bottle.

Two days after the last cease-fire, we went with my father for a three-day trip to the Caspian. In the opposite lane we saw streams of cars, Tehranis who had taken refuge by the sea returning home. All through the four-and-a-half-hour journey Father would stop, as he had when I was a child, to point out the unique wildflowers he spotted. I sat in the back with the children.

It was both a joyous and a sad trip for us, joyous because the war had really ended this time, and sad because it reminded us of the festive times we had spent there before the revolution. Now this exceptionally beautiful place looked as if it had been pillaged. Both nature and the revolution had taken their toll. The tide had advanced and overtaken many of the seaside villas. The walls to gardens were demolished and sometimes the houses were destroyed. On the beach we found scattered pieces of masonry, discarded shoes and clothing. The flourishing restaurants and resorts had been closed down. I remember one in particular, Motel Ghoo, the first of its kind in Iran, a large resort with dancing on the pier and bingo games at night and parties on the beach. It had been cordoned off by a clumsy wall and fence and was used as headquarters for the revolutionary guard. The small square that had been the center of the busy town during the tourist season with its movie theater, small shops, and coffeehouses now swarmed with morality patrols. Instead of popular music, military marches or religious incantations emanated from the loudspeakers in the corners of the square. The women and men, in their dark, somber clothes, looked incongruous against the backdrop of the sea.

My father had sold his beloved villa by the Caspian just before the revolution. At my insistence we paid it a visit. We parked the car at the corner and walked toward the house. The large garden had been divided and walled off. My best memories of my adolescence were of our trips to the Caspian. I loved the lush green, so close to the sea, the air, moist and seductive, soaking your body, the calm, the way the flowers looked bigger and brighter, as if illuminated from within. But after the revolution I hated going there. The Caspian region had been the target of the regime's anger and neglect. I did not want to see the beloved refuge of my imagination turned into such a shabby place.

the goddess of bad news

I WENT TO AUSTIN, TEXAS, AND THEN to Los Angeles in early 1990 for conferences. Two days after my return, Father came over for dinner. He came early, and seemed distracted and a little agitated. Negar ran into the living room, with the presents I had brought them, followed by Dara waving his Zorro costume like a flag. My father kissed them and said, "Now I need to talk to your mother for a few minutes. I have good news for her." We went to the library. I sat on the couch, he pulled up a chair, leaned toward me, and told me he had married Shahin.

I was flabbergasted. I knew they had vaguely talked of marriage, and we saw her every once in a while. She even gave me a few tips on decorating my house. But he never mentioned impending plans. He'd waited for me to leave the country to marry her—at least that is how I saw it. I said, "You hid it from me, you must have known before I left." He said he did it for me, that I'd told him I didn't want to have to lie to my mother anymore about his relationships with other women. Then he said, "I wouldn't have married her, I wouldn't have married anyone if I'd known you didn't like her. I had counted on your being friends." I think that is what made me doubt his sincerity. But how could I be blind for so many years and not see how my complicity in making up fictions to tell Mother might lead one day to his making up stories to appease me?

I believe Father was happier with Shahin than he had been with my mother, although their relationship followed a familiar pattern: he became her friend, her father, her accountant, and her caretaker. He did the shopping and helped around the house. He wrote letters to her addict brother, admonishing him on her behalf. He promised her that before he died he would provide her with the kind of life she deserved, which meant using his power of attorney to sell everything we had. In a desperate frenzy to get our confiscated lands back he would make deals with shady characters he had shunned all his life. And Shahin treated him in some ways much as my mother had. She never warmed up to his family and she snubbed my uncles and cousins. Whenever we went over, for Norooz (Persian New Year) or some other formal occasion, he was anxious that our children might spill something. We always felt ill at ease, sitting on the edge of our chairs, ready to take flight. She was both mean and absurdly conscious of titles and labels. Once a friend told me to look at a blouse Shahin had given me for my birthday; the label had been cut out and she had pinned a designer logo to the cuff. Father tried to defend her, reminding me of how much I had liked her, insisting he never would have married her without my approval. Sometimes he had tears in his eyes; he could not believe that I would not believe him. I had been his most trusted confidante, so it was natural that it would hurt when he lied to me.

"It was only in the last two years of his life," my best friend, Pari, told me, "that Mr. Nafisi was unhappy. Otherwise," she said—I surmise in order to calm me—"he had a good life with her." The last two years Shahin pressured him to sell one of the islands that had been in Mohammad and my names, which had been semiofficially confiscated by the government. She was worried that, should he die, the money would go either to the government or to us, and not to her. Even at that age, with his heart trouble, my father would travel to the Caspian sometimes twice a week to cajole and bribe the people who had occupied the island, the local Islamic revolutionary committees and clerics. I kept telling him to let that island be. "We don't need the money," I said, "and you don't need the headache." I couldn't bring myself to tell him that for someone who had boasted he would never bend to the Shah or any other power, it was demeaning to now try to appease these people for a piece of land.

Father loved Shahin, of that I am as certain as I can be of anything about him. She might have loved him in her own way. Unlike Mother she did acknowledge his devotion. But he never found the peace he had searched for. He would have dinner with us once a week. Always he arrived nervous and worried. He wanted me to love his wife, not just respect her but love her. ("Azi wants to talk to you," he would say, calling me from their home and giving her the receiver. I'd hear him say, "She misses talking to you.") And he worried about money.

All his life, until a few days before he died, he went to work almost every morning. He had enough money to live comfortably but that was insufficient for Shahin. "I told her I would take care of her," he said, "I made a promise." She had given up on the idea of fashion design and he helped her open a business as an interior decorator. He took me to the notary to renew his power of attorney, so that he could sell another piece of land. For some reason he and Shahin would try to convince us that she was the real breadwinner, that her decorating business had flourished to that extent.

He tried to decipher Shahin the way he had tried to understand my mother. In his last diary, written a few months before his death, there is a note: "For Shani: If you view reality the way it really is you will make fewer mistakes. Your problem is that you mistake your own dreams and desires for reality and then you become disillusioned." He might as well have written that note to himself.

Shahin appeared to share my mother's gift for fantasy, but she lacked Mother's vulnerabilities. She used her misfortunes for specific goals. The protection she sought was not a vague demand for love and acknowledgment, it was far more pointed and material. Her greed had little mystery about it, which may be why she got what she wanted and my mother never did.

A while ago a close relative told me, "There was really nothing wrong with what your father did. It isn't that other men don't have affairs. In fact, they tend to have them far more often than Ahmad did. But they keep them separate from their family and friends. They know how to be discreet. Ahmad's marriage made no sense. Men marry younger women either for sexual pleasures or to be taken care of in their old age. In that house, Ahmad did everything. He did the shopping, helped with the washing up, carried his wife's bag, and constantly sent her on vacations on her own so that she could rest." This man wanted to know why my father couldn't act more like a normal man. Why did his affairs have to turn into such messy dramas? In my more sober moments I wondered this myself. Would I have loved him more? I don't think so. I loved him because his faults were not ordinary, because he felt guilty and he wanted not to have affairs but to be in love. His last diary is filled with his worries about his "promise" to Shahin, which, after his death, we discovered he more than fulfilled, even at the expense of his own good name.

In personal life as in politics you either accept the rules or you openly and on principle rebel against them. In both cases there is a price to be paid. Fortunately, no one goes free. But what price? Not belonging to either camp, my father paid a double price. He had neither the comforts of convention nor the satisfaction that comes from breaking with what is expected of you. All through his diaries two opposite tendencies come up: the desire to break away, to embark on the life he wanted, coupled with a fear of what would happen to him if he did.

With tireless energy my mother pursued him, calling his place of business, asking friends and acquaintances about his activities, and accusing me of not protecting her, of selling her out to "that man and his floozy." She had started to call my friend Pari behind my back, in part to complain, and she commissioned her to get the deeds to the property. Once she discovered my father had married, she made life hell for all of us for many weeks. I told her I had nothing to do with it, that I sympathized with her and had made a pact, out of respect for her, not to see his new wife at our home. I was trying to be honest with her. But it did not work. Too many things had happened, too much mistrust had built up over the years. What amazed me was why a woman with her sense of pride and strict morality had not initiated a divorce a long time before. Was it because she was afraid that being divorced would be more humiliating than tolerating a bad marriage? Or could it be that despite what she claimed she really loved him?

She would say that she had known from the start he'd had "some other woman" in mind or he would not have broken up with Ziba Khanoom. At other times she would contradict herself and claim that, after extracting all the money she could from him, it was Ziba Khanoom who had left him. On calmer days she would try to make me part of her network of eyes and ears. She wanted me to give her their phone number. "I don't have it," I'd say, "I call him at his office." She asked Bijan, the children, friends; finally she found their number and would call them day and night, threatening them and leaving messages on their voice mail. Let it go, everyone advised her. Be happy with your children and grandchildren, be grateful they are healthy and loving. "Loving?" she would retort with a sour smile.

PEOPLE ARE COLLECTORS for different reasons, but usually there is some specific purpose or focus—an obsession with matchboxes, for example, or ashtrays, or art. They tend to target specific objects. My mother seemed to hoard more than to collect, and what she hoarded was of no use. When I was younger she would sometimes use her old fabrics to make clothes for herself or for me, but gradually she just stored them in trunks, folded meticulously, one on top of the other.

Her storage rooms were the heart of the house, its secret pulse: trunks filled with fabrics, clothes, presents she had bought for my father, my brother, and me, two trunks filled with silver, the china from her first marriage. Then, after the revolution and my father's departure, she started hoarding basic staples. She boasted that she had preserved rice and sugar from prerevolutionary times. She stockpiled butter, which she almost never used. The storage rooms must have given her a sense of security, but until the day she died she never knew how to integrate these things into her life: display the silver, eat off the best china, wear the fur coats, allow us children to lose or destroy our toys. Sometimes, suddenly and for no reason, she would give away the precious objects she had guarded for many years, not to us, as might seem natural, but to relative strangers. She had developed a tendency to deny me any object I was interested in; if anything, she tried to take back what she had previously given me.

She hoarded people as well as things. In the last years she took to collecting most avidly the stories of crimes committed by the Islamic regime. With these she was always generous. So many mornings we woke up to her knocking, or we found her at night when we returned home from a party, in the stairway. "Have you heard?" she would say, and then she would invariably tell us a tale of woe. Like the Goddess of Bad News, she worried lest we forgot. As soon as I glimpsed that sparkle in her eyes and heard the suppressed excitement in her voice, I knew we would soon be regaled with the tale of another murder. She was meticulous in her descriptions: in the ritual of stoning, men would be buried up to their waists, women to their necks; the stones had to be neither too large nor too small. One man had escaped and been forgiven because if you escape you will be pardoned. She reported with horror of street hangings where they hanged the culprit from a crane in order to make an example of him. Imagine Negar and Dara, she would say, coming upon such a scene on their way to school. And then there was the story of the man and woman who had been found beheaded in their garage (the woman's name has somehow stayed in my mind, Firoozeh Sanaii) and of the older woman robbed and murdered—a hint of her own situation, alone when we left for a few days' vacation, alone once we were gone for good.

All through the nineties, alongside the political openings, there was also a systematic harassment of dissidents and secular intellectuals. One by one writers, poets, and translators would be murdered as they went about their business, shopping, visiting friends. My mother had listened carefully to our dinner conversations about the mysterious disappearances of Ahmad Mir Alaii, one of our best translators, and of a wonderful colleague at the University of Tehran, a professor of ancient Persian languages and culture, Ahmad Tafazoli, and about the burning down of the bookstore Morghe Amin by Islamic vigilantes who objected to a book published by the novelist Shahrnoosh Parsipur. Have you heard? she would exclaim, barging in in the early morning, Have you heard Mr. Golshiri has been arrested? We already knew, had been woken up early in the morning to hear that the night before, Golshiri and five other writers had been arrested at the house of the German consul.

Every time I left Iran for a conference my mother would start a campaign a few days before my departure. Usually there would be a knock at the kitchen door and without waiting for an answer she would come in. "Don't forget to tell them," she'd say. "You must tell them everything." She wanted me to relate all the crimes committed by the regime. She avidly listened to foreign broadcasts, the BBC and the Voice of America, and reported their news back to us. "The British are at it again, muddying the waters," she would say. "They are in cahoots with the regime, never telling the truth." She even had a list of those assassinated by the regime outside Iran: the former prime minister Bakhtiar, his close associate Abdolrrahman Boroumand, Forough Farrokhzad's brother, Fereydoun. Sometimes she invited me for coffee and commanded me to listen carefully to what a friend or a perfect stranger had to say about the goings-on in the country. The first time she said tell them, I said, "Tell who, Mom?" "Those who invited you. Tell Mahnaz." Mahnaz Afkhami was the former minister for women's affairs under the Shah. We were related. Her younger sister Farah, who later, like me, became active in the Confederation of Iranian Students, had been a childhood friend. At one point both Farah and I would have demonstrated against Mahnaz, but now the sisters shared the same fate: Mahnaz having been responsible for initiating projects and implementing the laws protecting women in the seventies, was near the top of the regime's blacklist. Mahnaz lived in exile in the U.S., where Farah fled to, eight months pregnant and with a three-year-old daughter, after her husband, Faramarz, was executed. Every time I left for a conference my mother would ask me to give her regards to Mahnaz and to tell her that people knew about her good work and how they appreciated her. "You used to jeer at people like Mahnaz," Mother would say reproachfully, "you didn't appreciate her." I wanted to remind her that she herself did not approve of Mahnaz at the time. This feeling of admiration was relatively new. "They will listen to her," my mother would say.

I can still picture Mother early in the morning, standing by the garage door, ready to perform the parting rituals, holding a tray on which she had placed a copy of the Koran and a small bowl of water with a single flower floating in it. Before sprinkling the water after me for good luck and a safe journey, she takes a semi-crumpled piece of white paper out of her dressing gown pocket and hands it out to me. "I have written down a list of names of the people who are in jail or were killed. Give it to your friends. Make sure you do," she says, almost pleading. "Okay, Mom." "I hope this is not one of those okays you give when you have no intention of carrying out what I ask you," she says, as I get into the car and close the door.

SOMETIMES I FELT GRATEFUL that we lived in such close proximity to Mother. When Dara and Negar were small Mother often told them stories when they went to take their afternoon nap. She would spread a large blanket on the floor with three pillows and the three of them would lie in a row. I walked past their room and through the open door I could see Negar lying on her back, her thumb in her mouth, eyes focused on the ceiling, listening with that look of abstraction that children have when they leave the present reality for that other world. Dara, as usual, demanded his favorite objects from the picture books: "That moon," he would say, "that moon is what I want." When they grew up she taught them how to play cards. In the evening she would call them downstairs for a hand of passur, or rummy, or twenty-one. She would tell them how her father, a great gambler, would sometimes play with her and because there were only two of them, each would double as an absent partner—a complicated process I never really understood. She always made sure to lose and she paid the children with chocolates and money. I would often come home from visiting friends or meetings to the sound of laughter and find Mother, Negar, and Dara sitting around the kitchen table.

She bought them gifts, usually small jewelry for Negar and toys for Dara. I have in my drawer a long gold chain with little medallions: a tiny heart, a pomegranate, a slipper, keys, and several emblems of the winged Zoroastrian deities so much in demand after the revolution. She knit the children colorful socks, mittens, and scarves, and in the morning she would come halfway up the staircase and shout their names. "Come down and feed the birds!" she'd say. After we left Iran to live in the U.S. in 1997, every time I called, she would say, "Tell Dara I am taking care of his birds," her voice breaking as she spoke.

She loved both children, but Dara, our son, was her favorite. She often accused us of taking advantage of his good nature. She thought he looked like my brother, and that Negar looked like me, only of course her children were better looking. These were the light moments—their times together usually were light, except when she allowed her wrath toward my father to extend to them. I still have Negar's diaries from when she was eight: "Today Maman Nessi told us we should not visit her anymore," she wrote. "She said she is not our grandmother, someone named Shahin the Turk is our grandmother now. I cried, but she said, 'That's what your mother wants.' "

Sometimes she would come upstairs when we were not home and collect their "good toys"—presents from birthdays and other occasions—and hide them so they would not destroy them. I am still amazed as I write about this at how alien the concept of pleasure and play was to her; she was so threatened by it, as if it would inevitably lead to loss and sorrow. Once Tahmineh Khanoom, who knew every nook and cranny in my mother's apartment, as she helped her every once in a while, took Negar, Dara, and me downstairs when my mother was out. She opened a closet door and, lo and behold, the whole closet was filled with large teddy bears and stuffed animals, Barbie dolls, cars, and trucks Bijan's sisters had sent the children from America. This was so strange that it made the children laugh as we paid her in kind by reappropriating a few of their favorite toys—we didn't have the heart to take them all and leave her with nothing. "And you blamed us," Negar said, as we sneaked back upstairs, our hands full to overflowing, "for losing our toys!"

IN HER LATER YEARS my mother spent most of her time in a drawing room next to her bedroom. The room depressed me, despite the fact that it was sunny, with wide French windows opening onto a balcony facing the garden. This cheerful sunniness was overshadowed by photographs, which seemed to proliferate alarmingly on tabletops and all available surfaces and on the walls. They were arranged without regard for size or shape and almost none of them hung straight; they leaned toward one another like drunk strangers at a bar.

In this room she served her legendary coffee to guests, chosen as haphazardly as her photographs. Alongside the guards from the neighboring hospital, Saifi's relatives, my students, and our neighbors, were strangers she had come across at a friend's house, or, in two or three cases, met in a cab or on a bus. These assorted individuals could be found perched precariously on the edge of their chairs, as if wary of the stranger occupying the seat next to them. Sometimes

Mother in her final years, among her photographs.

she paid heavily for this indulgence, such as when, for a while, a shady character who looked like a handsome Kojak, named Ahmad Agha, was her favorite. For a long time Ahmad Agha visited her on a daily basis, supposedly reporting on clandestine activities by opponents of the regime. He had introduced himself to her as a political activist, and fed her fantastic stories about secret activities in the bazaar, mysterious uprisings in clerical schools, and grisly murders committed by the militia and revolutionary guards.

Every day Mother would repeat Ahmad Agha's stories, her expression brimming with excitement, with such heartbreaking trust that it was impossible for us to openly question the authenticity of his tales. We tried to find diplomatic ways to warn her, but she was, as she'd always been, deaf to criticism of the people she favored. Ahmad Agha coaxed money out of her, in the name of donations to victims of the regime and freedom fighters, and when he disappeared as suddenly as he had appeared, he took off with her silver, which included precious souvenirs from her mother and first husband, and two of her antique carpets. Like others who stole from her, he knew where she kept her good things, in the basement near the garage. It was easy to cheat her of her belongings, all you had to do was say the right things. If you were unconditionally and irrevocably against the Islamic regime, you were high on her list of favorites. If you took her side against my father, then you could get almost anything out of her. She felt she could trust people who agreed with her. It was to our credit— my brother's and mine—that we did not acquiesce in this arrangement, despite the personal cost of our sedition.

L ONG AFTER AUNT MINA had a falling-out with my mother, I continued to visit her. By the mid-eighties Aunt Mina was ill. I remember one day in particular, she was in a reminiscing mood and for the first time she decided to tell me her side of the story. "Your mother is a funny person," she said, getting up from her chair to bring me her photograph album. "She will accuse you of the worst crimes and break off all relations, and a few weeks later she'll expect you to act as if nothing has happened. I sometimes think she thrives on creating scenes and stirring emotions.

"The trouble with Nezhat," Aunt Mina went on, "is that she goes to extremes in everything she does. She is so kind and helpful that you know you can never repay her and then suddenly she becomes so overbearing, and demanding." Aunt Mina told me that they often quarreled about my mother's treatment of me. "So many times when you went back to England or America after your summer vacations, Nezhat was so mad at you that she would curse you and say she hoped your plane would crash.

"I don't know which was worse," Aunt Mina said, "her mother's suicide or her discovery that Saifi had a fatal disease on her wedding night." "Suicide?" This was the first time I had heard any suggestion that my grandmother's death had been from suicide. Surely someone would have mentioned it. She waved away my question. "I'm not sure what it was, there were rumors—childbirth, infection, even that your grandfather had killed her, there was also some speculation that she had been unhappy and committed suicide. You know that there were problems with her niece Fakhri, she suffered from some sort of mental illness, depression, I believe. I don't think Nezhat wanted to know the truth, and it's all water under the bridge now." I was as shocked by this piece of information as by Aunt Mina's casual way of mentioning it. It was one stray piece of a puzzle I had long been struggling to put together.

"I sometimes think that Saifi was very bad for your mother," Aunt Mina said. "She never recovered after his death. She wore black for a long time" (my father had written that when he first saw her, Mother was wearing black, "waves" of grief still crossing her face). "She never found her bounce again." The absence of love, my student had called it—perhaps that was my mother's illness. So many women seem to suffer from it. Aunt Mina herself, come to think of it, my grandmother, even some of my young students. "She turned that man into a god; no man deserves that," Aunt Mina said, with a mischievous smile. "I hope you have learned something from your mom."

There was no way that I could ask my mother if my grandmother had committed suicide, but I asked my father. "I don't know what it was," he said. "There were so many rumors. No one paid enough attention to the poor woman to find out." Over the years I asked my mother's cousins, but no one knew anything about her. So the only way I can deal with the fact that no one knew or remembered anything about my grandmother's life is to record what we do know about her for certain—and the fact that everyone forgot her. A friend once asked me why I thought truth mattered. "Truth," he said, "is not comforting, certainly not nearly so much as lying or forgetting."

Less than a year after that visit, Aunt Mina died. For a long time she had been suffering from cancer of the stomach. She had become very thin, which somehow made her look even more elegant and ladylike. Despite her illness she was always perfectly dressed and was very much in command and control of her beautiful apartment furnished with antiques. Unlike Mother's apartment, hers had order and harmony. My mother did not object to my visits to Aunt Mina, but she did not warm up to her when she was sick. Usually the way to make Mother forget her animosities was to inform her of someone's misfortune. But Aunt Mina was ill and dying, and Mother revealed no curiosity or sympathy. "I have heard," she'd say in a neutral tone, "that she cheats at rummy. I defended her," she added matter-of-factly, "but that is what they say, that she cheats and no one likes to play with her."

She used to pride herself on how she was "always there" for friends and relatives in times of grief, irritating me when she boasted that she seldom attended weddings but was always present at funerals. Yet when her stepmother died, although she was concerned for Aunt Nafiseh and spent most of her time with her, she showed little actual grief. At the mourning ceremonies she talked loudly and even laughed. Aunt Nafiseh's friends took great pleasure in shushing her, saying, "Nezhat Khanoom, *please* . . ."

When Aunt Mina was in the hospital I visited her regularly. The last few days they took her to the ICU. I remember standing behind the window of the ICU with her daughters, watching her. She was restless, she kept moving, and we stood there helpless; she was already beyond our reach. After she died, I went to the cemetery with

Layla, her younger daughter, and we watched from behind a window as she was washed and prepared for Muslim burial. When I told my mother, she was sitting on the couch in her faded pale-green dressing gown. She said nothing. "Layla was always a good girl," she said finally. "I like her."

After a while Mother got up, and as she walked toward the door, she said, "Would you like a cup of coffee?"

facing the world

FATHER HAD ACTED AS AN INTERMEDIARY between Mother and the world. Problems with the plumbing, the house or garden, the servants, whatever it was she would interrupt him at his office, in the middle of a meeting, and expect him to resolve the issue. If she wanted to travel, he secured her passport and tickets. If she felt insulted by a friend or acquaintance at a party she was furious if he did not "defend her." At the start of the revolution, when the new regime announced that former parliamentarians had to report to the courts and pay back their wages, Father went to the preliminary meetings on her behalf and paid the dues. The act of defending and protecting her, a woman so furiously in love with the idea of independence, was left first to my father and then to my brother and me.

As far as domestic and practical matters were concerned, now that Father was gone, Mother was dependent on us, which really meant on Bijan. Father had settled the financial aspects of her government case but then she was summoned to the court again for a second interrogation—more of a formality. How would she do this without him? I offered to accompany her, as did friends. But she adamantly refused our offers. "I hope," she said, "the day that I have to depend on anyone for anything will never come." When I insisted, she said, "Please do not trouble yourself, I am quite capable of taking care of myself. It is how I have lived all my life. That is my lot," she concluded coldly, and haughtily.

And as it turned out, she was right, she did not need me. She returned triumphantly, and revealed how she had defiantly told them that she had nothing to be ashamed of. She spoke with pride of her record in Parliament. They could not find fault with her record, as she had voted against the American capitulation law and the family protection law, both of which the new regime repudiated. She said, "I told them that if they had any sense, they would build a statue of me in gold, but we know better than to imagine that will ever happen! I told my interrogator—he was not a cleric, by the way—that I was a Muslim before he was born, I could be his mother. 'So,' I said, 'Please save your breath, don't preach to me about my religion. And don't think for a moment I believe in this garb you've forced on us, as if covering myself would make me more of a Muslim.' "

"What did he say, Mom?" I asked. "Oh, he wasn't like the others, maybe in his heart he is against the system. He laughed and said, 'I know you are a good Muslim and I know you don't mean what you say.' I said, 'Oh, I mean it all right, and if you come to my house for coffee I will explain it all to you.' " Before she left she told her examiner that her father gambled and drank but was far more of a Muslim than many of our present leaders because he practiced the basic tenet of Islam, charity toward others, which is more than she could say for them.

That day she was so excited, as if she had discovered some hidden potential. Yes, she did not need an intermediary between herself and the world. She had come to this realization a little too late, though, because by the time she told the story to Bijan she had already started spicing it up with accusations against my father, whom she blamed for maliciously reporting her to the officials he had become so chummy with. "Fancy that this man who claimed he would not bow to the Shah now toadies to these people, all because he needs to provide for that slut he calls his wife."

I FIRST TRAVELED TO THE United States and Europe for a conference a few days before New Year of 1990. We had our home and children, my husband had a job he loved, and I was by now an established critic in Iran. For almost two decades, from the early eighties until we left, in the summer of 1997, I had studied and written about Persian literature. Since childhood I had seen how Father moved in and out of fiction, turning to stories from the *Shahnameh* and classical literature to teach us about Iran, and now this had become almost a second nature to me. I searched modern fiction and poetry for clues to how we confronted and evaded reality, how we articulated our experience and turned to language not to reveal ourselves but to hide. I was as sure then as I am now that by looking at contemporary Iranian fiction I could gain access to a real understanding of political and social events.

But then, suddenly, I felt it was not enough to be a literary critic. It was easier, given the political climate, to write academically correct essays and articles—and this was also how you gained respect among the intellectual elite. But more and more I was becoming mischievous in my writing. I remember how excited I would get with my little nuggets of perceived truth, which I would gather up gingerly and take home to my nest. But the form was wrong: there seemed to be something artificial, something contrived about these eager ideas tamed and made to adhere to a sober language. I started writing about Vladimir Nabokov partly because of my students' enthusiasm for his works. I seemed to share some of the same obsessions he had: a preoccupation with exile, a firm belief in the portable world of the imagination, and the subversive power of literature, a belief that it is possible, through fiction, to turn anguish into a thing of enduring beauty.

Many of the things that are dangerous to a totalitarian mind-set can be found in Nabokov's novels: respect for the individual, erotic love, an appreciation for the complicated relationship between victim and oppressor. Nabokov understood that one could take control of reality through imagination.

My book *Anti-Terra* was published in 1994, and I resigned from my academic post a few months later. I enjoyed teaching, but the more popular my classes became, the more difficult the university officials made it for me to teach. For one thing, I had created a special speakers' program, inviting well-known writers, filmmakers, and artists to speak and engage with the students. The first speaker had been the famous director Abbas Kiarostami, who was giving his first public talk since the revolution. One of my students, Mr. Forsati, the head of the Islamic Students' Association and an avid fan of films, had worked on my behalf to make the series possible. Hundreds of people came to the large auditorium to hear him speak. The last event featured another prominent but controversial director, Bahram Beyzaii, who was outrageously frank in his criticism of the regime. At the start of the revolution he had written a hugely popular and critically acclaimed play about the death of the last king of the Persian Empire, Yazdegerd, who was killed by a miller right before the invasion of the Arabs. After the Beyzaii event, as Mr. Forsati and I were walking down the steps, he said, "You should know that these meetings will have to come to an end. Beyzaii was the last straw. The administration feels they have become too politically subversive."

Students from other universities started coming to listen in on my classes. I let them participate because I felt there were so few spaces in Tehran for open debate on literature. How could I refuse anyone who wanted to spend his or her free time discussing *Tom Jones* or *Wuthering Heights*? The dean of the faculty was less magnanimous. He decided to ban outsiders and instituted a new rule that whoever wanted to visit me had to get permission through his office. Every day there were new rules and restrictions. They would woo me and then restrict my activities. I felt at some point that I was spending more time fighting than doing my job. I resigned, but my resignation was not accepted for two years. They would have had no problem expelling me; but who did I think I was to resign? At least that is how I interpreted it. For the next two years I taught a private class to seven of my favorite female students and one man who would not be denied his rights.

It took my husband and me a long time to decide to leave Iran. For months we argued back and forth about our future, our children's future, and how we could best serve our country—such arguments were routine among our friends, family, and acquaintances. All our time in America, he reminded me, we had dreamed of return.

I wanted our children to have the same choices we had, to see the world and make their own decisions. I also wanted to be a writer and a teacher, something that seemed almost imperative to my own survival. Bijan's job was not directly involved with the regime. He was partner in an architectural firm with a group of colleagues he very much respected and liked, and the firm had been assigned exciting projects that made him feel wanted and appreciated. In addition, I reminded him, it made a difference that he was a man. He tried to make light of that by telling me how we bypassed the regime's laws, citing his own experience.

It is not that Bijan disagreed with me. Since my return to Tehran, I had, partly because of my sex and vocation, felt somewhat displaced, never wholly at home. He, on the other hand, felt very much at home, and with the same focus he put into every project, he set out to actualize his dream of a permanent home—a dream he had been living with ever since he left Iran at the age of seventeen. Eighteen years after our return, he had created a home, almost an island, populated with his family, friends, and colleagues. Leaving this home was very painful for him.

One night, past midnight, Bijan was stopped by the revolutionary militia as he was driving home from a party. They accused him of drinking, which he had been although he denied it. He was taken to the revolutionary committee headquarters, where he spent the night in a cell with addicts and other young men arrested for partying and other such offenses. In the morning he was taken to the committee head with some of his cellmates. The committee's catch was usually taken to the court in a minibus, but the officer in charge discreetly informed Bijan that he could go by bus or take a cab, in which case he'd have to pay for the cab, but he could also call home—a veiled hint that with the appropriate bribe Bijan could be let off. In the cab the officer reminded him that he would be required to take a blood test, and would he like to call someone, a family member or a friend, who might come and pick him up later? Bijan took the hint. The officer received his bribe, and a driver from Bijan's office took the blood test and Bijan got off. Of course not everyone was so lucky. We had friends who had been forced to clean toilets in jails, or were beaten and fined. We knew of two separate incidents of young men who had tried to escape the armed raids on their parties and been killed falling from the windows or from fire escapes.

When I complained about our complicity and silent acquiescence in all of this, Bijan would point out that many Iranians did not give in to the dictates of the regime. People agreed on the surface to the rules and went on breaking them, including the officials and government functionaries. It was a defiance that the government could do nothing about. There was a mischievousness to these acts of insubordination that I appreciated although with some misgivings: I was troubled by this particular form of disobedience because it implied a silent agreement between the regime and the people. It seemed to me dangerous to give in to that sort of complicity. It is important not just to disobey the rules but to acknowledge that it is one's right to do so, and to do so openly. "My mother did not allow us to do a lot of things," I told him, "but we did them anyway; we felt we were right to lie to her and did not feel bad about it" (although we did) "because she was being dictatorial. You think that made lying okay? It is an illness in our society, the way victims become complicit in the acts perpetrated against them. Because no matter what justifications we may give, you and I are liars and cheaters as long as we play their game, and, what is worse, we feel it is okay."

This habit of pretending to give in to the regime created a certain moral laxity, a spiritual laziness in all of us. You could see it in our male acquaintances who would say with a mocking expression, "Why make such a fuss over a piece of cloth?" Not understanding that first of all the veil was not just a piece of cloth; it had been invested with spiritual significance for many men and women, and besides, this was not about how I felt about the piece of cloth in question, although I should have been free to express my feelings. This was about the freedom of choice. No regime, no figure of authority, had the right to tell a woman how to relate or not relate to God.

Shahrnoosh Parsipur wrote about how when she was in jail she was instructed by her warden to pray. She told him she would pray without a veil because she believed that God had no specific gender, but if God were to have one it would be female, and so she had no need to veil herself from her God. Parsipur had no political affiliations and yet she was kept in jail and underwent terrible punishments because she refused to buckle under to authority. I think she must have believed, with John Locke, that all authority is error. But now secular, enlightened men chided us for making nuisances of ourselves by objecting to the mandatory veil. And they were perfectly happy to use the laws of the land to marry younger second wives or divorce their wives without their consent. One problem with a regime like this was that it offered so many temptations against your better judgment.

In the end both Bijan and I had our points. But the decision to leave or stay in Iran was very personal, and either way there would be a price to pay. I was lucky to have a portable profession. I could teach and write no matter where I lived. My guilt was in regard to my parents. I did not want to leave them. So many of their generation had been left behind, with no one to look after them. Father had remarried, but what about my mother?

I had discussed the possibility of our departure with my father many

times. He said it might be in our best interest to leave, at least for a few years. I told him I would miss him. He said, "I left my father when I was eighteen, this is the way of the world. You need to think of yourself." He told me that for a while now he had been thinking of maybe leaving Iran himself.

Me with Negar, Father, and Dara, in the early 1990s.

One morning, when it had become almost certain that we would go, I went to my mother's apartment. She was in the kitchen. I walked around the room, looking at the photos: Negar in her red dress standing by a tree; Dara, his cheeks still full and baby-fattish, a rakish expression on his face; Mohammad and me in black and white when I was about seven and he two. She came in with two coffees and biscuits. I started telling her about my last trip to the U.S. I said that I had been offered a fellowship for two years at Johns Hopkins University's School of Advanced International Studies. A pause. She said, "Well, this is good news." She reminded me of the time she had taken me to England. "Why shouldn't your children have the same opportunity?" She said, "It's not as if you'll be leaving forever." I said, "I don't want you to be alone, why don't you come with us?" She smiled sarcastically. "This is my home," she said. "And anyway, I cannot leave. That gentleman, your father, has made sure of that."

The question of her leaving the country had come up before. Mohammad and Shahran had left almost a decade earlier and they begged her to come visit them in England. No matter what excuse she used, Mother always remembered to mention my father's responsibilities, telling us that because they never had a real divorce, she could not leave the country without his notarized consent. "I would never ask him for anything, even if I were at death's door," she said. "It is tragic that I, who voted against the family protection law because of this very stricture about wives needing their husbands' consent, should be subjected to this humiliation." She spoke with such conviction that we believed her. But later we discovered that the divorce had been registered on her birth certificate: she was in fact free.

At other times she would say, "Anyway, I promised myself I would never ask anything from this regime, so I will not now beg for a passport, even if it means never seeing my beloved children and grandchildren again." "But Mom," I would say, trying to reason with her, "having a passport is your right. You wouldn't be begging, you'd be asking for what is rightfully yours." Such arguments always ended either in a positive refusal or in some vague allusion to having things to do, perhaps she would go when they were done. This time I was desperate. I thought, if we can get her to come and visit us or my brother it would be good for all of us. Finally she agreed to rethink her position, after she "had taken care of some important affairs first." "This is my country," she told us seriously—leading us to believe that highly sensitive political commitments prevented her from leaving Iran. "In a sense," she said, "this country is as important to me as my own children. I have my patriotic duties."

For a while Mother was excited about our departure. She talked about it to others. She would turn to me and ask, "At which university were you accepted?" "Johns Hopkins, Mom." On the phone I would hear her say, "Yes, that's the one. No, not the hospital, a university, a very good one; she has a fellowship." When she put the receiver down, she would turn to me. "What did you say this fellowship was?" She said, cryptically, "You will be back soon, perhaps in two years. Mark my word, Ahmad Agha was here yesterday and he told me people in the bazaar are very, very unhappy with this regime. Yes, you'll be back. This regime will be gone in two years." (As if one day the clerics would all pack their bags and say, "Well, we're off now. Maybe we'll see you later, maybe we won't.") "You can come back in two years, can't you?" "Yes, Mom," I would say with desperation.

Once I burst into tears. She said, "Why are you crying? Poor Azi, always moving from one place to another, never enjoying your life, never having a real home." She told me to tell the world about what was happening in Iran. "Do your patriotic duty. I will send you information," she said, in a confidential manner. "Of course we cannot talk on the phone freely. But we will devise a language. If I say, 'Agha is ill,' you will know I am talking about the regime."

As time went by and we started packing and preparing, she became more concerned, less buoyant. Without reason she would stop talking to me, or she would complain about being abandoned one more time, a woman all alone in this large apartment. I reminded her that Mohammad's mother-in-law lived upstairs in Mohammad's flat and that, out of consideration for my mother, we had rented our apartment to a colleague of Bijan's. "What will I do when you leave and I am at the mercy of this gentleman, your father?" "Mom, Pari is my lawyer and friend, you won't be needing anything." "Will you," she would then say, "bring me the deeds to the lands before you leave? Can I ask you to do this one simple thing?" "Of course," I would say, knowing full well that I would not have the courage to ask my father to give me the deeds. She said, "Well, what I remember is all those years ago when you were so young"—her voice would break—"and we lived in that big damp house in Lancaster, how scared you were. I spent hours finding the words for you in the dictionary. Now . . ." she trailed off.

As the time for our departure grew near I became almost frantic in my attempts to spend time with her. Long hours would elapse, sitting in that drawing room, as I tried to draw stories out of her. I would walk around the room and ask her about the photographs. "Mom, who is this?" "Oh, look at you and Aunt Mina." "Do you have any pictures of Saifi after you were married?" Her responses were perfunctory, and when I asked her about my grandmother or Saifi she repeated the same stories she had always told me, almost word for word.

One morning she brought out a small suitcase from the storage room. It was filled with old photographs, and we scattered them on the floor. I could hear Negar and Dara laughing out on the balcony. The French window was open and they were playing some nonsensical word game. Every once in a while one of them would say something particularly preposterous and they would break into peals of laughter. My mother would not sit down by me. As I went through the suitcase, she drifted in and out of the room, occasionally tossing off a comment about a photograph. I put some photos aside. I knew that there was no way I could preserve that moment: my children out on the balcony, my mother almost at peace with me, a feeling of comfort and intimacy I hadn't felt in so many decades. "Negar, Dara," she called as soon as she came in, carrying a tray in her hands, "your coffee and chocolate is ready." "Mom," I was going to say, "don't give them coffee, they are too young." But I knew she would only say, "You of all people don't need to tell me what is good or not good for the children!"

I had become obsessed with her past. I wanted to know her, to feel what it was that had made her so distant from us and yet so very close and vulnerable. It was difficult to communicate with her, to talk to her. I could never find the right words. I could not say, "Mom, I understand why you feel this way, and I am grateful to you for Lancaster and for other things, but I love Father as well." I could not tell her that most of all I had wanted her to love me. I wanted her to touch me, not out of pity but because she wanted to. "What do you want, Mom?" I wanted to ask. But there were so many things we left unsaid.

THOSE LAST MONTHS BEFORE we moved from Tehran had the texture of nostalgia, as if the present had already faded into the past. I remember one morning in particular, she had called me down for a cup of coffee. When I arrived in her apartment I found her in the kitchen and she told me to settle into the drawing room while she finished making coffee. Waiting for her, looking around me, I noticed certain changes about the room to which I had not paid much attention. She always liked to have a smaller room for casual entertainment. At first she had moved everything to her bedroom and turned the adjoining room, which had been my father's bedroom, into her drawing room. Then she had moved her bed into the new drawing room, turning it into a couch during the daytime and a bed at night. By now she practically lived all hours of the day and night in that room. The photographs on the walls had also undergone a transformation. Ever since I could remember she'd had pictures of the four of us—one of my father with the mayoral key and chain—together on one wall. There were other photos of us, a typical family portrait with my brother still in his teens. The photographer had tried to improve us and made my eyes so light they looked green. But now I noticed that my mother had removed all of the photos with my father in them.

The room was full of photographs of her children and grandchildren. Among the color snapshots of Negar, Dara, and Sanam, I spotted a black-and-white photo. It was of a young bride, sober and serious, and her light-haired, smiling groom. My mother and Saifi. On her bedside table were two books, both from my library. They were among my childhood favorites. One was a book I had been in love with when I was around eleven. Layla had given it to me for my birthday and I used to boast that I had read it twelve times. It was called *Désirée*. Written in diary form, it was a romanticized version of the life of Bernardine Eugénie Désirée Clary, the daughter of a wealthy merchant from Marseille who was befriended by Napoleon, to whom Napoleon was allegedly engaged when he was still poor, and whom he later betrayed to marry Josephine. She ended up marrying one of Napoleon's generals and later became the queen of Sweden. This book was adorned with pictures from the movie with Jean Simmons, Marlon Brando, and Merle Oberon; not surprisingly I forever identified them with their historical counterparts. The first sentence went something like this: "I think women with a prominent bosom are more attractive, so tomorrow I intend to stuff mine with handkerchiefs." My mother had picked up this book and another one of my childhood favorites, *Uncle Tom's Cabin*, and she read them as real history. I started telling her—as was obvious—that these books were novels, but she was determined to believe otherwise and I desisted. I told her about Harriet Beecher Stowe and women like her and their fight for women's rights and against slavery, and how I felt these women's struggles were so close to our own. I also told her about how when I first went to Paris I tried to find the bridge where Désirée's future husband found her contemplating suicide after she had discovered that Napoleon would marry Josephine.

I told her I was planning to write a book and dedicate it to her. "What will you call it?" she asked. "*Shameless Women*," I said. "And you think I will like a book with such a title?" "No, Mom, what I mean is that I remember you and Aunt Mina told us how they used to say that teaching women to read and write would make them worldly and would encourage them to write love letters to men and to be shameless. I want to write a book about that, about how frightened some people are of educating women." I told her about a story by Shahrnoosh Parsipur set near the end of the nineteenth century. One day, as the heroine's father, an *adib*, or poet-scholar, is walking down the street, deep in thought and oblivious to the world around him, a foreigner on horseback, probably an Englishman, runs him down.

The insolent foreigner, angry at the *adib*'s inattention, whips him across the face. This incident creates a big scandal. It is arranged that the foreigner should go to the scholar's house and apologize. This simple confrontation is probably a footnote in the life of the Englishman, but it transforms the scholar's life forever. The change is presented at first through small details. At that time very few Persian homes had chairs and furniture; even the well-off sat on the carpeted floor, leaning against huge cushions. In order to properly receive the foreigner, the scholar has to borrow Western-style furniture. This is the first sign of the foreign invasion. The Englishman breaks another rule. In most Persian houses it is still the custom to take one's shoes off when entering the house. The foreigner, ignorant or heedless of this custom, enters with his boots on. Thus the act of apology turns into a gesture of his superiority. The most important result of the encounter is the scholar's startling discovery of the roundness of the earth. Before, he had been vaguely aware of the earth's roundness but had preferred to ignore it. For several days he contemplates what his discovery means for him. Instinctively realizing the connection between the foreigner's presence, the roundness of the earth, and future changes and upheavals, he finally announces: "Yes, the earth is round; the women will start to think, and as soon as they begin to think, they will become shameless."

I told my mother, "That is what I mean when I talk about shameless women—women like you, Ameh Hamdam, your teacher Ozra Khanoom, how they fought to be educated. I want to write about this and about the fictional women in our literature."

I did not tell her that I also wanted to write about the hardheaded women like Rudabeh, Vis, and Forough, like Alam Taj, women who persisted in taking risks, in . . . how can I say it? Women who are not afraid of being sensual. I wanted to ask her if there was any discrepancy between being an educated woman, a medical doctor, say, and being a woman who loved to dance.

She was following her own train of thought. "I always wanted you to be educated," she said, "useful for your country. At least I achieved that. The parent who disciplines a child is always the one who is disliked. It is the indulgent one they want to spend time with." I should have said, "Yes, you did give me that, you gave us education, and where I am now I owe to you. You wanted your dreams for me." I should have acknowledged that. But somehow it was all a bit too late.

I would have liked to think that from that day on this was how our relationship would be. But the next day, or the day after, we resumed our normal relationship. She would open the door to my kitchen and start hurling insults at me, while in the living room my guests would try to continue their conversation as if they could not hear her. After she had caught me talking to Father on the phone, for the umpteenth time, she would ask for the documents to the lands she and my father had owned together and I would remain silent. And then she would remind me that she didn't expect much from me anyway, because I was made of those same rotten genes.

One day, about a week before we left Iran, she came up to our apartment early in the morning. She said there was something she wanted to show me. She looked irritated and handed me a big fat file. "You never thought of showing these to me," she said. She had all my articles, almost every single one of them. She even had a Xerox copy of the introduction I had written to the Persian translation of Richard Wright's *American Hunger*. She had framed letters and poems by my students. "The ones you threw away," she said. The copies I now have of my articles from Iran mainly comes from the file she gave me then. She said, "Your new book about this Russian, I don't understand. I don't understand why you have to write about him. But I am happy that you are doing what you want. This is my last contribution," she said. "I have no more money, thanks to that gentleman and his concubine, but I am glad I have left my children with something no one can take away from them."

THE LAST MORNING, as she came to the garage in her familiar faded, pale-green dressing gown to say good-bye, she looked angry and barely responded to our greetings. When I tried to kiss her good-bye, she turned away. She performed all the farewell rituals to ensure the traveler has a safe journey, bringing out, as she always did on such occasions, her small bowl of water with a single flower in it and the Koran. She poured the water behind us, in our footsteps as we left, for good luck. But what I remember most clearly is that expression of bitterness and hurt.

As the car drove off I reimagined my mother, a trick I had learned when I was very young—look at the view, close your eyes and reimagine it, and then open your eyes and look again. I turned and looked at her again, in her pale-green dressing gown, obscured by the shadows in the dark garage, and I was struck by how old she looked, the spots on her face, the still beautiful gray hair, the high cheekbones, and the lusterless eyes . . . Our parents' old age shocks us in the same manner that our children's growth to maturity does, but without the joy; there is only sadness. I thought suddenly how vulnerable she was and alone. Then a thought crept in and took root. I will soon lose her, I thought, but loss presupposes ownership. She and my father had both given me something to lose. I felt sorry for her—not so much for Father, who had in a broken way fulfilled his dream. But I felt sorry for her, because she had nothing to lose, she had lost her mother too early, and with my father's departure she had lost what was left of her home. This thought lurked for five years in a corner of my mind, until it suddenly hit home after her death.

We had left a little earlier than necessary. My father was waiting at the airport to see us off, and to help us with the luggage. He knew people at customs who could help in case something came up, and I constantly worried that something might come up. But nothing happened: no one harassed us. I kept thinking that all my life I have worried about my father's death, and now probably this was the last time I would see him.

Father had given me the stories, my portable home. With Mother it was more complicated. I had come to my books and my vocation and even my family both because of her and in spite of her. It was ironic that in the end I had become what Mother wanted me to be, or what she had wanted to become: a woman content with her family and her work. My daughter, Negar, became what Mother had aspired to: she went to medical school and is studying to be a doctor. She said, "Mom, I will be the first girl in our family to become a doctor. Maman Nessi would have loved that."

People need to be acknowledged for who they are, they need to be seen and loved as they are, in order to come fully into their own. How could we acknowledge her? My father's sins and his virtues were concrete and specific. We could love him, be mad at him, and acknowledge him. Not so with her. It was as if when she looked into the mirror she saw only a void. She turned us into mirrors, desperate to find an image she could not see. Sometimes I caught myself looking in the mirror and seeing my mother's face. I had never thought I looked like her, and when people told me I did, I would almost vehemently deny it. I looked like my father, I would tell them. Yet as the years went by I heard this remark more often, from my own daughter, in fact, who friends said looked like me. It was not that I was like my mother in coloring or the slant of my eyes; it went deeper than that. There was an expression, a ghostlike intimation, as if a shadow had passed over my face. There she was in the mirror, not kind or generous, but cold and relentless.

WHEN I LEFT IRAN I took with me a decaying piece of green cloth with the flourishing inscriptions of Mozafaredin Shah, the Qajar king. It had belonged to my mother's mother, a descendant of this Shah, and it would tear at the touch. More than the antique fabrics she had given me this decaying green cloth reminded me of the grandmother I had never seen. I also raided the old suitcase in the storage room and greedily took all the photographs I could get my hands on. When our family settled into our new life in the U.S. I got into the habit of taking them out and gazing at them for long stretches of time. I memorized each gesture, the kind of shoes my mother wore, the shape of her earrings, the way she had of leaning back in some photos.

—

A FEW YEARS AGO the colleague of Bijan's who rented our apartment in Tehran told us on a visit to D.C. how my mother would invite him and his family to have coffee with her. "It was interesting," he said. "Nezhat Khanoom kept telling us stories about her first husband and her family, about how kind her father was, preferring her to his other children. The strangest thing of all was that she kept saying, 'Don't believe anyone who tells you my stepmother mistreated me. My stepmother loved me like her own daughter, she treated me very well.'"

She was talking to a voice inside her own head. Now that Father had left her she needed to prop up her old mythology. She needed to know that she was wanted if not by the living, at least by the dead. I had wanted to know what made my mother stop dancing after that first dance with Saifi. I had my answer: she never let go of that first dance, just as she never let go of Saifi. What was it that Aunt Mina used to say: "Let go, Nezhat. Let it go." The first step in dancing is letting go, and she never did.

I had to let go as well, let go of her, stop resisting her at every turn. I impulsively turned to tell Bijan's colleague, as I had done under similar circumstances before, "No, it wasn't the way she told you, she was fantasizing again." But I said nothing. I began to think that perhaps at this stage the only way she could survive was to travel to that past which she loved, this time to rearrange and shape the world according to her liking. Let her live in this world where her father is kind to her, where her stepmother acts like a mother, where her sister is a friend, and where her husband forever dances with her. Round and round the room they go, in a house that no longer exists.

the last dance

WHEN MY MOTHER DIED, on January 2, 2003, I was writing the acknowledgments to my last book. I had already dedicated it to my parents and to my own family, and in a conventional way I had dutifully recognized my mother's encouragement and enthusiasm for my endeavors. Now I felt I had to change everything. How should I acknowledge my mother? If asked, what could I truthfully say about her?

For months before her death I had been mourning her as if she had already died. My friend Pari had called me from Tehran one day to say that she had been hospitalized. Pari's tone on the phone had sounded deliberately casual. "Everything's okay now," she said. "Mrs. Nafisi is her old self again, inviting the nurses to have Turkish coffee and chocolates with her. Would you believe it," she added, "we had to bring her coffeemaker and cups to the hospital, otherwise she threatened not to stay."

I was not consoled. As soon as I put down the receiver I thought, "She's dying." For a few days I roamed the house crying, and looked at the photographs I had taken with me when we left Tehran. My family became alarmed. They tiptoed around me and made no reference to the solitary hours I spent sitting on my bed, propped up against pillows, photographs scattered all around me while, magnifying glass in hand, I gazed at the old black-and-white pictures of my mother.

This is how the past comes to us, not neatly but like a knife, always unexpected. And it comes in fragments. You try to put the pieces together, but you can only really understand it if you accept its irretrievable and fragmentary nature.

THAT DAY I MOURNED my mother's death, although she was not yet dead, and every day I would call or be called from Tehran where I heard a report of her condition in the hospital. X-rays were taken, then she was transferred home. Someone was with her day and night. In her final days she was moved to the house of Tahmineh, our children's former nanny, who was now a good friend. I spoke to all manner of different people, all of whom tried to reassure me. I made impossible suggestions about returning home, getting her a passport, and bringing her to D.C. When I spoke to her on the telephone sometimes she recognized me and at other times she did not know whom she was talking to.

Her rancor and bitterness had passed almost as soon as we left Tehran. On the telephone she lavished the affection that she could not show me when I was home. She would say, "Although I am alone and I miss my children and grandchildren terribly, I am so glad none of you are here. I am proud to have educated two dedicated and principled children." Sometimes she said, "I heard you the other night"— an interview I had given to the Voice of America or the BBC. She lowered her voice in a conspiratorial tone, saying, "What you say is heard. Do you understand?" "Yes, Mom." "Always tell the truth. I have taught my children to never, never lie."

"Soon I shall have more news for you," she went on. "That person, remember?" "Yes, of course." I was sure that if anyone was eavesdropping on us, they too would figure out that "that person" was the regime. "You know who I'm talking about?" "Yes, Mom." "Well, he is very sick, very, very sick." "Is he?" "Yes, my friends tell me they have no hope for him."

"How is Dara?" she would say with a sudden change of tone. "Tell him I feed the birds for him. Now that he is alone there don't hurt the poor child." At the end of each and every phone call she would say, "What shall I send you? Walnuts? Do you need anything?" Sometimes a visitor from Tehran would bring me walnuts or dried cherries, some small gold medallion for the children.

This time when I talked to her at the hospital she sounded different. She complained a little, but she forgot to ask me what I wanted her to send me. I said, "Mom, listen to the doctors." "Tell Dara I feed the birds," she said. "Don't hurt Dara, that poor boy, all alone, none of you appreciate him." She said, "I am alone, yes, but I am proud to have two such children, educated, with high principles. I am glad you never caved in," she said. "Please send me dried cherries," I said. She said, "And walnuts?" "Yes, yes, walnuts, I would love walnuts."

The last time I called her she was weaker, but there was a lift to her voice. She sounded so happy to hear from me. She said, "Azi, is that you?" "It's me, Mom." I said, "Mom, we miss you. Mom, I owe you so much." She said, "What?" I said, "I owe so much to you. You came to Lancaster, you sat up nights." But she had drifted and she was no longer listening. She said, "What do you want me to send you? Do you still have nuts?" "Yes, Mom, yes, please Mom . . ." Could I tell her, Please Mom, don't die? But her voice trailed off—she did not need that acknowledgment anymore. When I used to call, she talked so much and I wanted her not to talk so much, and now that I wanted her to talk, she wouldn't. She must have been so lonely and now she didn't need us anymore.

O N THE ACTUAL DAY when the news of her death arrived it was snowing. I was alone, waiting for a friend to pick me up to go to work when the phone rang. After I hung up I did nothing. I had imagined her death for so many months, but now I could not dwell on it. What was it that Désirée, my favorite childhood fictional character, had said? It is no consolation when you are told that death lies at everyone's door. I thought, Father will also die.

Why don't we pay more attention to those we love? Why don't we ask them more about every little detail, about their childhood, about how they feel, what they dream of, and if they are tired or don't want to talk, why don't we insist? Why don't we keep every photograph, take notes, why don't we ask others about what they know, those who were there before us, those who know things we don't?

I was overcome by the unreasonable fear of having to talk to others about my mother's death. I did not even want to call my brother in London or tell my husband and children. There were things I needed to know before I was ready to acknowledge her death.

Then there were the invisible inhabitants of that parallel world she had created out of her past, for whose loss she somehow had made us feel responsible. It was inevitable that they would come out, those apparitions kept at bay for decades; they too will demand their own separate story the way I demanded mine. And now every time I tried to write the acknowledgments for my book, beginning with "And my mother, Nezhat," those ghostly presences stepped out of the shadows, challenging me, "What about your mother, Nezhat? Come on, give us the truth for once."

Did she die the way she lived, steeped in her illusions? Those illusions which in life had been destructive, came to her rescue in the end. Pari told me that near the end they told her that the regime was gone and that soon I would return with our family. Mother had asked about specific people in the regime. She wanted to know what had happened to Rafsanjani, the former president, and to the Supreme Leader, Ayatollah Khamenei. They told her that they were both awaiting trial. They said, all will end well, everything has happened the way you said it would. Hearing all this I thought, at least to the end she refused to accept what she did not want, forever resisting "the unwanted."

In the weeks after my mother's death I would go up to our bedroom and scatter her pictures around me on the bed, scrutinizing them with a magnifying glass, an act that worried my family although it was strangely soothing to me. One night Negar and Dara joined me. I remember the flickers of anxiety in their eyes that belied the light tone of their voices as they tried to get me to go downstairs and watch *Seinfeld* with them, as was our habit. Unable to persuade me, they sat on the edge of the bed and started picking up the pictures, commenting on them, exclaiming how young and how different Maman Nessi looked. Dara told us that he missed feeding the birds with her, although it had really been her idea and that he had done it to humor her. "More than feeding the birds," he said, "Maman Nessi fed me, giving me chocolates and candy." "That's because you were her favorite," Negar said. "I was Babaii's favorite; he used to call me 'Little Azi' and tell me stories from the *Shahnameh* and plant flowers with me in the garden. Maman Nessi also told us stories. Many of them were fairy tales, but the one I liked best was about her first meeting with Saifi." Negar asked me if I remembered how Mother would repeat that story, telling us about her beautiful clothes and dancing with Saifi. "Round and round the room," Negar said, motioning with her hands. Of course I remembered. And once more I tried to retrieve that special tone of my mother's voice, the one that seemed to come from some faraway place, while she repeated the story of that magical day, now as frozen in time as the fairy tales she liked to tell my children:

"I met him at my uncle's wedding. I was only nineteen and looked very beautiful. There were two celebrations, one in midmorning, when I had on my crepe de chine dress, and then in the evening, when I wore a dress made of duchess satin. Saifi was very handsome, son of the prime minister and like me a descendant of the Qajar kings. He kept looking at me, but while my father was present he did not dare to come closer. No other man did, except my uncle, with whom I had the first dance. As soon as my father left Saifi asked me to dance, again and again, four times, until my uncle started to glare at us. The next day he and his family came to our house to ask for my hand . . ."

the perils of love

WHEN WE LEFT TEHRAN, I tried to preserve the image of my father at the airport as he stood there, watching us as we waited in line to go through. I thought, I will never see him again. I missed him terribly when we were in America, living in Potomac, Maryland, but he was the one who would call and leave messages on our voice mail, and I could hear not in his actual words but in his tone that he was hurt. "I just wanted to hear your voice," he would say, or "It's Negar's birthday," or "I keep hearing you on Voice of America and the BBC but I cannot hear you on the telephone." When *Reading Lolita in Tehran* was published I at first did not send him a copy. "I heard about your book," he said in one voice mail. "Other people ask me about it and I don't know what to tell them. It seems your father is the last one to know." It broke my heart, his voice, but I still could not respond properly.

Every once in a while I called him back—he mainly called me from his office and I telephoned him there. We talked for a long time and hearing his voice I missed him and promised to write. I told him I'd send him articles about my book. Sometimes he sent a fax, asking me to be kind to his wife, saying that he really loved her, that he always thought I also loved her, and that we were friends. I called him usually after these faxes. "Are you really happy?" I would anxiously ask.

I DID SEE HIM one last time, in the summer of 2003 in London, when we all gathered for a family reunion. Shahran and Mohammad had divorced and Mohammad had married another wonderful woman, Georgie. We all remained friends and Shahran also lived in London. That summer Father looked so frail. Even then, he was very dapper and alert and charming, but he looked vulnerable. When we met, we both broke into tears and over the next six days whenever we talked at some point or another he burst into tears. I wanted to make sure that he was happy, despite the fact that he reassured me every time we spoke. He seemed so anxious. He said he needed to sell the land. He had promised Shahin that he would bring her security. He said he was assured of the fact that his children were fine, financially sound, and that they had loving families, but she, Shahin, had no one. Apart from her mother who had recently died no one had treated her the way she deserved, and even her mother had loved her son more, a son who never took care of her. Had these words not been familiar to me, had he not repeated similar words almost all through his life with Mother, I might have believed him. He also said that he wanted to leave Iran, to spend his last years with us. In that we both, my brother and I, encouraged him. When he left, Mohammad said he would begin the process of bringing him, and later his wife, to England.

Father with Mohammad's son, Sina, in 2002.

We were in Finsbury Park, my brother was playing with his son, and Father and I walked around the lake. He said, "I was not a womanizer. The only times I was really unfaithful to your mother were with Ziba and with Shahin. Your mother was a good-hearted woman, that is why it was so difficult to leave her. I tried, I tried everything, but she was lost to me, everything that was important to her had already happened before we met."

I N THE FALL OF 2004, my brother and Georgie arranged to spend Christmas vacation with us. They wanted us all to go to New Orleans. Suddenly, in November, Mohammad called to say they had to cancel because Father was ill, he had had a heart attack. Mohammad was going to Tehran immediately. Unlike with my mother's illness, I took this calmly at first. All my life I had been afraid of losing him. I felt my anxiety protect me, as if my desire to keep him alive forever would cast a charm around him, and save him from death. Until the day he went to the hospital he had gone to work every day early in the morning, and had traveled to the Caspian sometimes twice a week, to sell the lands his wife was so keen on selling. He fought and reasoned with the revolutionary committees, the locals who had taken over the land after the revolution, the local clerics, anyone who would be bribed or enlisted to his side. His last diary is filled with notes about his anxiety over the land. There is a reference to Mohammad, Georgie, and her mother visiting Tehran, and a hopeful entry written in shaky handwriting about Mohammad and me wanting him to leave Iran and live with Mohammad in London. He wrote that this was what he desired most in life. And just as in his prison diaries he wrote about Iran and Iranians, about where the country was headed.

I called him at the hospital. I said, "Hello, Dad." He said, "Is that you, Mohammad?" "No, it's me, Azi." "Oh, Azi," he said, "I was just reading your book. I have read one hundred fifty pages of it." ("*Anti-Terra* and *Reading Lolita in Tehran*: Azar's books," he wrote at the top corner of a page in his diary.) He said he was feeling better. He would soon return home. And yes, as soon as the doctor allowed, he would leave for London.

A few days after my father was dismissed from the hospital my brother returned to London to prepare for his arrival. Their house had many steps. They sold that place and bought another in great haste and at some financial disadvantage so that it would be convenient for Father. Mohammad called to say that Father would be with them in January, and I should make plans to go to London. I had a great deal to do and I remember I kept telling myself I wish it were another time, maybe in two months' time, how am I going to go to London in the middle of all this work? I talked to Father on the phone and he said he was feeling better. He said, "I will see you soon." Two days later Mohammad called again. The day after the doctor had told my father he was well enough to leave for London he had died.

My mother's last days and moments had been relayed to me meticulously by trusted friends. I did not hear how Father spent his last hours. All through his illness he had been tended by my uncle and cousin, who were medical doctors. They had sent me the medical reports and diagnosis. Father had gone to work even after he left the hospital. My uncle said the stress and his travels to the Caspian had worsened his situation, but at least he did not suffer long. He never wanted to have the kind of illness that would cause others trouble. Always that. Maybe he died because he did not want to inconvenience his daughter's plans.

After he left the hospital he stayed in a spare room because he did not want to disturb his wife in the middle of the night. The night he died he had felt sick around midnight, but it was some time before his wife discovered it. By six in the morning he was declared dead.

I go over those hours, those days, and try to imagine how he felt. Was he afraid, as he suggested in one sentence in his last diary when he complained of memory lapses, of dear Shahin's pressuring him about the land in the north, and of his fear of death? Was he at peace as he declared so many times and in the poem he composed for his own tombstone?

I have been told several times that it was not my fault for not being there when my parents died. None of this is a consolation. I don't feel better because it was really politics that prevented me from seeing my parents, nor do I feel consoled that other daughters have had to suffer so much more, like my old school principal's children who were away when their mother was wrapped in a sack and hanged or killed by a firing squad. I curse the totalitarian regimes for holding their citizens by their heartstrings. The revolution taught me not to be consoled by other people's miseries, not to feel thankful because so many others had suffered more. Pain and loss, like love and joy, are unique and personal; they cannot be modified by comparison to others.

As it turned out, I did go to London. In their new London home, Mohammad and Georgie gave me my father's room. It was the only room in the place that had been fully furnished: there were still boxes in the living room. It was a small room on the first floor, with a dresser, a vase of flowers, a window looking out at a small garden. The bed took up most of the room. When I said good-bye to my brother at the airport, Mohammad said, "Well, here we are. We are the elders now."

AFTER MY FATHER'S DEATH Mohammad returned to Tehran to be at his funeral and other ceremonies. He called me to say that it was up to us to maintain a friendly and cordial relationship with Shahin Khanoom. After all, Father loved her and expected that we show her every consideration. I called her to offer my condolences and we had a long conversation during which she told me how in his last moments he had held on to her hand, telling her how much he loved her and thanking her for all she had done for him. I also asked her to give Mohammad copies of Father's poems, some of which we did not have, especially the ones dedicated to our mother, and a few of his paintings—these had been returned to my father after Mother's death and included his portraits of Mother, Mohammad, and myself. She promised she would. A few days later she called me, her tone exceptionally kind and commiserating. She wanted a copy of my birth certificate, which she needed in order to obtain Father's pension. I again asked for copies of Father's poems and some of his paintings. I also asked for a few personal mementos. Once she received a copy of my birth certificate she sent me his glasses, two ties, and a belt. She refused to give us copies of his poems and his paintings. The meanness in this gesture severed any fragile ties we had to her.

In my first real confrontation with my mother so many decades

ago, when, at the age of four, I instinctively and with some desperation realized that I did not even have the power to move my bed to my
favorite spot in my room, my father taught me to regain control by
traveling to that other world no one could take away from me. After
the Islamic Revolution I came to realize the fragility of our mundane
existence, the ease with which all that you call home, all that gives you
an identity, a sense of self and belonging, *can* be taken away from you.
I learned that what my father had given me through his stories was a
way to make a home for myself that was not dependent on geography
or nationality or anything that other people can take away from me.
These stories could not guard me against the pain I felt at my parents'
loss; they did not offer consolation or closure. It was only after their
deaths that I came to realize that they each in their own way had given
me a portable home that safeguards memory and is a constant resistance against the tyranny of man and of time.

THIS BOOK IS DEDICATED to the memory of my parents, Nezhat and Ahmad Nafisi—with love and appreciation. I'd like to acknowledge my brother, Mohammad, a considerate, meticulous, and generous sibling, who is in no way responsible for the content of this book; my husband, best friend, and critic, Bijan Naderi, and our children, Negar and Dara Naderi, for their love, patience, and support, for stories we shared, and for making it possible to imagine the impossible; and Bryce Nafisi Naderi for so many hours of wonderful companionship.

I would also like to acknowledge my beloved niece and nephew, Sanam Banoo Nafisi, with whom I shared so many stories; Sina Nafisi, the new storyteller in our family; and my good friend and sister-in-law, Georgiana Perry-Crooke (remembering always the room with the flowers). And Shahran Tabari, who read the manuscript with her usual care and enthusiasm. I am grateful for her insights and suggestions and, as always, for her friendship and love.

Then there are other members of our family whose support made the writing of this book easier: my good friends and in-laws Mani and Q Aghazadeh, Taraneh Shamszad, and, in memory of our beloved friend Mohammad Shamszad, for his generosity, tenderness, and curiosity. My cousin Hamid Naficy, who read an early draft of the manuscript, for his time and his wonderful insights. And our good friend "Faryar."

For their affection, support, and the magic of their company and conversation I would like to thank: Joanne Leedom Ackerman, Ladan Boroumand and my cousin Abdi Naficy (for making me feel that I am in Paris, no matter where I live), Farah Ebrahimi, my uncle and aunt

Reza and Ashraf Naficy, my cousins Nader and Koroush Naficy, Samantha Power, Alberto Manguel, "Pari," Sophie Benini Pietromarche, Jacki Lyden, Haideh Daragahi, Steven Barclay, and the wonderful people at the Steven Barclay Agency, including the newest member, Milo.

My thanks to friends, colleagues, and the institutions that helped me with the research for the background material: Foundation for Iranian Studies, and my good friend Mahnaz Afkhami, for her support and for providing access to the files and the library at the Foundation. My friend and colleague Hormoz Hekmat, the editor in chief of *Iran Nameh*, was very generous with his time and resources, providing me with books, valuable information, and help on the historical time line. I am also grateful to my friend Azar Ashraf, special collections assistant at the Princeton University Library, for providing me with documents and sources.

Massumeh Farhad, the curator at the Freer and Sackler Galleries at the Smithsonian, was, as always, not only generous with her friendship, insights, and support but also provided access to the wonderful photo archives of the old Tehran and the Qajar period. I am also grateful to her and my good friend Roya Boroumand, for once more reminding me that style and substance are inseparable. I would like to thank Roya and the Boroumand Foundation for Promotion of Democracy in Iran for providing me with information regarding the tragedy at the cinema Rex in Abadan.

Haleh Esfandiari generously supplied me with information and contacts regarding Saifi and my mother's youth. Fanny Esfandiari is "the lovely Austrian lady" of my story.

Majid Naficy, for quotations from his personal essay "Love and the Revolution" published on January 3, 2008, at http://www.iranian.com/main/2008/love-and-revolution, and the copy of the text of his late wife, Ezatt Tabiian's will, translated from his book in Persian *raftam golat bechinam* (Stockholm, Sweden: Baran Publishers, 2000).

Dr. Farokhrou Parsay's biographer, Mansoureh Pirnia, for information and the photograph of Dr. Parsay.

The translations of poems from Ferdowsi's *Shahnameh* are taken from Dick Davis, the incomparable interpreter and translator of some of the best works of Persian classical literature. Translations of poems by Forough Farrokhzad are taken from Michael Hillmann's biography, *A Lonely Woman*. Said Nafisi's memoirs are from the *Bih Rivayat-i Said Nafisi: Khatirat-i Siyasi, Adabi, Javani*. I am thankful to Baqer Moin's *Khomeini: Life of the Ayatollah* for information related to the Islamic Revolution.

I would also like to thank the SAIS Mason Library at Johns Hopkins University, Gelman Library at the George Washington University–SAIS, the DC Public Library (West End branch), Politics and Prose, and Bridgestreet Books.

My agent, Sarah Chalfant, has been a rare friend and wise consul ever since our first conversation about Henry James. I have benefited greatly from the fierce commitment shown by Sarah and other colleagues at the Wylie Agency to that elusive but essential element in a book—its quality.

I would like to once more express my gratitude to Johns Hopkins–SAIS for providing me with the space and time to work on this book as well as on my other projects at SAIS. My thanks especially to Dean Jessica Einhorn, and to Tom Keaney, the former director of the Foreign Policy Institute, as well as its present director, Ted Baker. A grant from the Smith Richardson Foundation made it possible for me to sustain writing this book while at Johns Hopkins–SAIS. I am thankful for their generosity.

Leila Austin started working with me as my assistant, but over the past three years our relationship has developed into a cherished friendship and a valuable collaboration. She did her best to provide me with the space to write my book against not only intrusions from the outside but from those of my own making. She helped at different stages with the research and background for this book as well as on the glossary and time line, performing these tasks with the same sense of intellectual curiosity and personal integrity that she performs every other undertaking.

At Random House, Kate Medina supported this book and saw it through thick and thin with so much grace, care, and patience. I am very grateful to know that my book is in such good hands. My thanks also to Millicent Bennett for her support at all hours of the day and night, and for her patience with an author reluctant to hand in her manuscript at every step of the way. We seldom appreciate the work and dedication of so many individuals behind the scenes who make the publication of one small book possible. I would like to especially acknowledge my publisher, Gina Centrello, and the wonderful staff at Random House: Tom Perry, Sally Marvin, London King, Benjamin Dreyer, Vincent La Scala, Carol Schneider, Sanyu Dillon, Avideh Bashirrad, Claire Tisne, Rachel Bernstein, Elizabeth Paulson, Debbie Aroff, Anna Bauer, Gene Mydlowski, Laura Goldin, Deborah Foley, Richard Elman, Barbara Bachman, Maria Braeckel, Frankie Jones, Rachel Omansky, Kate Norris, Allison Merrill, Jillian Schiavi, Jennifer Smith, and Carol Poticny.

Joy de Menil has been, throughout difficult years, both the ideal editor and a good friend. I cannot express my gratitude for her support, her sense of commitment, and her invaluable insights and suggestions. I will always associate and celebrate the birth of this book with the birth of Joy's daughter, the miraculous Cecily Louise Reed.

Among my most cherished and well-remembered memories related to the writing of this book are the times I spent as a writer-in-residence at the American Academy in Rome in the spring and summer of 2005 and at the Corporation of Yaddo in June of 2007. To these two great institutions and to their guardian ghosts I would like to express my gratitude.

Finally, a great portion of this book was written in different places around my hometown of Washington, D.C. I would like to acknowledge the most frequented ones: The Phillips Collection and the National Gallery of Art and their cafés, the Soho Café, the Starbucks on the Waterfront, Barnes & Noble in Georgetown, and the Borders on 18th and L.

THE FOLLOWING IS A SELECTION of literary works mentioned in or closely related to my memoir that are available in translation.

POETRY

Simin Behbahani, *A Cup of Sin: Selected Poems*
(translated by Farzaneh Milani and Kaveh Safa)

Forough Farrokhzad, *Sin: Selected Poems of Forough Farrokhzad*
(translated by Sholeh Wolpe) and *Bride of Acacias:
Selected Poems of Forough Farrokhzad* (Modern Persian
literature series)

Fakhredin Gorgani, *Vis and Ramin* (translated by Dick Davis)

Abolqasem Ferdowsi, *Shahnameh: The Persian Book of Kings*
(translated by Dick Davis)

Hafez

Majid Naficy, *Muddy Shoes*

Rubayiat of Omar Khayyam (translated by Edward Fitzgerald)

Rumi

Saadi (translated by Ralph Waldo Emerson)

Sohrab Sepehri, *The Lover Is Always Alone*
(translated by Karim Emami)

Ahmad Shamlu, *The Love Poems of Shamlu* (translated by
Firoozeh Papin-Matin and Arthur Lane)

FICTION

Simin Daneshvar, *Suvashun* (translated by M. Ghanounparvar)

Houshang Golshiri, *The Prince* (translated by James Buchan)

Sadegh Hedayat, *The Blind Owl*

Manuchehr Irani (Golshiri's pen name), *King of the Benighted* (translated by Abbas Milani)

Shahrnoosh Parsipur, *Women Without Men* (translated by Kamran Talattof and Jocelyn Sharlet)

Iraj Pezeshkzad, *My Uncle Napoleon* (translated by Dick Davis)

Strange Times, My Dear, the PEN Anthology of Contemporary Iranian Literature (edited by Nahid Mozaffari and Ahmad Karimi Hakkak)

Goli Taraghi, *A Mansion in the Sky* (translated by Faridoun Farrokh)

Obeyd-e Zakani, *Ethics of the Aristocrats and Other Satirical Works*

NONFICTION

Abbas Amanat (ed.), *Crowning Anguish: Diary of Taj al-Saltana*

Paul Auster, *The Invention of Solitude*

Najmieh Batmanglij, *From Persia to Napa: Wine at the Persian Table*

Edmund Gosse, *Father and Son*

Michael Hillmann, *A Lonely Woman: Forugh Farrokhzad and Her Poetry*

Nigel Nicholson, *Portrait of a Marriage*

Lorna Sage, *Bad Blood*

Leon Wieseltier, *Kaddish*

THE FOLLOWING ARE selected moments in twentieth-century Iranian history that provide a context for this book.

1905–11: The Qajar king Mozafaredin Shah signs the Constitutional Charter—the first of its kind in the Middle East—in response to widespread protests against the despotic monarchical system. The protests are led by discontented members of the clergy, bazaar merchants, and the Iranian intelligentsia, including women. The resulting constitution sharply limits the power of the Shah, calling for the establishment of a Parliament, and officially placing the Shah under the rule of law. In 1909, Sheikh Fazlollah Noori, a conservative cleric who resisted these reforms, is hanged for opposing the constitution's curtailment of clerical authority. He is later considered a martyr by Ayatollah Khomeini and religious conservatives.

1921: In an atmosphere of internal political instability, economic decline, and foreign intrusion into the internal affairs of Iran, a colonel in the Russian-trained Persian Cossack Brigade named Reza Khan leads a successful coup against the Qajar dynasty. He becomes army commander and minister of war under a new prime minister, Sayyid Zia od-Din Tabatabai.

1925: Reza Khan is crowned as Reza Shah Pahlavi, founder of the Pahlavi Dynasty. In his sixteen years of authoritarian rule, he focuses primarily on the creation of a strong central government, bolstering Iran's territorial integrity and independence, and creating the administrative, juridical, and educational institutions required for Iran's entry into the modern world. He is considered a Westernizer, and cracks down on the clergy and any aspect of Iranian society he deems "backward."

1935: Under Reza Shah's rule, the country's name is officially changed from Persia to Iran. In an effort to swiftly modernize Iran, a government decree bans the wearing of the veil in public in 1936, one of several moves against religious dictates. This decree is later repealed, in 1941, due to popular pressure. Iran's first Western-style university, the University of Tehran, is established.

1941: British and Russian interests, historically at odds in Iran, join forces during World War II and occupy the country to fend off German influence over Iranian oil resources. Reza Shah, whose mistrust of the British and Russians had led to closer associations with Germany, is forced to abdicate in favor of his son Mohammad Reza Pahlavi. He is exiled to Johannesburg, where he dies in 1944.

1943: Iran declares war on Germany, which qualifies it for membership in the United Nations. U.S. president Franklin D. Roosevelt, British prime minister Winston Churchill, and Russian general secretary Joseph Stalin gather in Tehran in November, reassuring the Shah that they are committed to Iranian independence.

1945–46: Although the 1943 Tehran Tripartite Declaration by the Allied powers guarantees Iran's territorial independence at the end of the war, in 1945 the Russians refuse to withdraw from the country's northern border, instead instigating resistance that leads to two separatist movements in the northern regions of Azerbaijan and Kurdistan. In 1946 these pro-Soviet autonomous governments are overthrown as a result of pressure from the U.N. Security Council and the United States. Saham Soltan (Saifi's father) serves as prime minister, briefly, in early 1945.

1951–53: Mohammad Mossadegh becomes prime minister and successfully nationalizes the oil industry, over British protests. Mossadegh clashes with the Shah, and in 1952 the Shah removes Mossadegh from power, but then reinstates him because of his overwhelming popularity; Mossadegh also forces the Shah into an equally brief exile to Rome in 1953. In the fall of 1953 Mossadegh is overthrown in a CIA-supported coup, and the Shah returns to power.

1961: The author's father becomes mayor of Tehran.

1962: As part of a larger social and economic reform package, and under the rubric of his "White Revolution," the Shah announces a bill that includes a land reform program granting suffrage to women and allowing non-Muslims to serve in Parliament.

1963: Hassan Ali Mansour is appointed prime minister. The author's mother is one of six women elected to Parliament, as a result of the White Revolution reforms that allow women increasing access to political and administrative arenas for the first time in Iran's history. The author's school principal, Dr. Parsay, becomes a senator and is later appointed minister of education. As part of a larger clerical resistance to the White Revolution, Ayatollah Khomeini instigates protests against the secular nature of the government's reforms. Khomeini is jailed after the protests, which come to be known as the June 5th uprising. The author's father is jailed in December.

1964: The capitulation law decrees that American soldiers have diplomatic immunity inside Iran. This causes nationalist furor and further antigovernment sentiment. The incarcerated ayatollah Khomeini is exiled to Turkey. Eventually, he takes up residence in the neighboring country of Iraq.

1965: Prime Minister Mansour is assassinated on his way to Parliament.

1967: The family protection law is passed, which gives greater freedom to women and grants them more legal control over their children. The trial of the author's father runs from September to November. He is exonerated of all charges.

Dr. Farokhrou Parsay is appointed minister of education. Dr. Parsay spent her career advocating for gender equality in Iran. After obtaining a medical degree, she taught biology at Tehran's Jeanne d'Arc School for girls. In 1963, Dr. Parsay was elected to Parliament and started petitioning for women's suffrage and encouraging legislation that amended laws pertaining to women and families. In 1965, she was appointed deputy minister of education, and in 1968 became the first woman to occupy a cabinet position as minister of education. Farokhrou Parsay was executed in 1980 by the Islamic Republic.

1971: The Iranian monarchy hosts the lavish celebrations of the twenty-five-hundredth anniversary of the founding of the Persian Empire by Cyrus the Great. The festivities at Persepolis, which took ten years to plan and cost up to $120 million, attract worldwide attention and are attended by international royalty and dignitaries. This is met with wide domestic and foreign criticism.

1975: The creation of the single-party system, under the Rastakhiz (Rebirth) party, is officially announced by the Shah. However, this attempt to unite the country under the guise of a more participatory government is met with little public enthusiasm. In effect, while becoming more socially liberal, Iran is becoming increasingly closed politically, leading to the alienation of the middle class.

1976: The Shah changes the Iranian solar calendar from an Islamic one based on the prophet Mohammad's migration from Mecca to Medina (Hijra) to one based on the pre-Islamic establishment of the Persian Empire in 558 B.C. This attempt to emphasize Iran's pre-

slamic past further angers the clergy against the monarchy. Mahnaz
fkhami becomes minister of women's affairs. Mahnaz Afkhami's ca-
eer advocating for women's rights dates back to her leadership of the
Vomen's Organization of Iran (WOI) in 1970. During her tenure as
ead of WOI, she worked toward revising the family protection law.
n 1976, she was appointed minister of women's affairs, a post she filled
ntil the 1978 Islamic Revolution. During this time such women's
ights as equal pay for equal work, half time work with full-time ben-
fit for mothers of young children, and the creation of child care cen-
rs in the workplace were obtained. In 1978 she was asked to oversee
committee to monitor progress toward women's full participation in
ccord with the National Plan of Action.

1977: U.S. president Jimmy Carter establishes the office of
uman rights in the U.S. State Department, sparking a wave of human
ights demands against the Iranian government. Some political pris-
ners are released as a result of this pressure. The Shah makes an
fficial state visit to America and is met with protests and demonstra-
ions. The author is among the protesters.

1978: Widespread domestic opposition to the Shah creates tur-
oil across the country, setting the stage for the Islamic Revolution.
n August, the Cinema Rex in Abadan is set on fire by Khomeini's fol-
wers, killing 430 people. The fire is falsely blamed on the Shah's se-
ret police, SAVAK. The misplaced blame for this incident further
flames public emotion against the monarchy, paving the way for a
erical uprising that is supported by most secular intellectuals. Iraq
xpells Khomeini, and he moves to Paris where he continues to re-
eive global attention for his revolutionary message against the
egime.

1979: In response to mounting protests, the Shah leaves Iran in
anuary, appointing Shahpoor Bakhtiar as prime minister. Bakhtiar
timately fails to gain control of the situation, however. Khomeini
rrives in Tehran in February and the Islamic Revolution begins in

earnest, changing the country from 2,500 years of monarchy to an I lamic republic under the Ayatollah's rule. Islamic *Sharia* laws are r instated, the family protection law is revoked, and Western influenc are banned. The Islamic Republic is established on April 1. Bakhti goes into hiding in April, and is eventually assassinated in Paris 1991. Evin Prison is occupied by revolutionaries. In a breach of th capitulation law granting diplomatic immunity, U.S. embassy dipl mats are seized as hostages in November. This sparks internation outrage, but the hostages will not be released until 1981.

1980–88: In September 1980, Iraqi forces led by President Sa dam Hussein invade a portion of western Iran in an attempt to sei control of the rich oil-producing province of Khuzistan and to asse Iraqi control over both sides of the Shatt al Arab waterway, which li on the border between the two countries. After brief occupation of th Iranian city of Khorramshahr, Iraqi forces are pushed back to the bo der by 1982, after which both nations engage in sporadic air and mi sile attacks against each other's cities and military and oil installation In 1988, after eight years of war, Iraq agrees to Iranian terms for se tlement of the war: the withdrawal of Iraqi troops from occupie Iranian territory, division of sovereignty over the Shatt al Arab wate way, and a prisoner-of-war exchange.

1989: Ayatollah Khomeini dies one year after the end of the Irar Iraq war.

ACHAEMENIDS refers to the Achaemenid Empire, dating 550–330 c., which was the first of the Persian empires to rule over significant ortions of Greater Iran. Initiated by Cyrus the Great, the Achaemenid a is considered a relatively tranquil period in Middle Eastern history, ue to the fusion of many different cultures spanning three continents and verse religious beliefs and practices. The Achaemenids, under Cyrus d Darius the Great, were also known for their progressive planning and ganizational skills, both on the administrative and military fronts, as ell as for their humanistic worldview.

ADIB Persian word meaning a man of letters, poet-scholar, learned.

AMEH paternal aunt in Persian.

AMOO paternal uncle in Persian.

BAHA'I a follower of Bahá'u'lláh and the Baha'i faith, a religion unded in nineteenth-century Persia, emphasizing the spiritual unity of humankind. Characterized by the notion that throughout history the ajor world's religions have been engaged in an ongoing dialogue, the aha'is believe that all of the divine messengers of religious faith are in-rconnected, and ultimately emphasize the collective evolution of hu-anity. This sect, which is an offshoot of Shia Islam, is the focus of rsecution in the Islamic Republic, mainly because of their claim that

Bahá'u'lláh is the personification of the "Hidden Imam." This is consi
ered as heresy in orthodox Shiism.

BAHMAN the eleventh month of the year in the Persian solar calenda

BAZAARIS an Iranian social group consisting of merchants, guild
and artisans involved in traditional trades surrounding the bazaar (ma
ket). This group has been historically tied to the clergy, mainly throug
intermarriage. The bazaaris were major participants in the 1979 Islami
Revolution.

CHADOR an outer garment or open cloak worn by some Irania
women in public spaces. A full-length semicircle of fabric open down t
front, a chador is thrown over the head and held closed in front by t
hands.

ESFAHAN the capital of Esfahan province and Iran's third large
city, located approximately 340 km south of Tehran. A historical capit
of Iran for two hundred years, it is most famous for its beautiful Islami
architecture, satiated with many covered bridges, palaces, mosques, an
minarets. It has been designated by UNESCO as a World Heritage Site

EVIN PRISON a prison in Tehran notorious for its political priso
ers' wing. Many notable political prisoners have been held at Evin befo
and after the revolution.

HAJI AGHA the title for a man (*Agha*) who has made a pilgrimage
Mecca (*Haji*).

HAMEDAN the capital city of Iran's Hamedan province, built b
tween 3000 and 1100 B.C.; believed to be among the oldest cities in Iran
well as the world.

IRAN-E JAVAN (THE YOUNG IRAN CLUB) a political activi
group made up mainly of writers and intellectuals, founded in 1921, wi

the mission to bring about a democratic Iran. The organization's first official vehicle was *Ayandeh* (the Future), a journal that encompassed the group's manifesto, expressing the urgent need for a "national unity" of Iran, mainly in regards to a national language.

JAN a term of endearment, following someone's name, meaning "my dear." The colloquial version of the same term is *Joon.*

"JIMOCRACY" refers to President Jimmy Carter's term in office, and the changes he made to U.S. foreign policy that would inevitably affect Iran's view of human rights at home and abroad.

KARBALLA in Iraq, located about 100 km southwest of Baghdad, it is considered by the Shia Muslims to be one of the holiest cities in Islam after Mecca, Medina, Jerusalem, and Najaf. This is the site for the battle of Karballa, where Shiisms' second Imam, Hussein, was martyred. *Muharram* represents the annual remembrance of this tragic day.

KHAN title equivalent to "Mr."

KHANDANYHA a weekly publication of critical political analysis founded in 1940 by Ali Asghar Amirani. Most of its content consisted of extracts and collections of foreign and Persian articles as well as commentary by Amirani himself, thereby resonating profoundly with many intellectuals in Iran.

KHANOOM title equivalent to "Mrs."

MAKTABS small, cramped rooms that served as Muslim elementary schools, where boys were instructed in Koran recitation and reading, writing, and grammar, often by less than qualified teachers or low-ranking cleric.

MULLAH Muslim title commonly given to local Islamic clerics or mosque leaders in Iran. It may also serve as a derogatory title given to some Islamic clergy who are not as well educated and well versed within the clerical hierarchy.

NOROOZ the traditional Iranian/Persian New Year holiday, marking the first day of spring and the beginning of the Persian calendar. This celebration predates Islam and begins on the day of the astronomical vernal equinox, usually on or before/after March 21st.

OMID IRAN popular Iranian magazine in the 1960s.

PAHLAVIS refers to the Pahlavi dynasty that ruled the Imperial nation of Iran, from the crowning of Reza Shah Pahlavi in 1925 to the overthrow of his son Mohammad Reza Pahlavi in the Islamic Revolution of 1979. Reza Shah led Iran through large-scale modernization and reform and the centralization of government. Mohammad Reza Shah continued these reform policies while building a strong army and maintaining friendly relations with the West during the Cold War. The demise of the Pahlavi dynasty marks the end of the ancient tradition of the Iranian monarchy. Please see "Moments in Twentieth-Century Iranian History" for more information.

PASSUR an Iranian fishing card game for four players.

QAJARS refers to the Qajar dynasty, which ruled Iran from 1794 to 1945. One of the most notable events during this time was the Constitutional Revolution, providing, within limits, freedoms of the press, speech, and association, and security of life and property, marking the end of the medieval period in Persia. Following the occupation of Persia during World War I, Soltan Ahmad Shah's rule dissipated with the arrival of a new Shah, Reza Pahlavi, in 1925, and the Qajar dynasty was declared terminated.

QASR PRISON located in Tehran, one of Iran's oldest political prisons and the first in which prisoners got their legal advantages.

RAMADAN a Muslim religious observance that takes place during the ninth month of the Islamic lunar calendar, during which time it is believed the Koran was revealed to the Angel Gabriel to deliver it to the prophet Mohammad. During Ramadan, participating Muslims do not eat or drink anything from dawn until sunset, a practice that is meant to teach patience, sacrifice, and humility. This is also a time for heightened prayer and reverence to God for past sins and guidance in the future.

RASTAKHIZ the "Resurrection" party, established on March 2, 1975, by Mohammad Reza Pahlavi as a new single political party to which all Iranians were required to belong. This was an attempt to appease the population through a limited form of political participation. This single-party system was short-lived, ending in 1978 as the Iranian Revolution gained ground, and today the Rastakhiz party exists in exile as an Iranian monarchist party opposing the Islamic Republic.

SAFAVIDS an Iranian Shia dynasty that ruled Persia from the early 1500s to 1722. During this period, the Safavids established Shia Islam as the official religion of their empire, one of their many efforts to unify the existing, diverse Iran.

SEFID ROOD one of the main branch rivers of the Tajan River, which runs through Garmsar, Iran. The name also refers to an area on the river.

SEPID SEYAH a major Iranian publication, existing in the mid-1960s.

SHAYKHIS an Islamic sect existing in Iran, dating from 1826 to the early 1900s. Led by Ahaykh Ahmad al-Asa'I, it introduced certain innovation on Shia thought, challenging the nature of religious authority and the notion of the occultation of the last Shia Imam, a central tenet of Shiism.

SHIA the second largest branch of Islam, differing from the Sunni sect in its rejection of the authority of the first three caliphs (leaders). The

Shia believe that the prophet's family and descendants (known as Imams) are his true successors. This distinction has led to spiritual differences such as the Shia veneration of the Imams as sinless, and different accounts of the prophet's life and traditions. The largest branch of Shiism, the Twelvers, who dominate Iran, also ascribe to the concept of *Occultation*, which refers to the disappearance of the messianic figure of the *Mahdi*, an Imam who is said to return on Judgment Day to fill the world with justice.

SUNNI the largest group in Islam, meaning "principle" or "path." They believe that the first four caliphs of the Muslim community were the rightful successors to Mohammad, and they hold that because God has not specified any subsequent leaders of the Muslim community, elections of such are necessary. Accordingly, Sunnis recognize four major legal traditions: Maliki, Shaf'i, Hanafi, and Hanbali.

TUDEH PARTY an Iranian communist party closely related to the Communist party of the Soviet Union, formed in 1941.

TUMAN currency of Iran until 1932. Although in 1932 the rial replaced the tuman at a rate of 1 tuman = 10 rials, many Iranians still employ the term *tuman* in everyday transactions.

ZAYANDEH ROOD one of the most important rivers of the central plateau of Iran, located in Esfahan.

ZOORKHANEH a traditional Iranian gymnasium with historical ties to training "pahlavans" (a charitable man of physical and moral strength). The ritual training sessions are accompanied by drums and rhythmic chants from the *Shahnameh* by Ferdowsi, which recounts legendary stories of the kings and warriors of ancient Persia. Women are traditionally prohibited from entering and participating in sporting events.

ZOROASTRIANISM founding religion of the Persians, Zoroastrianism is based on the philosophy and teachings of the prophet Zoroaster, who saw the universe as the cosmic struggle between truth and lies. His religious philosophy hinged on the idea that the purpose of humankind, like that of all other creations, is to sustain *aša* (a combination of creation, existence, and free will). For humankind, this occurs through active participation in life and the exercise of good thoughts, words, and deeds. Once the dominant religion of much of greater Iran until the Arab conquest and the advent of Islam, the number of Zoroastrians has since diminished to no more than 200,000 worldwide.

GRATEFUL ACKNOWLEDGMENT is made to the following for permission to reprint previously published material:

The Belknap Press of Harvard University Press: Epigraph for Part 2, "Prose Fragment 22" [Rev 91] from *The Letters of Emily Dickinson,* Thomas H. Johnson, ed., p. 915, Cambridge, Mass.: The Belknap Press of Harvard University Press, copyright © 1958, 1986, the President and Fellows of Harvard College; 1914, 1924, 1932, 1942 by Martha Dickinson Bianchi; 1952 by Alfred Leete Hampson; 1960 by Mary L. Hampson. Reprinted by permission of the publishers.

The Belknap Press of Harvard University Press and the Trustees of Amherst College: Epigraph for Part 3 is from *The Poems of Emily Dickinson,* Thomas H. Johnson, ed., Cambridge, Mass.: The Belknap Press of Harvard University Press, copyright © 1951, 1955, 1979, 1983 by the President and Fellows of Harvard College. Reprinted by permission of the publishers and the Trustees of Amherst College.

Farrar, Straus & Giroux, LLC.: Excerpt from "A Part of Speech" from *A Part of Speech* by Joseph Brodsky, translation copyright © 1980 by Farrar, Straus and Giroux, LLC. Reprinted by permission of Farrar, Straus and Giroux, LLC.

Mage Publishers: Quotes from Forugh Farrokhzad on pages 168–69 and 181–82 are from: *A Lonely Woman: Forugh Farrokhzad and Her Poetry* by

AZAR NAFISI is a visiting professor and the director of the Dialogue Project at the Foreign Policy Institute of Johns Hopkins University. She has taught Western literature at the University of Tehran, the Free Islamic University, and the University of Allameh Tabatabai in Iran. In 1981 she was expelled from the University of Tehran after refusing to wear the veil. In 1994 she won a teaching fellowship from Oxford University, and in 1997 she and her family left Iran for America. She has written for *The New York Times, The Washington Post, The Wall Street Journal,* and *The New Republic* and has appeared on countless radio and television programs. She lives in Washington, D.C., with her husband and two children.

www.azarnafisi.com

This book is set in Fournier, a typeface named for Pierre Simon Fournier, the youngest son of a French printing family. Pierre Simon first studied watercolor painting, but became involved in type design through work that he did for his eldest brother. Starting with engraving woodblocks and large capitals, he later moved on to fonts of type. In 1736 he began his own foundry, and published the first version of his point system the following year. He made several important contributions in the field of type design; he cut and founded all the types himself, pioneered the concepts of the type family, and is said to have cut sixty thousand punches for 147 alphabets of his own design. He also created new printers' ornaments.

RACHEL HEATH

The Finest Type of English Womanhood

It is 1946, and seventeen-year-old Laura Trelling is stagnating in her dilapidated Sussex family home, while her eccentric parents slip further into isolation. A chance encounter with Paul Lovell offers her the opportunity to alter the course of her destiny – and to embark on a new life in South Africa.

Many miles north, sixteen-year-old Gay Gibson is desperate to escape Birkenhead. When the girls' paths cross in Johannesburg, Laura is exposed to Gay's wild life of parties and inappropriate liaisons. Each in her own world, but thrown together, the girls find their lives inextricably entangled, with fatal consequences ...

DAVID LOYN

Butcher & Bolt

'Excellent'
MAX HASTINGS, SUNDAY TIMES

'Gripping ...A timely and important book'
JOHN CROSSLAND, DAILY MAIL

Afghanistan has been a strategic prize for more than 200 years. Foreign invaders have continually fought across its beautiful and inhospitable terrain, in conflicts variously ruthless, misguided and bloody. A century ago, the common sneer about how British soldiers treated Afghan tribesmen was that they would 'butcher' them, then 'bolt'.

Butcher & Bolt recounts this violent history, beginning in 1809 with the very first British mission – an encounter that ushered in two centuries of conflict littered with misunderstandings and broken promises, in which the British, the Russians and later the Americans repeatedly underestimated the ability of the Afghans and the power of the Frontier tribes.

In a new final chapter, Loyn examines the emerging threat of the Pakistani Taliban and the challenges faced by those fighting on the most dangerous frontier in the world.

'Superb ... Few Western journalists know Afghanistan better than Loyn'
SAUL DAVID, DAILY TELEGRAPH

'Impressive ... Should be required reading for everyone in the Foreign Office'
JOAN BAKEWELL, SUNDAY TELEGRAPH

LIAQUAT AHAMED

Lords of Finance
1929, The Great Depression, and the Bankers who Broke the World

Shortlisted for the BBC Samuel Johnson Prize for
Non-fiction and winner of the *Financial Times* /
Goldman Sachs Business Book of the Year Award

'*Compelling and convincing ... humanises the world's descent into economic chaos*'
ROBERT PESTON

The current economic crisis has only one parallel: the Wall
Street Crash of 1929 and subsequent Great Depression of the
1930s, which crippled the future of an entire generation and
set the stage for the horrors of the Second World War. Yet this
financial meltdown could have been avoided, had it not been
for the decisions taken by a small number of central bankers.

In *Lords of Finance*, we meet these men – the four bankers who
truly broke the world. Their names were lost to history, their
lives and actions forgotten, until now. Ahamed tells their story
in vivid and gripping detail, in a timely and arresting reminder
that individuals – their ambitions, limitations and human
nature – lie at the very heart of global catastrophe.

'*Highly readable ... he cannot have foreseen how timely his book would be*'
NIALL FERGUSON

'*Has immense importance to modern policymaking ... a fascinating and even
a great book*'
THE TIMES

'*Brilliant and Timely*'
GUARDIAN

BARRY UNSWORTH

Land of Marvels

'A richly imagined novel squarely in the tradition of his Booker-Prize triumph
Sacred Hunger'
GERALDINE BROOKS

1914, and an English archaeologist called Somerville is fulfilling a lifelong dream: to direct an excavation in the desert of
Mesopotamia. Yet forces beyond his control threaten his work.

The Great War is looming, and various interest groups are
vying for control over the land and its many prizes. And
Somerville, whose intention is purely to discover and preserve
the land's ancient treasures, finds his idealism sorely tested.
Naked ambition, treachery and greed are at play in this
thrilling adventure from the master of the historical novel.

'The reader is caught up in the excitement of Somerville's discoveries. Richly
peopled, fast-moving, cleverly plotted, written with economy and elegance, this
novel has the satisfying density and sweep of a book twice its length.'
SUNDAY TIMES

'Though Unsworth's fiction is historical, its themes — mainly concerning the
power of self-deception — are universal ... Unsworth's tale has the slow burn of
a professionally laid fuse burning towards an explosive finale.'
DAILY TELEGRAPH

'The historical novel should do three things: make tangible the period in ques-
tion; reflect it in to the modern world; and, like all novels, entertain. Barry
Unsworth is a master of all three concerns.'
TIMES LITERARY SUPPLEMENT

Jo Marchant

Decoding the Heavens
Solving the Mystery of the World's
First Computer

Shortlisted for the 2009 Royal Society Prize
for Science Books

'Dizzyingly brilliant'
DAILY TELEGRAPH

In 1900 a group of sponge divers blown off course in the
Mediterranean discovered an Ancient Greek shipwreck dating
from around 70 BC.

Lying unnoticed for months amongst their hard-won haul was
what appeared to be a formless lump of corroded rock, which
turned out to be the most stunning scientific artefact we have
from antiquity. For more than a century this 'Antikythera
mechanism' puzzled academics, but now, more than 2000
years after the device was lost at sea, scientists have pieced
together its intricate workings.

In *Decoding the Heavens*, Jo Marchant tells for the first time the story
of the 100-year quest to understand this ancient computer.
Along the way she unearths a diverse cast of remarkable characters – ranging from Archimedes to Jacques Cousteau – and
explores the deep roots of modern technology in Ancient
Greece, the Islamic world and medieval Europe.

'*The tale of a wondrous relic . . . sounds like pulp fiction: But it is all true.*'
INDEPENDENT

THE POWER OF READING

Visit the Random House website and get connected with information on all our books and authors

EXTRACTS from our recently published books and selected backlist titles

COMPETITIONS AND PRIZE DRAWS Win signed books, audiobooks and more

AUTHOR EVENTS Find out which of our authors are on tour and where you can meet them

LATEST NEWS on bestsellers, awards and new publications

MINISITES with exclusive special features dedicated to our authors and their titles

READING GROUPS Reading guides, special features and all the information you need for your reading group

LISTEN to extracts from the latest audiobook publications

WATCH video clips of interviews and readings with our authors

RANDOM HOUSE INFORMATION including advice for writers, job vacancies and all your general queries answered

Come home to Random House

www.rbooks.co.uk